Haciendas and *Ayllus*

Haciendas and *Ayllus*

Rural Society in the Bolivian Andes in the
Eighteenth and Nineteenth Centuries

HERBERT S. KLEIN

Stanford University Press
Stanford, California
1993

Stanford University Press
Stanford, California

© 1993 by the Board of Trustees of the
Leland Stanford Junior University

Printed in the United States of America

Library of Congress Cataloging-in-Publication Data

Klein, Herbert S.
  Haciendas and ayllus : rural society in the Bolivian Andes in the
eighteenth and nineteenth centuries / Herbert S. Klein.
      p.   cm.
  Includes bibliographical references (p.   ) and index.
  ISBN 0-8047-2057-6 (cloth : alk. paper)
  1. Land tenure—Bolivia—La Paz (Dept.)—History—18th century.
  2. Land tenure—Bolivia—La Paz (Dept.)—History—19th century.
  3. Haciendas—Bolivia—La Paz (Dept.)—History—18th century.
  4. Haciendas—Bolivia—La Paz (Dept.)—History—19th century.
  5. Landowners—Bolivia—La Paz (Dept.)—History—18th century.
  6. Landowners—Bolivia—La Paz (Dept.)—History—19th century.
  7. Indians of South America—Bolivia—La Paz (Dept.)—Land tenure—
History—18th century.   8. Indians of South America—Bolivia—La
Paz (Dept.)—Land tenure—History—19th century.   I. Title.
  HD489.L3K57 1993
  305.5'0984'12—dc20
  92-19596 CIP

To Maria Lígia Coelho Prado

Preface

THIS STUDY is based primarily on two principal sources: the local notarial records of the province of La Paz; and the *revisitas* or *padrones de indios*, which were the special Indian tribute censuses carried out by the colonial and republican governments of Bolivia with some regularity from early in the colonial period until the end of the nineteenth century. Unfortunately, in numerous periods of research in the archives of Bolivia, Argentina, and Spain, I have encountered none of the private correspondence or account books (*libros de caja*) of individual hacendados, nor the financial accounts of the *comunidades* (*caja de comunidad*), which are cited in the notarial records and government documents. (The only known remaining papers of this kind are in private hands. I have had access to some of these, which I cite later in the work.) The nature of the surviving records has thus forced me to stress the general patterns and larger structural forces, rather than provide a detailed accounting of the economies of individual units of production. While this focus on macrostructural change is common to some of the literature on the rural economy of Latin America, the stress on the demographic structure of the work force is not. Very few hacienda studies have examined the demographic characteristics of the labor force itself, and there is a dearth of studies on the Indian communities and their demographic makeup. For this reason, I believe that the general conclusions reached in this study will provide not only a basic framework in which any possible microanalytical studies of the La Paz haciendas and *comunidades* can be placed, but a model for studies on the peasant populations of haciendas and Indian communities in other regions of Latin America in the premodern period.

It has taken me some two decades of archival research and computer-assisted analysis to make sense of these complex accounts. In the process, I wrote the following series of articles, the first appearing in 1980 and the last published in 1990: "Peasant Response to the Market and the Land Question in 18th and 19th Century Bolivia," *Nova Americana* (Turin, Italy), V (1983); "Accumulation and Inheritance among the Landed Elite of Bolivia: The Case of Don Tadeo Diez de Medina," *Jahrbuch für Geschichte von Staat, Wirtschaft und Gesellschaft Lateinamerikas* (Cologne), 22 (1985), pp. 199–226; "The Structure of the Hacendado Class in late Eighteenth Century Alto Peru: The Intendencia de La Paz," *Hispanic American Historical Review*, 60, no. 2 (May 1980), pp. 191–212; and "The Distribution of Landed Wealth in Late 19th Century Bolivia: The Hacendados of the Department of La Paz in 1881–1882," in Mats Lundhal and Thommy Svensson, eds., *Agrarian Society in History: Essays in Honor of Magnus Mörner* (London, 1990), pp. 71–88. These essays were in almost every case preliminary statements of the themes treated here, and in writing this book I have had to reformulate all of them. This has involved both a reanalysis of the original data and a redefinition of many of the conclusions. Thus readers of my earlier work will find that many of my preliminary hypotheses have been refined and put into a new framework.

Given the many years of archival research, data coding, and reflection that this project required, I have an unusually long list of persons and institutions to thank for making this study possible. Nicolás Sánchez-Albornoz, Silvia Rivera, Erwin Greishaber, Ana Maria Lema, Daniel Santamaria, Tristan Platt, Eric Langer, Brooke Larson, Ricardo Godoy, Thierry Saignes, Nathan Wachtel, and Thérèse Bouysse-Cassagne kindly and patiently spent many hours discussing their own research findings with me and often permitted me to read their unpublished manuscripts and documentary collections. I am especially indebted to the late Germán Colmenares for his instruction in colonial legal history when we shared drinks together in the bars of Sevilla. Xavier Albó has always served as my mentor in Bolivia and was instrumental in obtaining access for me to the Cathedral Church archives, whose director, Monsignor Alberto Aramayo, eventually gave his full support to my work. Private archival documents were generously made available to me by María Luisa Soux Muñoz Reyes from her family collection, and Philip Parkerson and Alberto Crespo provided me with partial access to the rich documents on Bolivian economic history in the still closed Tejada Sorzano collection. Like any researcher, foreign or national, who has worked in the Archivo Nacional in Sucre, I am under special obligation for the many acts of kindness shown to me by Don Gunnar Mendoza, its indefatigable director. In the newly created Archivo de La Paz, Roberto Choque and Mary Money were extremely helpful in guiding me through the notarial documents and *padron de indios* collection (the latter of which Choque has ably cataloged), as was Florencia Romano, who aided my work when she directed this center. My former Bolivian students Antonio Mitre, Clara Lopez, Manuel Contreras, and Ana Maria Echalar have made my innumerable stays in Bolivia a worthwhile experience and have been crucial in orienting me to new developments in the political, economic, and social evolution in the country. I also am indebted to Eric Van Young, Stuart Schwartz, and Stephen Haber for constantly sharing with me their comparative knowledge of the economic and social history of Latin America.

In the tedious copying of the censuses and in their coding, I have been assisted by a loyal band of students and friends. At various times Clara Lopez, Antonio Mitre, Juan Herbert Jauregui, Lilliana Lewinski, Alicia Crespo Parkerson, and Eileen Keremitsis joined me in the archives. My Peruvian students Maria Emma Mannarelli, Marcos Cueto, and Gerardo Renique aided in the complex task of coding of the *padrones*, as did Gail Triner and Daniel C. Klein.

Parts of the manuscript were critically read for me by Stanley Engerman, Karen Spalding, and the anonymous reader for Stanford University Press, all of whom provided helpful suggestions. I would also like to thank the American Philosophical Society, the Social Science Research Council, the National Science Foundation, and Columbia University for the grants which made research in three countries possible.

H.S.K.

Contents

Introduction   1

1. The Hacendado Class in the Late
   Eighteenth Century   6

2. Commerce and Landed Wealth: The Life
   of Don Tadeo Diez de Medina   34

3. The Structure of the Indian Communities
   in the Late Eighteenth Century   56

4. The Mining Crisis and the Peasant Populations
   of Chulumani and Pacajes, 1786–1838   84

5. Peasant Response to the Market and the
   Land Question in the Nineteenth Century   112

6. The Hacendado Class in the Late
   Nineteenth Century   133

Conclusion   160

Appendix A   169   Appendix B   179   Appendix C   183
Notes   187   Bibliography   217   Index   225

Tables and Figures

TABLES

1.1. The Indian Population of the Audiencia of Charcas (Upper Peru) According to the Last Colonial Revisitas   8

1.2. Haciendas and Yanaconas in the Intendencia of La Paz, 1786–97   18

1.3. Size Distribution of Haciendas by District, Ranked According to Size of Yanacona Population, Intendencia of La Paz, 1786–97   19

1.4. Distribution of Haciendas in the Intendencia of La Paz, 1786–97   20

1.5. Distribution of Hacendados by Size of Yanacona Population, Intendencia of La Paz, 1786–97   21

1.6. The Top Ten Percent of Hacendados of the Intendencia of La Paz, 1786–97   24

1.7. Location of Haciendas of Multiple-District Hacendados   26

1.8. Mean Ratio of Tributarios to Total Yanacona Population on the Haciendas of the Intendencia of La Paz, 1786–97   27

1.9. Characteristics of the Hacendado Class in the Intendencia of La Paz, 1786–97   28

2.1. The Joint Estate of Don Tadeo Diez de Medina and Doña Antonia Solis at the Time of Its Liquidation in 1789   46

3.1. Average Indian Population by Property Type in Chulumani in 1786   64

3.2. Average Indian Population by Property Type in Pacajes in 1786   65

3.3. The Economically Active Indian Population in Chulumani in 1786   66

3.4. The Economically Active Indian Population in Pacajes in 1786   66

3.5. Sex Ratios of the Indians in Chulumani in 1786   68

3.6. Sex Ratios of the Indians in Pacajes in 1786   68

3.7. The Children-to-Women Ratios of the Indians in Chulumani in 1786   70

3.8. The Children-to-Women Ratios of the Indians in Pacajes in 1786   70

3.9. The Indian Population of Chulumani in 1786, by Sex and Age   73

3.10. The Indian Population of Pacajes in 1786, by Sex and Age   73

3.11. Characteristics of the Hacendados Who Owned Land in Chulumani in 1786   75

3.12. Yanaconas, Tributarios, and the Adult Male Economically Active Population on the Haciendas of Chulumani and Pacajes in 1786   77

3.13. Coca Production in the Yungas in 1796   78

3.14. Demographic Characteristics of the Hacienda and Ayllu Populations of the Major Districts of the Province of La Paz in 1786   80

3.15. The Tribute Tax Rate Charged Against Originarios in the Major Districts of the Province of La Paz, Late Eighteenth and Early Nineteenth Centuries   82

4.1. Estimated Capital Outflows of the Bolivian Economy, 1825–45   87

4.2. Total Indian Population in the Pueblos of Chulumani, 1786–1838   91

4.3. Population Change by Category of Indians in Chulumani, 1786–1838   91

4.4. Population Growth Rates by Category of Indians in Chulumani, 1786–1838   91

4.5. Changes in the Haciendas of Chulumani, 1786–1838   93

4.6. Multiple Ownership Among Hacendados of Chulumani, 1786–1838   94

4.7. Number of Haciendas and Average Yanacona Population per Hacienda by Pueblo, Chulumani, 1786–1838   96

4.8. Total Forastero Population by Pueblo, Chulumani, 1786–1838   97

4.9. Total Ayllu Population by Pueblo, Chulumani, 1786–1838   98

4.10. Basic Indicators of Population Structure in Chulumani, by Tributary Category, 1786–1838   101

4.11. The Indian Tributary Population in Pacajes, by Pueblo, 1786–1838   103

4.12. Population Change by Category of Indians in Pacajes, 1786–1838   104

4.13. Population Growth Rates by Category of Indians in Pacajes, 1786–1838   104

4.14. Average Tributario and Average Total Population per Unit in Pacajes, 1786–1838   105

4.15. Basic Indicators of Population Structure in Pacajes, by Tributary Category, 1786–1838   107

4.16. Yanaconas as a Percentage of Total Population by Pueblo, Pacajes, 1786–1838   108

4.17. Forasteros as a Percentage of Total Ayllu Population by Pueblo, Pacajes, 1786–1838   109

5.1. Estimates of Tribute as a Percent of Total Government Revenues, 1827–80   114

5.2. The Change in the Number of Ayllus and Haciendas in the Department of La Paz, 1846 and 1941   119

5.3. Tributary Population of the Department of La Paz by Category, 1786–1877   122

5.4. Average Number of Male Tributarios (Originarios and Forasteros) per Ayllu, Department of La Paz, 1786–1877   123

5.5. Average Number of Male Yanaconas per Hacienda, Department of La Paz, 1786–1877   124

5.6. Ratio of Forasteros to Originarios in the Department of La Paz, 1786–1877   125

5.7. Annual Growth Rates of the Tributary Population in the Department of La Paz, 1786–1877   125

6.1. Value of Haciendas in the Department of La Paz by Province, 1881–82   137

6.2. Distribution of Estate Values in the Department of La Paz by Province, 1881–82   138

6.3. The Relative Importance of the Wealthiest Estates (≥ 10,000 Bs.) in the Department of La Paz, by Province, 1881–82   140

6.4. Rural Land Sales and Rentals in the Department of La Paz, 1888 and 1889   142

6.5. Minga Wages for Coca Production on the Hacienda of Chimasi, 1803–4   146

6.6. The Richest Five Percent of Hacendados in the Department of La Paz, 1881–82   150–52

6.7. Value and Number of Estates Owned by Each Hacendado in the Seven Provinces of the Department of La Paz Combined   152

6.8. Number of Provinces in Which Multiple Estate Owners Held Estates, Department of La Paz, 1881–82   153

6.9. Estate Ownership by Sex and Institution   154

6.10. Sale of Communal Indian Plots (Sayañas) in the Department of La Paz, 1881–1920   157

6.11. Breakdown of Farm Area and Cultivated Fields by Type of Ownership, Department of La Paz, 1950   158

APPENDIX TABLES

A1. The Value of Rural Properties Owned by Don Tadeo Diez de Medina   170

A2. The Value of Urban Properties Owned by Don Tadeo Diez de Medina   171

A3. Assessments of Some Rural Properties of Don Tadeo Diez de Medina   172–73

A4. Output of the Coca Haciendas of Don Tadeo Diez de Medina, 1782–92   174

A5. Prices of Coca Received by Don Tadeo Diez de Medina, 1782–92   175

A6. Output of the Foodstuffs Haciendas of Don Tadeo Diez de Medina, 1782–92   176–77

A7. Selected Yungas Haciendas, Their Values and Mortgages   178

B1. Complete Population Statistics on Chulumani, 1786–1838   180

B2. Complete Population Statistics on Pacajes, 1786–1838   181

C1. Adult Male Tributarios of All Categories in the Department of La Paz, 1852–77   184

C2. The Male Tributary Population of Bolivia, 1838   184

C3. The Male Tributary Population of Bolivia, 1858   185

C4. The Male Tributary Population of Bolivia, 1877   185

FIGURES

2.1. The Family of Don Tadeo Diez de Medina   40

4.1. Bolivian Silver Production, 1754–1854   86

Haciendas and *Ayllus*

Introduction

THE EXISTENCE OF a Spanish landed elite and an Indian peasant mass was the distinguishing feature of most of the Amerindian societies of the Western Hemisphere until the mid-twentieth century. In Mexico, Guatemala, Ecuador, Peru, and Bolivia, the dominant theme in rural life from the period of the conquest until well into the twentieth century was the interaction of these two classes and the relationship between the hacienda and the self-governing Indian landed communities. Yet for all the importance of these classes and institutions, relatively little detailed information exists on this subject. This has not prevented scholars from proposing several stereotypical models that have gained wide currency in the literature until quite recently. In the nineteenth century, liberal reformers posited an anticapitalist corporate Indian mentality and sought to transform the Indians into a European-style landed peasantry. Most recently *indigenista* and Marxist reformers have suggested a socialist or cooperative model, in which an anticapitalist mentality is also presumed.

The large landed estate has found both its supporters and its detractors from early in the nineteenth century. While there was initially some sympathy for this institution, in our century historians have attacked these privately held estates and suggested the ideal of a feudal, anticapitalist, and all powerful hacienda "world," using the western European feudal manor as a model. It was also assumed that these "feudal" estates dominated Spanish American rural life from the early colonial period through to the twentieth century.[1] Recently various Marxian schools of his-

torical analysis have accepted the idea of a market-oriented hacienda economy, but have stressed a precapitalist or "feudal"
mentality of the landed class.[2] Common to most of these theo-
ries has been the idea of an immobile and passive peasantry constantly exploited and capable of defending its interests only
through spasmodic acts of rebellion or through passive forms of
resistance.

But these various models of non-market-oriented and immobile landed elites or passive and exploited Indian peasantries
have begun to be challenged through detailed regional studies
of rural society. Many areas of Mexico have been shown to have
maintained powerful free Indian communities until the end of
the colonial period and even well beyond. The idea of a non-
market- and non-profit-oriented hacienda owned by a socially
and economically immobile hacienda class has also come under
serious challenge.[3] Others have suggested a positive Indian response to the arrival of the market economy and a powerful and
active legal role of the communities and their leaders in the defense of their rights and privileges.[4] Even the belief that hacienda labor systems were organized exclusively in a nonmarket
fashion and were based principally on force has recently been
questioned.[5]

In the case of Bolivia, ideas about both the nature of the hacienda and the relative importance and continuity of the free
Indian communities (or *ayllus*) are coming under increasing
scrutiny.[6] Careful reconstruction of Andean rural history by a
dynamic group of Bolivian, European, and North American
scholars in the last decade has completely revised our under-
standing of rural society, in terms both of the Indian communities and, to a lesser extent, of the haciendas. Highland Bolivian communities not only survived the initial shock of conquest
but were able to dominate rural society into the late nineteenth
century. Haciendas proved to be responsive to market incentives, and even the landless labor force is seen to have evolved in
a largely market-oriented manner. All this new research has un-
dermined the long-held belief that the rural world was a change-
less one and that the Indian peasants were a passive and down-

trodden mass held in subjugation by a feudal Spanish elite until the social revolutions of the twentieth century.[7]

It was in the context of this ongoing reevaluation of Andean rural society that I decided to explore in detail the workings of the haciendas and *ayllus* in the province of La Paz in the eighteenth and nineteenth centuries. I selected La Paz, the ecologically complex agricultural region just south of Lake Titicaca, because it was the most densely populated and richest agricultural zone in Bolivia and the southern Andean highlands during those centuries. Its 139,000 square kilometers (8 percent of the total area of Bolivia) encompassed a native Indian peasant population of some 230,000 in the 1780's and accounted for just under half of all the Amerindian peasants of the region of Upper Peru (Audiencia of Charcas), which in turn would become the Republic of Bolivia. By the time of the first national census in 1900, this Indian peasant population had grown to 430,000 and represented a slightly smaller percentage of the Bolivian peasant population.[8] This was a region whose principal center of gravity was the high plateau flatlands to the east and south of Lake Titicaca. At 10,000 to 14,000 feet above sea level, the region near the lake was an excellent zone for high Andean agricultural production of traditional root crops (potatoes, quinoa, etc.) and meat, wool, and cheese from sheep, llamas, alpacas, and vicuñas. It was one of the richest agricultural zones in the South American empire of Spain and was the home region of the Aymara Indians.

Intimately associated with this highland zone (known as the *altiplano*) were eastern Andean escarpment valleys going from the semitropical climates at 5,000 to 10,000 feet above sea level to the totally tropical zones below 5,000 feet. In these valleys crops that could not be produced in the highlands were grown. This included corn, wheat, barley, and other mediterranean grains in the upper valleys, as well as coca, citrus fruits, and innumerable spices and other tropical products in the lower ones.

From well before the Spanish Conquest all these zones were intimately connected, with highland populations sending colonists to work the lower valleys in collaboration with the local populations. Thus a complex network of multi-ecological agri-

cultural interchange existed well before the arrival of the Spaniards and continued in place, though in a far more attenuated
manner, even until the twentieth century. While the market appeared in the colonial period to move goods between zones,
many highland communities continued to own upper valley and
tropical valley estates, preferring ownership and complex exchange mechanisms to the cash nexus to move goods between
zones and to complement the rigidly limited highland output.

In the center of this vast, complex, and highly integrated agricultural zone stood the city of La Paz. It emerged as the largest
city of Upper Peru by the late eighteenth century, and would become the effective capital of the country by the end of the nineteenth century, with its population going from 40,000 to 60,000
during this same period. This city was the commercial and political capital of the republic, and the construction of an international rail network between the Pacific and Atlantic coasts in
the late nineteenth and early twentieth centuries guaranteed its
premier role, which it has retained to the present day. It was the
elite of this city that owned the haciendas of the rural hinterland, and it was these white and *cholo* (white and Indian mixture) landlords who slowly spread their domination over the
rural peasant masses. The Indians in turn resisted this domination in their *ayllus* and multi-*ayllu* communities, which fought
until the twentieth century to maintain their control over the
land and economy of rural *paceña* society. In this long and complex struggle, the nature of the free communities and of the haciendas which opposed them, and the changes in both over
time, are the central themes of this work.

In this complex geographic setting, I am concerned with describing the origins, size, structure, distribution, relative wealth,
control over resources, and patterns of mobility of the hacienda
class. This will be studied both from the perspective of the class
as a whole and from the viewpoint of one of its most powerful
members in the late colonial period, Don Tadeo Diez de Medina.
This analysis of the world of the hacienda will be matched by a
study of the changing size and characteristics of the free Indian
communities in both the poorest and the wealthiest districts of

the province (Pacajes and Chulumani, respectively), which included both highland and valley zones. An analysis of the response of these communities to economic contraction in the national market in the first third of the nineteenth century will be followed by a study of their response to booming markets in the last two-thirds of that century. Finally, the major state attack on communal property at the end of the nineteenth century and the nature of hacienda organization that replaced an important part of it will be examined so as to define the nature of the system that emerged from the late nineteenth century and lasted until the middle decade of the twentieth century. As is obvious from any study of contemporary rural Bolivia, the history of this long and complex struggle between hacienda and *ayllu* continues to define the La Paz countryside even today, well after the revolutionary reorganization of the Land Reform of 1953 and the definitive destruction of the haciendas in the zone of La Paz.

CHAPTER ONE

The Hacendado Class in the Late Eighteenth Century

THE RURAL WORLD of eighteenth-century La Paz was defined by two basic institutions, the hacienda and the *ayllu*. To understand the first of these two crucial institutions, it is necessary to understand the makeup of the class that organized these large landed estates. In this first chapter, I will determine the numbers, distribution, relative wealth, and composition of the non-Indian *hacendados* in the province (or Intendencia as it was then called) of La Paz.

By the last two decades of the eighteenth century, the Intendencia of La Paz was organized into seven districts (or *partidas*): six core Andean areas, and a newly created seventh frontier zone of recently missionized lowland Indians.[1] Within the six Andean districts—Larecaja, Omasyuos, Sicasica, Pacajes, Chulumani, and the three rural parishes of the city of La Paz itself— there were over 200,000 Indian peasants, and they represented almost half of the Indian peasants in the region of what was then called Upper Peru or the Audiencia of Charcas (see Table 1.1).

The province was the most important center of rural Amerindian life in the Peruvian Andes, containing as it did the largest number of Indian peasants in any province of Upper or Lower Peru at this time.[2] Some of its Indians were also among the wealthiest in both Perus, and it thus produced the largest amount of tribute of any Peruvian province. It was also a major source of forced draft (or *mita*) labor for the mines of Potosí. Along with its dense population, the province was of paramount importance as the core area of Aymara civilization. While Quechua speakers were scattered throughout the pueblos of the districts of Omasuyos and Larecaja, the Indians of the province were predominantly Aymara speakers. It also contained close to half of the known Uru speakers in its lakeshore and Desaguadero River areas.[3]

In the late eighteenth century, the hacienda was still a minority institution, though a growing one. The majority of the Indian peasant population of the region was distributed among the 491 free land-owning Indian communities, or *ayllus*. The 1,099 haciendas, owned by 721 hacendados, contained only some 83,000 peasant workers, or about 40 percent of the provincial total, yet they were the dominant element in commercial agricultural production. Moreover, their numbers were growing steadily throughout the late eighteenth century.

As I noted in the Introduction, the Intendencia of La Paz incorporated all of the major ecological zones of the Andes except the Pacific coastal valleys. It was a major producer of all the traditional Andean agricultural and animal products, and formed a coherent and relatively self-contained market region, though it was also a key provisioning area for the southern Andean mines of Oruro and Potosí. The six principal districts of the province covered the region to the south and east of Lake Titicaca, in an area of some 138,000 square kilometers.[4] From north to south the Intendencia extended along the central highland plateau known as the *altiplano,* from the southern and eastern shores of Lake Titicaca to the relatively sparsely settled arid plains just north of the city of Oruro. In its eastern reaches the province included all the major settled upper- and lower-altitude semitropical and tropical valleys of the eastern Andean escarpment.

In pre-Hispanic times these districts formed a cohesive economic area producing high-altitude root crops, grains, meats, and textiles, as well as more tropical products such as citrus fruits and coca, plus temperate crops such as corn. This area had historically experienced a complex interchange of goods among the different ecological zones, with many of the *altiplano* communities maintaining colonies in the lower valleys.[5] These con-

TABLE 1.1

The Indian Population of the Audiencia of Charcas (Upper Peru) According to the Last Colonial Revisitas

Province and district	Year of census	Indian population		
		Men	Women	Total
La Paz				
La Paz[a]	1804	5,104	2,709	7,813
Larecaja	1803	26,320	16,663	42,983
Omasuyos	1803	30,244	28,135	58,379
Sicasica	1803	21,710	19,981	41,691
Chulumani	1803	13,972	11,884	25,856
Pacajes	1807	24,625	23,817	48,442
Caupolican	1803	3,432	3,136	6,568
Total		125,407	106,325	231,732
La Plata				
Llamparaes	1807	6,451	5,817	12,268
Tomina	1806	3,553	2,583	6,136
Oruro	1786	3,527	3,353	6,880
Paria	1795	13,873	13,538	27,411
Carangas	1803	6,844	7,861	14,705
Sinti	1805	5,332	4,877	10,209
Total		39,580	38,029	77,609
Cochabamba				
Cochabamba	1803	2,090	2,202	4,292
Clisa	1803	8,101	9,258	17,359
Tapacari	1803	8,092	8,728	16,820
Arque	1803	6,281	6,864	13,145
Ayopaya	1803	3,244	2,970	6,214
Sacaba	1803	706	219	925
Misque	1803	4,050	4,337	8,387
Valle Grande	1803	373	242	615
Santa Cruz	1807	1,302	1,311	2,613
Total		34,239	36,131	70,370
Potosí				
Potosí	1789	6,218	5,995	12,213
Chicas	1804	6,608	6,245	12,853
Atacama	1804	1,391	1,176	2,567
Lipez	1804	2,257	1,979	4,236
Chayanta	1805	17,812	16,340	34,152
Porco	1805	14,333	14,001	28,334
Total		48,619	45,736	94,355
Total Audiencia		247,845	226,221	474,066

SOURCE: AGN, 9-9-7-7, "Estado de la poblacion que por las ultimas Revisitas que existen. . . ," Buenos Aires, Nov. 24, 1812.

[a]The three rural parishes of the city of La Paz.

nections were modified by the Spanish conquest and by the subsequent forced community resettlements and reorganizations of the sixteenth century, but they were nevertheless still of vital importance until the end of the nineteenth century. In the colonial period the regional variation within the zone continued to provide for a very diversified agriculture. Thus Pacajes and Omasuyos along the southern and eastern shores of Lake Titicaca were classic *altiplano* centers of potatoes and quinoa, as well as of the meat, hides, and wool of llamas, alpacas, and the Spanish-introduced herds of sheep. At the other extreme was the newly created district of Chulumani, which was completely contained within the steep intermountain valleys of the eastern Andes and became the primary coca-producing zone as well as a major source of tropical fruits.

Sharing both the *altiplano* region and some of the more temperate high eastern escarpment Andean valleys were the two districts of Larecaja (close to the lake) and Sicasica (to the south). Both were producers of all the standard root products, as well as of important corn and wheat crops in their temperate valleys. These same eastern escarpment valleys were also centers of temperate fruit production, and there were even some vineyards planted in parts of Sicasica. Finally, the three rural parishes (or *parroquias*) just south of and below the city of La Paz were important centers for the growing of temperate fruits.[6]

The center of this important and representative agricultural region was the Spanish-created city of La Paz, with a population estimated at approximately 40,000 persons at the end of the eighteenth century.[7] It was the capital of the Intendencia, the home of a thriving commercial community, and the center of an important network of interregional and international trade routes. It was here that the overwhelming majority of the absentee landed elite resided, and it was from the commerce and royal treasury of this center that much of the wealth was generated for investment in the rural zones of the Intendencia. Finally, given the volume of its commerce, the wealth of its agriculture, and the size of its Indian population, the capital and its provincial hinterland were one of the wealthiest tax-producing areas in all of the Andes.[8]

Before analyzing how haciendas were distributed and how their owners exercised control over peasants, certain limitations of the data upon which this study is based should be clarified. To begin with, it is worthwhile analyzing the basic source that will be used both in this chapter and in all later sections of this book, the Indian tribute census.

The origins of the systematic royal tribute census lists called the *padron de indios*, or *revisita*, go back to the earliest times of the Spanish conquest. Justifying a special head tax on Indians as a repayment for Christianization and education, and for use of what were now its lands, the Crown demanded an annual income from all male heads of households in the Indian peasant communities. At first collected in kind and given to a representative of the Crown in the form of a Spanish *encomendero*, most tribute tax by the end of the sixteenth century was collected directly for the Crown and was paid for in specie.

By forcing the Indians in the communities to pay their tribute (*tributo*) tax in money instead of kind, the Crown was of course also forcing them into the market to obtain cash for their tax payments. Thus from the mid-sixteenth century on, the Indian communities were forced to either sell their products on the urban and Spanish markets for cash, and/or sell their labor on the Spanish-controlled labor markets. Since the *kurakas*, or Indian nobility, and the *jilakatas*, or village leaders, were made responsible by the Crown for the collection of the tribute, as well as the organization of any forced draft labor required by the government or private individuals (e.g., the *mita*, or forced labor for the mines), the entire tribute system reinforced self-government and the independent rule of the free communities. Although the head tax was made to correspond to the number of landowning heads of households in the community, the tax was in fact collected only from the leaders of the community as a corporate body.

Because of the sixteenth- and seventeenth-century demographic crisis, the number of Indians declined until the early

1700's and thus the tax base was constantly shrinking. Between Indian protests of overtaxation because of outdated lists and Crown complaints about falling incomes, the royal bureaucracy decided to collect census information on taxable Indians by carrying out a periodic census of heads of household who were present in any given year. Thus, early on, systematic censuses were collected, so that by the latter part of the eighteenth century, especially after the reform of the census in 1786, the *padrones* became modern-style censuses of all persons living in the community.

At first the Crown charged the tribute tax only on landholding heads of households (the so-called *originarios*) in the communities. But the relative delay in adjustment of the tax burden on the declining population put tremendous pressure on the landholding Indian peasants, and by the early seventeenth century many peasants were attempting to escape these onerous obligations of both taxation and mine or other forced labor. Many Indians fled to the distant lowland frontiers, and some escaped into the cities, there to form a new socially intermediate class of persons known as cholos or mestizos. But the majority of peasants attempting to escape originario burdens remained in the regions they knew and continued their traditional work roles. They did this either by leaving their home communities and residing on the communities of other Indians as landless laborers (or *forasteros*), or by going to work for the Spaniards who were organizing private agricultural estates on the empty lands left by the Indians. These Indians were called *yanaconas* in the southern Andean region of La Paz, though they were also known by the general term of *colonos* or *pongos* in other regions, in recognition of the type of labor performed in exchange for land access on the private estates (the *colonato* or *ponguaje*). This was the origin of the forasteros and the yanacona class. By 1734 the Crown found these groups important enough to include in the tribute tax collections, and henceforth they were registered in all the tribute censuses.[9] Given their lack of direct ownership of land, they were uniformly charged a flat 5 pesos (of 8 reales) per annum for their tribute.[10] This immediately relieved the pressure on the originarios in the communities, but added a new tax burden on the community itself.[11]

Although no concrete data exist on what occurred in the communities after 1734, it can be inferred from later evidence that the role of the forasteros was changed by this decree. More and more they appear as fixed to their new community, almost as much as the originarios. Soon there occurs in the colonial and republican documents distinctions between forasteros with some access to lands and forasteros with no access whatsoever, or even referred to as later arrivals. Some forasteros marry into the originario class; second sons inherit a semi-landed forastero status when land becomes too tight for originario fathers to endow all their children with land; and others assume special obligations within the community that give them more rights to land than the normal forasteros.[12] As for the yanaconas on the haciendas of non-Indians, these in turn seemed to have their taxes paid for them by the hacendados as a further inducement to settle on these estates.

Since the Crown demanded a tribute payment, or head tax, from every adult Indian male living in a free Indian community, it was necessary to maintain up-to-date tribute lists. Since only originario males aged 18–50 who resided on the free communities (or *ayllus*) were subject to this tax until late in the colonial period, most early lists simply provided the age and names of these adult male heads of households, given by the name of the *ayllu* in which they resided, and its district and pueblo location. Any Indians who resided on these estates and did not have full land rights (usually called *agregados* or forasteros) were simply ignored, as were all Indians living as landless workers on the estates of the non-Indian hacendado elite.

After the 1734 reform, both Indians working on the private estates of Spaniards and the agregados on the *ayllus* with fewer land rights, or none at all, also became subject to tribute taxation. The lists during the eighteenth century became progressively more complex and complete, by the 1770's including all female and male adults as well as their children. Variations in recording methods were finally resolved in 1784 when a formal census schedule was worked out by royal officials.[13] This new system, which went into effect in the Intendencia of La Paz with the census of 1786, required the listing of all Indians in each district, with their place of residence, their family structure, their work status, and the age of all males and of all females to 14. It also listed the names of all haciendas and their Spanish owners. Unfortunately, while most of the rules of recording were followed in the years after 1784, that of providing the full names of the hacendados was not always observed. Thus in the tables that follow, the data are of necessity taken from several different census years covering the eleven-year period from 1786 to 1797.[14]

Although this is a long period, in actual fact 74 percent of the 1,099 haciendas recorded are from the census carried out in 1786. Adding in the census of 1792 brings the total up to 92 percent. The universe of haciendas which I have created, while obviously subject to some margin of error because of the time spread, is nevertheless a reasonably accurate reflection of the population of haciendas, hacendados, and estate workers in the Intendencia of La Paz at the end of the eighteenth century. Where the time factor does have more of an impact is the relative ranking of the leading hacendados, and in the problem of fully recording their combined interdistrict holdings at any given moment in time.

Another serious deficiency with the censuses is that they provide only the name of the hacienda, its location and ownership, and the number of Indians living on it. There is no indication of the physical size, monetary worth, or crop production of the individual estates. Thus, the "wealth" distribution measures I will use are based on the number of Indian peasant workers "controlled" by the hacendado and not on the size, value, or productivity of his or her estate. The use of the number of Indians on an estate as a proxy for "wealth" and size gives a reasonable, if very rough, estimate of actual estate value in monetary terms. Since uncleared land was a relatively cheap commodity, and the investment in tools and seeds was relatively low, the most important productive element in the farm system was the labor of the Indians.

That labor was obtained through a complex combination of market and nonmarket incentives, which varied from region to region. Heavy tribute taxes collected in silver specie and corvée labor obligations (especially the *mita*, or labor draft, for the mines of Potosí) were important push factors forcing Indians off the *ayllus*.[15] Given the continuation of these push factors throughout the colonial and early republican periods, it might be argued that Chayanov's model of the special constraints of a "family labor farm system" operated to some extent in the Andean context, with the *ayllu* peasants reducing their labor input (and their participation in the Spanish market) once their needs were satisfied. Given the extensive private and communal resources available to *ayllu* members, these "family demand satisfactions" might be relatively easily met, especially as land was in this period an abundant resource.[16] For this reason, the only way to force originarios onto the market was through extralegal pressures such as the tribute tax and the forced labor drafts of the various local *repartamientos* for roads and public works and the unpaid seasonal *mita* labor for the miners in Potosí.

But there were also positive attractions offered by the latifundistas, who drew laborers to their estates by providing them with substantial quantities of usufruct estate lands in return for their labor on the demesne; by providing wages for special work tasks; by paying their tribute obligations, and finally by guaranteeing them exemption from *mita* mine labor.[17] Variable qualities of usufruct estate land given to the Indians resulted in varying work obligations for them on the parcels of the hacendado (the system being known in the period as the *colonato*), though the average obligations per individual tended to be three days per week. In some cases households offered only the labor of their heads, while in others both spouses worked.[18] As studies in later periods have made clear, the actual amount of land worked on behalf of the hacendado—though obviously the best land on the estate—represented only a minority of the fields cultivated on any given hacienda. The commercial crops were the basic product of the demesne, but these could be and often were grown on the parcels of these colonos, peones, or yanaconas, as these non-landowning Indians were variously called.[19]

Almost all estates, whether in the coca-growing valleys of Chulumani known as the Yungas or in the highland plains known as the *puna*, used both this resident labor as well as hired daily or even weekly labor. For example, in the account books for a wheat farm (called Sayani) and a sheep ranch (named Tahana) in the village of Caracato of the district of Sicasica, it was reported in 1799 that to sow the wheat it was necessary to pay four day laborers (*jornaleros*) and eight Indians from off the estate a daily wage of two reales "for lack of sufficient resident workers."[20] These jornaleros—or *mingas* as they were called in the Yungas—received a daily wage in money for work performed. They sometimes came from outside the zone, as was typical on the coca estates, or from neighboring haciendas where they were resident yanaconas but often went out to work as wage laborers for short periods of time.[21] Though the use of these wage laborers is surprisingly widespread, they were primarily employed as an addition to the resident population and only for special labor-intensive occasions, such as harvesting and clearing new lands.[22]

Aside from land or wages, estate workers were also granted a daily ration of food and coca when they worked on the lands of the hacendado.[23] For daily wage workers the owners paid wages in coin, but discounted the costs of all food supplied to the workers or their families; these foods, which were usually imported from other zones, were charged to the workers at an estimated 50-percent markup beyond the original purchase price and transportation costs.[24] This pattern of exploitation would seem propitious for creating a system of debt peonage, but the resulting debts incurred by estate colonos do not seem to have been large enough to have created a major debt peonage group on the estates.[25] Similar findings of both the low number of debtors (on average less than half of the resident labor force) and the relatively low level of debt in relationship to the earning capacity of estate workers was found in a sample of Guadalajara (Mexico) hacienda records for the eighteenth century.[26] Mexican hacendados also paid their workers in combinations of cash and food, with maize being the primary foodstuff, and supplied small advances of both cash and goods as well. But in all studies of the principal agricultural hacienda zones of central and southern Mexico in the eighteenth century, the weight of evidence shows that credit was advanced mainly to attract workers and that debt was not a major influence in hacendado-peon relations.[27] In neither the southern Andes nor central and southern Mexico was debt peonage a significant institution, nor did it affect labor mobility.

The actual organization of life for the colonos on the estate lands was not that different from what the Indians had known on their *ayllus*. They were organized into household groups and were represented by their own leaders, called here as well as in the villages by the term *jilakatas*, the traditional pre-Colombian name for village elders. Whereas the *jilakatas* on the *ayllus* were elected by the members of the community, on the estates it would appear that the hacendado had more choice in their selection. In contrast to the free communities, too, the non-Indian overseer, or *mayordomo*, and the owner determined land rights and land distribution, rather than *ayllu* elders. But all work negotiations and all representation to superior authority was done through the *jilakatas*. On some estates in the late nineteenth century, *jilakatas* even acted as *mayordomos*. It was also these elders who organized the special task work required by the hacendado above and beyond his usual claims, which often involved the hacendado paying resident colonos both extra wages and rentals for some of their equipment.[28]

In terms of actual land usage, the colonos differed little from the originarios on the *ayllus*. Each family had its own residence and corral for immediate family animals, as well as its fixed *sayaña*, or cultivable field, directly attached to the household. They also had individual claims on numerous plots (*qallpas*) scattered throughout the cultivable/fallow zones of the hacienda (the so-called *aynuqas* fields where use by person and crop were determined by the community elders on the *ayllu* and by the hacendado and the community elders on the haciendas). Finally, they shared common pasture lands. The major difference from the community lands aside from the decision-making authority over land access was that the hacendado also shared these fallow/cultivable plots (invariably the best lands) and also used the common pasture lands for his or her own flocks. Given this complex use of land for payment for labor, it is not surprising that the majority of the lands on the haciendas were used by the colonos.[29]

But aside from land, rations, and even wages paid for labor, the hacendados traditionally extracted personal service from their estate workers. This much-hated unpaid labor was known as *pongueaje*, and required labor in the houses of the *mayordomos* and hacendados.[30] It also included the obligation to provide free transport of the owner's crops to market. Finally, when working on the demesne lands, the resident estate Indians also provided their own tools to work the owner's lands.

Given the cheapness of land, the need for intensive labor, and the lack of investment in tools and equipment, the production on the estates was based primarily on the number of workers employed and the relative quality of the soil and the climate. Together with the high incidence of absenteeism and the relative freedom of colonos to migrate, the failure of the individual farm unit to maintain production always resulted in a loss of workers, as these latter sought better opportunities in either the newer frontier zones, more lucrative haciendas, or their traditional villages.[31] Moreover, the continued existence on these estates of male tributaries required the payment of substantial taxes on the part of the hacendados. Thus there were few if any cases of nonproductive estates retaining large numbers of yanacona Indians. The number of workers employed is therefore as reasonable a proxy for wealth as can be obtained.[32]

In examining the universe of the La Paz haciendas in terms of their spatial distribution, there appear to be obvious zones of concentration. The distribution of the haciendas in the province was clearly related to the quality of soil and the potential marketability of crops (see Table 1.2). Thus Chulumani with its fer-

TABLE 1.2
Haciendas and Yanaconas in the Intendencia of La Paz, 1786–97

Districts	Census date	No. of haciendas	No. of yanaconas	Total Indian population
Omasuyos	1786	169	20,487	43,075
Chulumani	1786	336	18,786	31,004
Sicasica	1792	206	17,190	41,542
Larecaja	1786	270	14,669	39,946
Pacajes	1796	90	8,875	44,777
La Paz[a]	1786/92	28	2,458	7,025
Total		1,099	82,465	207,369

SOURCES: AGN (Buenos Aires), Sala XIII, in the following locations: Chulumani (1786) in 13-17-6-5, libro 2; Omasuyos (1786) in 13-17-5-4, libros 1,2,3; Pacajes (1796) in 13-17-8-3, libro 1, and 13-17-8-4; Larecaja (1786) in 13-17-6-3, libros 1,2; 13-17-6-2, libro 2; and 13-17-7-1, libro 1; Sicasica (1792) in 13-17-7-2, libros 1,2; Parroquias de La Paz (1786) in 13-17-6-3, libro 1 for names of hacendados and for population; (1792) 13-17-7-3, libro 1.
[a]The three rural parishes of the city of La Paz.

tile valleys was unusually well-suited for the production of high-quality coca leaf and was therefore a major zone of hacendado activity. Most of the lands in these very steep semitropical valleys were newly developed, terraced estates that had been open or vacant lands prior to the arrival of the Spanish hacendados. They thus provided an area for attractive investment without conflicting with traditional Indian community land claims. The proximity of the valleys to the city of La Paz also gave rise to a pattern of absentee landownership, for Chulumani landowners tended to reside in the capital city.[33]

While no other district attained the high level of workers concentrated on haciendas achieved by Chulumani (63 percent), three other districts had approximately half of their Indian peasants living on haciendas. Omasuyos, though in the *altiplano*, contained much productive lakeshore land, and Larecaja and Sicasica had a whole series of semitropical valleys along the eastern escarpment of the Andes. Where the hacienda was least in evidence was in the most traditional and densely populated of all the districts, that of Pacajes in the heartland of the Aymara nation. Here the *ayllus* remained dominant and the relatively poor soil made the region unattractive for hacendados interested in creating new farm units. Whatever the district, however, it is important to realize that the free community was still predominant within the entire province at the end of the colonial period. In fact, this domination would last in most regions until the end of the nineteenth century.

The size distribution of haciendas by district also showed some interesting variations by resident population size (see Table 1.3). Because of physical constraints of land availability, Chulumani had 84 percent of the province's small estates (those with 1–9 yanaconas). Yet it was still able to show a median estate population of 20–49 yanaconas—the same as that of the province as a whole—because of its substantial number of large haciendas. For the other districts, land was not as restricted and therefore there was a more direct relation between relative wealth and size of work force. Omasuyos had the largest estates, with the category of 100–199 Indians being both its median and modal size. The other districts essentially fell between these two in terms of mean size of estates, with the median for most districts being in the 50–99 population range.

TABLE 1.3

Size Distribution of Haciendas by District, Ranked According to Size of Yanacona Population, Intendencia of La Paz, 1786–97

Hacienda size (no. of yanaconas)	No. of haciendas						
	Oma-suyos	Chulu-mani	Sicasica	Larecaja	Pacajes	La Paz[a]	Total
1–9	1	64	2	6	2	1	76
10–19	1	49	17	42	5	–	114
20–49	30	95	67	105	17	7	321
50–99	52	69	59	81	32	11	304
100–199	58	46	48	33	26	7	218
200–299	20	12	10	2	6	2	52
300–499	7	–	2	1	2	–	12
500–999	–	1	1	–	–	–	2
Total	169	336	206	270	90	28	1,099
Mean population per estate	121	56	83	54	99	88	75
(Standard deviation)	(86)	(65)	(75)	(42)	(71)	(60)	(71)

SOURCE: Same as for Table 1.2.

[a]Three rural parishes of the city of La Paz.

TABLE 1.4

Distribution of Haciendas in the Intendencia of La Paz, 1786–97

No. of haciendas per owner	No. of owners	Total yana- conas	Total male tribu- tarios
1	555	35,233	7,646
2	88	14,771	3,070
3	31	7,334	1,600
4	19	5,446	1,109
5	10	4,892	1,107
6	6	3,290	632
7	6	3,838	784
8	2	1,072	239
10	1	1,086	227
11	1	1,423	276
12	1	1,324	251
22	1	2,756	551
Total	721	82,465	17,492
Mean population per hacendado		114	24
(Standard deviation)		(182)	(38)

SOURCE: Same as for Table 1.2.

Just as there was a geographic concentration of the haciendas in the province at the end of the eighteenth century, similarly within the hacendado class there were also well-defined patterns of wealth concentration. The hacendado class as such was small, probably accounting for no more than 6 percent of the total number of whites in the province.[34] But even within the ranks of this small class, wealth was not evenly distributed. Looking at the 721 individual hacendados in the province in this period, we find that the overwhelming majority owned just one estate (see Table 1.4). Moreover, this majority on average held fewer yanaconas per estate than the hacendados who held more than one hacienda, and they thus controlled far fewer workers than their numbers would seem to warrant. Single estate owners made up more than three quarters of the hacendado class, but they controlled only 43 percent of the yanaconas living on haciendas. Amounting to only 23 percent of the 721 hacendados, multiple estate owners held 50 percent of the estates and 57 percent of the yanaconas.

This skewed distribution becomes even more pronounced

when the owners are viewed not in terms of the number of estates they controlled, but in terms of the number of their yanaconas. When the hacendados are grouped according to the total number of Indians on their properties (see Table 1.5), the bias in the distribution becomes even more clearly delineated. Thus, while those who controlled fewer than 100 Indians made up 65 percent of the total number of hacendados, they possessed only 23 percent of the Indians working on haciendas in the province. Even considering the poorest 80 percent of the hacendados, the ratio of control only rises to approximately a fourth of the yanacona population.

Thus the hacendado class was not an undifferentiated elite, but exhibited important variations. It contained a complex layering of both local resident and absentee landlords, as well as small single-hacendado farmers with relatively few Indians along with multiple owners whose holdings spread over vast stretches of the province.

That size and number of estates were the distinguishing features in terms of stratification are evident when examining the very elite of the hacendado class, or those who made up the top

TABLE 1.5
Distribution of Hacendados by Size of Yanacona Population,
Intendencia of La Paz, 1786–97

Yanaconas per hacendado	No. of hacen- dados	No. of haci- endas	No. of yana- conas	No. of tribu- tarios
1–9	59	60	304	111
10–19	68	69	989	290
20–49	186	198	6,181	1,407
50–99	161	182	11,519	2,363
100–199	142	224	19,964	4,431
200–299	49	105	11,692	2,355
300–499	38	126	14,995	3,061
500–999	13	73	9,157	1,932
1,000+	5	62	7,664	1,542
Total	721	1,099	82,465	17,492
Mean per hacendado		1.5	114	24
(Standard deviation)		(1.5)	(182)	(38)

SOURCE: Same as for Table 1.2.

10 percent of the landowning group. Unlike the majority of hacendados, these powerful landowners were predominantly multiple estate owners. Of the 73 hacendados who made up this elite, 61 held more than one estate, and the average was four estates per person (see Table 1.6). Moreover, this elite was a powerful one since it controlled fully 42 percent of all Indians on haciendas. In a broader comparative perspective, it would appear that this distribution of wealth among elite landowners was similar to other comparable commercial agricultural areas in eighteenth-century America. For the Southern United States in 1790, for example, the top 5 percent of the planters controlled 27.8 percent of the slave labor force in the five major slave states of the U.S. South.[35] The 37 largest hacendados who made up the top 5 percent of the La Paz hacendado class controlled 31.3 percent of the landless estate workers in the province. When the entire class of slave owners and hacienda owners are compared, there is virtually no difference between the two groups in terms of wealth concentration, since the GINI coefficients which measure these disparities were virtually the same in both cases.[36]

The pattern of wealth concentration in the La Paz districts was thus similar to the patterns to be found in the most advanced commercial agricultural zones in the Americas, which suggests that access to land and wealth among the non-Indian minority was as open as such a capitalist system permitted. This in turn challenges the generally held belief that Bolivia was and remained a rigidly stratified "traditional," almost caste-like society—especially in terms of land ownership—until well into the twentieth century. Just as recent research has tended to show a much more stratified pattern of wealth distribution among Indians than previously assumed, so too it would appear on the basis of this evidence that there was also much more differentiation among the landed whites and cholos than previously supposed. This finding, together with evidence that will be examined in later chapters about land sales and the changing size of the Indian labor force on the estates over time, supports the idea that the landed elite of La Paz was an open one greatly influenced by changing market conditions.

In examining the various levels of wealth among the hacendados, it is evident that the upper elite could more readily afford to practice Andean systems of multi-ecological farming. These wealthy landowners not only held more yanaconas per estate but also owned more estates per capita, and were also far more likely than the middling and poorer hacendados to hold estates in more than one district of the province. The very fact that they held estates far apart meant that most of these multiple-district landowners were absentee landlords, the overwhelming majority of whom lived in La Paz. These individuals clearly had the resources to diversify their holdings and, in imitation of the more advanced *ayllus*, to vary their crops with a mix of products from sharply different ecological zones. Of the 65 hacendados who held land in more than one district, some 30 were on the list of the top 10 percent of the hacendados in the province, and they controlled 58 percent of the estates in this category. Among these interdistrict owners, there was the same tendency toward concentration as noted in the province as a whole. Here the lowest category of multiple-estate-owners—those owning two estates—made up a third of the 65 hacendados but only controlled 16 percent of the Indian labor force on the estates.

Chulumani was the dominant zone of investment for those holding multiple estates (see Table 1.7). The Rio Abajo zone of the three parishes close to the city of La Paz was also a prime zone of investment for major landholders, since over half of the haciendas here were held by those who owned land elsewhere. This was a region of fruit orchards and vacation homes at a much lower altitude than La Paz, which made it especially attractive to the *paceño* elite. The *altiplano* province of Omasuyos, not surprisingly, was the second most preferred zone for multiple-district landowners. Containing the best lands along the southern shores of Lake Titicaca, it was the premier region for highland agricultural products. Equally important, it was close to the markets of the capital by easy transport. It was here that the La Paz latifundistas held most of their secondary farms producing traditional root crops, and here that they grazed their animals, especially their sheep herds.

TABLE 1.6
The Top Ten Percent of the Hacendados of the Intendencia of La Paz, 1786–97

(n = 73)

| Name | No. of | | | | Multiple |
	Yana-conas	Tribu-tarios	Estates	Sex	district holdings
Mon. del Purissimo Concepción	2,756	551	22	–	Y
Valdez, Jose Josef	1,423	276	11	M	Y
Diez de Medina, Tadeo	1,324	251	12	M	Y
Penaranda, Vicente	1,086	227	10	M	Y
Roxas, Ramon	1,075	237	7	M	Y
Convento de S. Agustin (Oruro)	956	168	3	–	N
Trucios, Joaquin	909	226	7	M	Y
Montes, Dionicio	834	171	6	M	Y
Yndaburu, Juan Pedro	819	194	5	M	Y
Shrine of Las Batallas	797	173	5	M	N
Simbron, Eulalia	795	124	7	F	Y
Rojas, Vicente	709	164	5	M	Y
Salinas, Jose	650	138	6	M	Y
Comunidad de Viacha	589	138	2	–	N
Monasterio de Santa Teresa	546	109	8	–	Y
Barrios, Cristobal	526	130	8	M	Y
Loayza de la Vega, Felipe	519	88	6	M	Y
Santiago, Marquez	508	109	5	M	N
Gongora, Maria Antonia	485	87	6	F	Y
Penaranda, Micaela	478	105	2	F	Y
Unknown	478	90	1	–	N
Suazo, Manuel	475	83	2	M	N
San Felipe, ?	471	85	4	–	N
Diez de Medina, Francisco Tadeo	470	95	6	M	Y
Conv. de Padres Buena Muerte	466	76	4	–	Y
Jofre, Ipolito	461	80	2	M	N
Bilbao la Vieja, Antonio	461	105	4	M	Y
Aliaga, Nicolas	446	74	7	M	N
Sagarnaga, Manuel	443	71	5	M	Y
Comunidad de Copacabana	441	87	4	–	N
Landaeta, Arsedino (hds.)	427	76	7	M	N
Sanes, Josefa	418	79	3	F	N
Loayza, Josefa	410	144	3	F	N
Monge, Juan de Dios	409	105	5	M	Y
Saavedra, Juan Domingo	408	92	5	M	N
Salinas, de	404	49	2	–	N
Cachicatari, Roque	404	87	2	M	N
Bravo de Saravia, Maria Josefa	400	81	2	F	N
Salazar, Junta	393	78	3	F	N
Monasterio de Carmen	378	77	4	–	N
Sangines, Andres	378	111	2	M	Y

TABLE 1.6 (continued)

| Name | No. of | | | Sex | Multiple district holdings? |
	Yana-conas	Tribu-tarios	Estates		
Telleria, Juan Manuel	358	86	3	M	N
Pinedo, Ignacio	356	80	3	M	Y
Valverde, Benito	353	63	1	M	N
Paredes, Jose	349	82	2	M	Y
Santamaria, Bernardo	349	54	4	M	N
Carreno, Antonio	344	61	1	M	N
Pisarrozo, Eusebio	337	72	3	M	N
Rada, Baltazar	332	53	6	M	N
Villanueva, Angela	326	67	2	F	N
Armentia, Protacio	320	84	5	M	Y
Bilbao, Antonio	318	91	2	M	N
Calderon, Maria	317	67	4	F	Y
Iglesia local de Carabuco	313	72	1	–	N
Gutierrez, Francisco	312	56	1	M	N
Vera y Paredes, Maria	307	56	3	F	N
Duran, Francisco (hds.)	299	54	1	M	Y
Machicado, Fernando	299	47	3	M	N
Ulloa, Jose Diego	298	50	1	M	N
Duran, Mateo	289	58	2	M	Y
Nolasco Crespo, Pedro	284	56	5	M	Y
Contreras, Tomasa	283	53	1	F	N
Convento de N.S. de Mercedes	281	52	1	–	N
Ayoroa, Josefa	278	75	2	F	Y
Torre, Manuel	275	52	2	M	Y
Meza, Jose Mariano	273	45	1	M	N
Zapata, Luiz de	271	50	4	M	N
Ortiz de Toronda, Juan Antonio	269	65	4	M	Y
Comunidad de Jesus de Machaca	267	46	2	–	N
Herrera, Jose	264	69	3	M	Y
Convento de San Agustin	260	57	2	–	Y
Zavala, Miguel Ignacio	253	51	1	M	N
Ayoroa, Antonio de	250	48	2	M	N
Totals	36,509	7,463	298		
Mean	500	102	4		
(Standard deviation)	(364)	(74)	(3)		

SOURCE: Same as for Table 1.2.

NOTE: The abbreviation "hds." (for "herederos") signifies the inheritors of the estate of a deceased parent or relative.

TABLE 1.7
Location of Haciendas of Multiple-District Hacendados

District	Total haciendas in the district	No. of haciendas controlled by multiple-district hacendados	Pct. of all haciendas in the district
Chulumani	336	102	30%
Omasuyos	169	64	38
Larecaja	270	37	14
Sicasica	206	36	17
Pacajes	90	25	28
La Paz[a]	28	18	64
Total	1,099	282	26%

SOURCE: Same as for Table 1.2.
[a]Three rural parishes of the city of La Paz.

Paradoxically, there was a significant difference in the ratio of workers to total population between resident landless workers on large estates and those on smaller ones. The relative importance of tributarios in terms of the total population shows a decline of the economically active male population as size increases.[37] In the entire province of La Paz, there was a moderate negative correlation between size of estate and ratio of economically active adult males (see Table 1.8). This factor suggests the existence of more dependent persons on larger estates and thus larger family size among the landless workers. This may be due to the capacity of the larger haciendas to provide more usufruct lands for their workers, who were in turn able to maintain larger families on the basis of the lands they worked. It also supports a finding made in a study of Bolivian haciendas in the pre-reform period of the twentieth century showing that the larger estates had a surprisingly small ratio of the land devoted to the crops of the hacendado. Only about 13 percent of the cultivated land on haciendas of 1,000 hectares and above was worked by the owner, whereas 87 percent was farmed by the yanaconas.[38] Moreover, on these twentieth-century latifundias, the plots of the colonos were scattered all over the hacienda, just as were the parcels of the hacendado. The hacendados and campesinos were obviously responding to the ecological constraints that forced cultiva-

TABLE 1.8
*Mean Ratio of Tributarios to Total Yanacona Population on the Haciendas of
the Intendencia of La Paz, 1786–97*

Hacienda size (no. of yanaconas)	No. of haciendas	Mean yanacona pop. (s.d.)	Mean tributario pop. (s.d.)	Mean ratio of adult male E.A.P. (s.d.)
1–9	76	5 (2)	2 (1)	40% (20%)
10–19	114	15 (3)	4 (2)	28 (13)
20–49	321	34 (8)	8 (3)	23 (8)
50–99	304	72 (14)	15 (5)	21 (7)
100–199	218	135 (28)	29 (15)	22 (12)
200–299	52	244 (30)	50 (12)	21 (4)
300–499	12	366 (57)	69 (17)	19 (4)
500–999	2	600 (8)	128 (33)	21 (6)
Total	1,099	82,465	17,492	
Mean		75 (71)	16 (16)	23% (12%)

SOURCE: Same as for Table 1.2.
   NOTES: Figures in parentheses are standard deviations. "E.A.P." stands for the "economically active population," which is defined here as the ratio of tributarios to total
population.

tion of lands of different qualities at different altitudes to maintain food balance.[39]

While the distribution of estates and landless peasants among
the hacendados was quite unequal and showed evident biases,
can these same differences be found when the hacendado class
is broken down into its basic components and the sex, education, and institutional affiliation of the hacendados themselves
are examined? From what is known about colonial Hispanic society and the nature of its sexual division of labor, men clearly
predominated in the landholding elite. But, surprisingly, we
find that in the La Paz hacendado class, not only are women an
important minority, but their relative wealth quite closely ap-
proximated their total class representation (see Table 1.9). The
124 women hacendados accounted for 17 percent of the total
number of landlords, owned 17 percent of the estates, and controlled 15 percent of the yanaconas.[40] From these figures it could
be argued that, although women were obviously less numerous
as landowners than their participation in the total population
would warrant, there was no special discrimination against

TABLE 1.9
Characteristics of the Hacendado Class in the Intendencia of La Paz, 1786–97

Type of hacendado	No. of individuals	No. of haciendas	Total yanaconas	Total tributarios
Men	490	758	54,355	11,653
Untitled	368	523	33,853	7,453
Licenciado	54	89	7,681	1,513
Doctor	29	69	6,607	1,440
Priest	6	10	732	144
Military officer	14	32	2,692	542
Presbyter	1	1	70	16
Titled noble	2	9	979	194
Cacique	1	3	187	56
Inheritors[a]	15	22	1,554	295
Women	124	186	12,512	2,653
Untitled	122	184	12,293	2,607
Titled noble	1	1	133	34
Inheritors[a]	1	1	86	12
Corporations, etc.	82	130	13,487	2,714
Multiple owners[b]	39	39	3,099	620
Parish churches	18	18	1,543	289
Monasteries	14	57	7,040	1,404
Comunidades	11	16	1,805	401
Status unknown	25	25	2,111	472
Total	721	1,099	82,465	17,492

SOURCE: Same as for Table 1.2.
[a]All these inheritors were families of deceased individual males and females, so I have listed them under their original owners and distinguish them from the multiple-owner estates.
[b]Multiple owners for one estate.

them once they did achieve the status of landowners, since their holdings in land and labor averaged the same relative ratios as their male counterparts. This role of the woman as independent hacendado is, moreover, strongly supported by the evidence of the padrones and the notarial records. Women were listed as estate owners over many censuses and bought and sold estates in their own names. This means that they were not a type of temporary owner who occasionally held control as a result of the death of male kin. This La Paz pattern is in sharp contrast to the very temporary and quite limited role assumed by women in controlling merchant wealth in the viceregal capital of Buenos Aires during this same period.[41]

When examining the relative importance of other groups within the hacendado class, it appears that the distribution of resources is not as equalized as it was among the women. The group that clearly distinguishes itself beyond its numbers was that of males with titles, whether those titles stemmed from a university education, the church, the military, or the nobility. Though accounting for only 14 percent of the hacendados, and just 17 percent of the estates, these titled males controlled 23 percent of the total yanaconas. On average, then, a title conferred by government, church, or university clearly gave one something of an advantage in the race for wealth and power in eighteenth-century Alto Peru. In contrast, untitled males, though constituting the largest single group, accounted for 54 percent of the hacendados, held 50 percent of the estates, and just 43 percent of the yanaconas. Thus possession of titles (especially that of Doctor, which refered to individuals with degrees in canon or civil law) gave something of an advantage in controlling larger estates. But given the limited number of such titles, and their very small share of estates and Indians, it can be argued that overall there was surprisingly little differentiation of access to yanaconas based on one's sex, educational or professional title, or even institutional affiliation. This relatively open quality of access to resources among different types of owners would seem to imply that more purely economic criteria had the most dramatic effect on wealth distribution. Thus there were rich and poor women hacendados as well as rich and poor untitled males, with no particular designation inordinately favoring or hindering mobility. This suggests that the rural landed elite was a relatively open one to whites and some cholos within Bolivian society—again a finding not in accordance with the usual assumptions that a rigid status system primarily governs access to resources in a "traditional" premodern society.

Some surprises also occur when examining the other groups within the hacendado class. To begin with, there were 11 *ayllus* that owned their own haciendas. Those of Pacajes were especially noteworthy in holding haciendas in both their own local pueblos and distant semitropical lower valleys, especially in Larecaja. Apparently these 17 haciendas were the much diminished residue of a far larger collection of farms. These were held by the *cajas* (or treasuries) of the communities and were used by them as sources of revenue to pay for their tribute and to provide alternative goods—especially corn and tropical fruits—unavailable in the home communities. At one time early in the seventeenth century they numbered well over 100 units, but they were either usurped as private property by the local caciques or sold by the caciques to Spaniards.[42]

Another institutional landowner whose role is somewhat different than might have been expected is the Catholic church. Though the church, like the titled males, controlled more yanaconas than it did holdings (4 percent of the hacendados and 10 percent of the yanaconas), it was nevertheless much less important than is usually assumed. This relative weakness as a direct landowner is even more apparent when the local church lands are withdrawn. Thus, 14 local parish churches held local haciendas for their benefices, and only 13 church institutions could be considered as major, intraprovincial landholders. Of these monasteries and convents, all but two were located in La Paz, the other two being monasteries in the city of Oruro. Given the important role played by the church in providing mortgage money for the hacendado class and the penchant for the latter to create *capellanías*, or permanent rents on their lands that were destined to the church for masses or benefices of clergy, the fact that the church possessed so few estates (or 75 out of 1,099) would seem to suggest a relatively healthy economic state for the La Paz hacendados.

A final landed group of some importance worth noting were the multiple owners of single haciendas. The landed estates owned by two or more individuals were concentrated in Sicasica and to a lesser extent in Larecaja. These multiple-owner farms are difficult to analyze and would appear to represent different economic circumstances. In Chulumani, where they also appeared in other periods, they seem to represent initial investment in undeveloped lands on the part of newly expanding haciendas. Usually one bought at low cost a parcel of unterraced land on another owner's undeveloped property. Workers were then brought in to terrace the land and plant the coca bushes. Once production and profit occurred, the more dynamic partner bought out the rest of the available lands from his or her previous partners. In other cases, these lands were set aside for relatives by the major hacendado for their maintenance or as an opportunity to invest in a family enterprise.

In poorer zones such as Larecaja and Sicasica, however, it may have been that once quite wealthy estates, while retaining their borders intact, were slowly dividing up the parcels of land because of the economic failure of the initial owner. This, in fact, was the pattern that would create a whole class of small properties out of initial renters and purchasers of small parcels in the declining economy of the valley of Cochabamba.[43] The case of the canton of Ayata in the district of Larecaja in 1795 may be considered typical. In the tribute census of 1797 this zone was listed as having only 16 haciendas with 256 tributarios and a total resident yanacona population of 1,094 persons.[44] In a dispute over local support for the church, the 41 owners of the parcels of land on what in 1795 were 18 haciendas were assessed the value of their properties and the various mortgages that were loaned to them.[45] Of these estates, six had multiple owners.[46] Whereas the 12 undivided estates were worth an average of 6,475 pesos, the six divided ones averaged only 390 pesos.[47] When just the 23 secondary owners on these multiple estates are examined, the average value of their parcels goes down to 235 pesos (standard deviation of 218 pesos) per parcel.[48] Thus it was clearly only the poorest estates that were in the process of subdivision.

The fact that this type of holding accounted for only 5 percent of the farms would suggest that in most cases this was a temporary or transitional form of landholding and tended to end in the permanent division of the estates into smaller haciendas, or the complete takeover by one of the several landowners. There were also cases of haciendas without Indians, and these were often so listed in the *padrones*. These represented no more than another 2–5 percent of the farms beyond the 1,099 given, and were clearly failed haciendas which either had gone out of production or were in the process of becoming small freehold farms run by their own white or cholo owners. In most cases, the names of these haciendas either disappeared from the census in later years, or appeared with new owners and with Indian laborers.

Finally, there existed on a few haciendas, as attested by the account books, some individuals who rented small parcels. This minifundia class of renters most likely came from the class of richer peasants, *mayordomos* and even *jilakatas*.[49] How extensive this class was is difficult to estimate without a larger sample of private hacienda records. This group, along with the parcel owners on estates, may have formed the basis of a substantial small landowner class. But even as late as the first republican agricultural census of 1950, the zone of La Paz was defined by haciendas and *ayllus*, and was the department of the republic with the fewest minifundia.[50] It can be assumed, then, that in the eighteenth and nineteenth centuries the rural world of the province of La Paz was primarily defined by these two contending large landed institutions.

In terms of its organization, its multiplicity of patterns, and its changing structural features, the hacendado class of the province of La Paz thus emerges as a relatively enterprising and thriving group. Persons with interregional holdings—and therefore a mix of complementary commercial activities—were important leaders of this class. Though the size of this elite was quite restricted, even by contemporary standards, its patterns of wealth concentration point to an internal class structure similar to that in other advanced commercial agricultural zones in the Americas. Women had an important and independent participation in this class—in contradistinction to their contemporary role in commerce. The church, though an important source of credit and active in the role of its few powerful convents, was nevertheless a small sector of the hacendado class, indicating that lay society was able to maintain a thriving and independent leadership in agriculture despite its financial dependence on the Church. Though title seems to have conferred some advantage, overall status seems to have played little role in determining access to wealth. Though there is clearly unequal distribution of wealth, no one social group had any particular monopoly. All of these features point to standard economic forces having a primary function in determining the nature of the system.

To determine fully the extent of social mobility and the entrepreneurial activity of this class, however, it is necessary to go beyond this general survey to study the actual careers of leading hacendados. For this reason, the following chapter will analyze in detail the economic history of the third-largest hacendado in the entire province, Don Tadeo Diez de Medina, in an attempt to resolve questions about the origins, structure, and long-term mobility of the landed elite of Bolivia.

CHAPTER TWO

Commerce and Landed Wealth: The Life of Don Tadeo Diez de Medina

THE TRADITIONAL VIEW of rural society in colonial Latin America has stressed the socioeconomic immobility and paternalism of the white landed elite. Some authors take this position to the extreme of postulating a hacendado class with an anticommercial mentality directing an autocratic, manorial-type system. Recent research has challenged this feudal model and stressed the direct connection between the large landed estate and the market. But there still remains serious debate about the landed elite itself, and many recent commentators have returned to a modified "feudal" version, stressing the nonmarket orientation of the landed class, especially in its relationship to labor and land.[1]

Unfortunately for this debate, there are still few systematic studies of the economic activities of the landed elite. It is for this reason that I have chosen to analyze in detail the career of one of Alto Peru's most powerful hacendados in the late colonial period. In examining this one career I hope to deal with the issues of the origins of this class, its relationship to commercial capital, and its social and economic orientation. Although the wealth of this one individual makes him an atypical example of the class as a whole, in his creation of a landed empire, in the wealth he generated, and in the way he maintained and transferred this empire, he was in fact typical of the wealthiest elements in this society. An analysis of his economic career therefore provides an important vision of the limits and patterns common to the world of the landed elite in the late colonial Andes.

Don Tadeo Diez de Medina was one of the 721 *paceña* hacendados analyzed in the previous chapter. With some 15 estates and over 1,700 peons, he was the third-wealthiest hacendado in the province.[2] Like the preconquest Indian *ayllus*, he incorporated within his productive empire all the major ecological zones in a vertically integrated system, the aim of which was the supply of foodstuffs, meat, and wool to the major urban market of La Paz.[3]

Don Tadeo Diez de Medina was born in La Paz sometime in the 1730's and died sometime in the first decade of the nineteenth century.[4] His life thus spanned the last great colonial boom and a major epoch of growth of his native city of La Paz, which by the end of his life had emerged as the premier city of Bolivia. While La Paz from its foundation in 1548 had always been an important commercial and administrative center serving the most densely populated agricultural hinterland of the Andean region, it nevertheless had been eclipsed in power and importance by the southern mining cities of Potosí and Oruro. During the first century of the famous silver boom, which ended in approximately the late 1650's, these mining centers had the larger populations and controlled more of the economic life of the region. It was here that the administrative center of the region was established, and the city of Potosí may have reached a population five to six times larger than La Paz. With the almost century-long depression in silver production that ended in the 1750's, the relative importance of the urban centers of Bolivia changed considerably, and by the middle of the eighteenth century La Paz was emerging as the premier trade center and the most populous city in the region. The growth of La Paz had come simultaneously with the resurgence of silver mining, but also with the very important growth of its Indian populations in the surrounding countryside. In all districts there was a secular trend upward of natural growth of population such that a much larger labor pool became available for the development of such hitherto neglected zones as the eastern tropical valleys, which were now opened to major development by *altiplano* labor and capital.

Don Tadeo de Medina was therefore well placed to take advantage of this second Andean silver boom and the growth of the La Paz region. From the evidence presented in both his formal petition for an entailed estate (or *mayorazgo*) and his final will and testament, it appears that he came from a solid but relatively undistinguished and landless merchant family.[5] At the time of his marriage to Doña Antonia de Ulloa y Solis in 1752 he admitted to owning no land whatsoever, and listed his fortune of 22,000 pesos as being in commercial goods only.[6] Clearly he was not of the same landed class as his wife, whose father and uncle were both very prominent landowners. Despite his father-in-law's wealth and prominence (he owned the position of life councilman, or *regidor perpetuo*, on the city council), he offered his son-in-law only 10,721 pesos in lands and cash as a dowry. Unfortunately for the young landless merchant, his father-in-law never fully paid him this sum, and Don Tadeo in the end estimated that he collected only some 2,250 pesos in all of this bequest.[7] Nevertheless Don Tadeo seems to have been closely linked with his father-in-law's brother, an important cleric in the cathedral chapter of La Paz. Eventually Don Tadeo would become an executor and trustee of his wife's uncle's rather large fortune, and his wife in turn would become an important inheritor of her uncle's lands and estate. Most of his father-in-law's property, however, seems to have gone to his numerous other children.[8]

While the dowry that Don Tadeo finally received included only 500 pesos in cash, it did contain the unimproved *estancia* called Capire in the pueblo of Laxa in the nearby district of Larecaja. The promised flocks of sheep that went along with this land were removed by his father-in-law, to the bitter complaint of the new bridegroom. Nevertheless, this was the young urban merchant's first holding in rural real estate, and he quickly invested large sums of money in both improving the lands and stocking the herds, and he also began buying other rural income-producing properties.

While continuing an active career in local and international trade, Don Tadeo slowly began to create a thriving and diversified rural empire that eventually made him one of the major landowners and farmers in the entire province of La Paz. From this first *estancia* on the *altiplano*, he began investing in the rich agricultural lands of sub-*puna* valleys of Larecaja, in which he grew maize and vegetables. But Don Tadeo also seems to have been one of the earliest investors in the coca-producing valleys of the district of Chulumani, or the so-called Yungas. The development of this region was intimately tied to the rapid growth of silver production in the second half of the eighteenth century. Though the area had produced some coca since precolonial times, most of it remained inaccessible and undeveloped steep, semitropical valleys that would require extensive investments in clearing, terracing, and constructing complex drainage works to become productive. It was the impetus of the late colonial mining boom that finally provided the capital to fully exploit this marginal coca zone. By the end of the century the Yungas were the primary centers for the production of high-quality coca leaf in Alto Peru. From the record of his investments, it would appear that Don Tadeo was one of the earliest of the new investors to open up this region. By the time that Chulumani achieved its status as a district independent from Sicasica and held its first complete Indian census in 1786, Don Tadeo was unqualifiedly the wealthiest landowner in the territory as measured by the number of peons he controlled.

Although the early period of this development is still unknown, it was evident that Don Tadeo's rural career got off to a very rapid start. In 1756, for example, he was able to purchase one half of the coca-producing plantation (or *hacienda de cocales*) Chicalulo in the town of Pacallo in the Chulumani district for some 4,890 pesos. In 1773 he purchased the other half of the estate, bringing his total costs to 9,800 pesos.[9] As he noted in his will, this sum bought him only the undeveloped lands, with no *cocales* (coca bushes), no Indians, and no buildings. Investing several thousands of pesos during the next several years, he was able to introduce some 184 yanaconas and enough coca bushes to produce 1,500 *cestos* (baskets) of coca per annum, so that his coca output brought in 12,000 pesos annual income. By the 1780's the total value of this estate, its coca bushes, improvements, and implements came to 65,000 pesos, making it among the top 10 percent of the coca haciendas in the zone, and the second most important rural property in his portfolio.[10]

Given the fact that the lands he obtained from his father-in-law and this new estate were both unimproved farms, it is obvious that Diez de Medina generated the bulk of his capital in these early years from his continued and intense activity in La Paz commerce. This activity consisted in direct importation of European goods for local sale, purchase of cattle and foodstuffs in interior markets for sale in La Paz, extensive loans to merchants for short-term credits for the importation and sale of goods, and finally general loans to leading officials and *vecinos* (leading citizens of La Paz) for their own various needs. He also invested in *censos* (mortgages) on rural and urban properties and collected annual interest on these same mortgage loans.[11]

A classic area for leading merchants to invest in was tax farming, both directly as a farmer or indirectly as a *fiador* (or guarantor) for someone collecting the taxes.[12] While the records have yet to be encountered, it can be assumed that Diez de Medina was also engaged in this activity. The fact that this young merchant already was rapidly accumulating political titles would suggest that he was not indifferent to this important source of funding. As early as 1764, Viceroy Manuel de Amat of Lima appointed him to be a captain of militia in La Paz.[13] This largely honorific title was converted into a real command in the Indian rebellion in 1780 when Diez de Medina fought in the nearby rural districts of both Pacajes and Sicasica. He also loaned the hard-pressed local treasury 2,100 pesos in cash at the height of the rebellion. He was elected *alcalde ordinario* in the municipal government of La Paz for several years, and in 1771 he purchased his title of *regidor perpetuo* in the same municipal government for 910 pesos.[14]

The enormous size of his wealth became especially manifest on the marriage of his daughters. In the early 1770's his first daughter, Maria Josefa, married a young merchant by the name of Diego Carazo. Though Carazo only had a capital of 2,000 pesos, he must have been intimately associated with Don Tadeo, for the latter granted him a *dote* (or wife's dowry) of 25,000 pesos. While this daughter seems to have died shortly after the marriage, Don Tadeo continued to pay out the assigned *dote*, since the two men continued in active partnership. He paid the first part of the dowry (some 9,000 pesos in cash) on the date of the marriage, by the 1790's had some 8,000 pesos in stock in his son-in-law's store in La Paz, and in his will of 1792 agreed that he still owed 5,224 pesos (having just paid another 3,375 to him quite recently). When two other daughters married in 1774 and 1776, he granted to each of his new sons-in-law approximately 26,000 pesos in dowry. To María Carmen, who married the Spanish-born army captain Don Juan Fernando Iturralde, he gave 10,000 pesos in cash, a hacienda named Elena in the Chulumani district, and some 6,000 pesos in jewels, slaves, silver plate, and dresses. The same occurred when his daughter Doña Francisca Paula married Fernando Retana, another merchant and partner of Don Tadeo: Retana obtained as his dowry the Yungas hacienda San Francisco de Paulo del Monte, and the same amounts in cash, jewels, and clothes.[15]

Although the records clearly indicate that these dowries were not paid in full at the time of the marriage, they were recognized as legal, long-term obligations. Don Tadeo usually gave some immediate cash down payment, along with rich personal effects for his daughters, and minimal rights to the estates, most of which were still listed in his own name by the time of the census of 1786. In the case of at least four of his five sons-in-law (one of his four marrying daughters married twice) there also were extensive financial arrangements in terms of joint commercial ventures not directly related to the *dotes*. (For a kinship chart of Don Tadeo's family, see Figure 2.1.) Aside from the 8,000 pesos' worth of goods in Carazo's store at the time he made his will in 1792, Don Tadeo was still clearing accounts on a joint venture with his deceased son-in-law Ramón Guillen for some 500 head of cattle they had purchased together in the valley of Aquile in

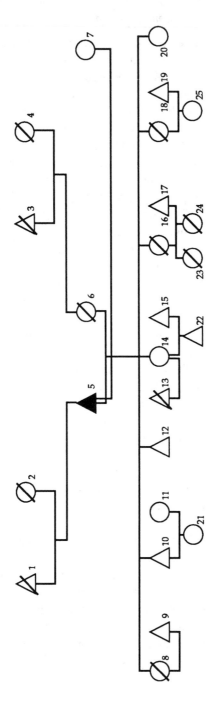

Figure 2.1. The Family of Don Tadeo Diez de Medina. Family members who had died as of 1793 are marked with a /. The names of the family members are as follows: 1, Ermenegido Diez de Medina; 2, Paula de Mena y Contrera; 3, Mateo de Ulloa y Solis; 4, unknown; 5, Tadeo Diez de Medina; 6, Antonia de Ulloa y Solis; 7, Manuela Mireles; 8, Maria Josefa Diez de Medina; 9, Diego Fernandez Carazo; 10, Juan Josef Diez de Medina (d.1814); 11, Francisca Ugarte (m. 1805); 12, Tadeo Antonio Diez de Medina; 13, Fernando Retana; 14, Francisca Paula Diez de Medina; 15, Francisco Guillen; 16, Maria del Carmen Diez de Medina; 17, Capt. Juan Fernando Iturralde; 18, Maria Antonia Diez de Medina; 19, Francisco Xavier Eguino; 20, Maria Magdalena Diez de Medina; 21, Maria de la Concepcion; 22, Protasio Guillen; 23, Maria Rafaela de Iturralde Medina; 24, Ana Maria de Iturralde Medina; 25, Maria Vicencia Eguino.

the province of Misque (in the Cochabamba Valley region) for use on Guillen's hacienda Vilavila in the Chulumani town of Irupana. At the same time, he had an arrangement with another son-in-law, Fernando Retana, for purchasing 200 *fanegas* of wheat from the Cochabamba Valley (this was, as he put it, only part of "several thousands of pesos [that we] sent to the Valley of Cochabamba").[16] He even made the son-in-law of his already deceased daughter María Antonia, Don Francisco Xavier Eguino, a trustee (*albacea*) and the sole executor of his will and temporary manager of his estates, until the return of his eldest son, who was then (in 1792) residing in Spain.[17]

Relations thus appear to have been close with all his sons-in-law, except Captain Iturralde, with whom he fought several long and very bitter judicial conflicts. These conflicts, which have produced a very extensive archival literature in the Audiencia of Charcas records, began in the early 1790's and went on for over a decade.[18] The basic thrust of this conflict had to do with the complaints from Iturralde that he had been cheated on the dowry in terms of the evaluations of the various properties he received. As a result, he challenged the accuracy of the original evaluations of the first division of the maternal and paternal estates, and he demanded an accounting of the profits from the rural estates of Don Tadeo for a ten-year period. It would appear that Iturralde won most of the earlier judgments but lost some lands back to Don Tadeo by the end. But so bitter did the conflict become, and so complex the genealogy, that the last records show Don Tadeo in litigation against Doña Gertruides Machicado, who was Iturralde's widow (she had married Iturralde after Don Tadeo's own daughter Doña María Carmen and her two daughters—Don Tadeo's grandchildren—had died).

In the early 1790's this conflict appeared to be for control over the *tambo* (or combined market and inn) that Don Tadeo owned in La Paz. Apparently Iturralde was demanding and got, by judicial decree, half-ownership in the inn, which was worth 29,200 pesos. This was besides the 13,002 pesos he had obtained in the dowry upon his marriage. It can be assumed from the bitter tone of Don Tadeo's comments on this affair that this was a falling-out among commercial partners.[19] Moreover, despite his Spanish birth and military title, Iturralde in his declaration of *capital*—that is, his worth at the time of his marriage—claimed in 1755 that his entire estate of 6,500 pesos was made up of imported goods (*efectos de castilla*) he held in Lima.[20]

Though the 1792 will suggests that the resolution of the *tambo* issue ended the dispute, later documents show that Iturralde went on to claim that his former mother-in-law's estate was not properly evaluated and that the five children inheriting had not been treated equally. In particular, he charged that the shares of his brothers- and sisters-in-law were allocated to the detriment of his own wife's inheritance. This led to a set of documents drawn up in 1794 that evaluated the production of the majority of Don Tadeo's rural haciendas in 1782–92 (see Appendix A and the tables there). The result of these new challenges was that in the mid-1790's Iturralde got some lands taken from the neighboring coca hacienda of Chicalulo and added to his Elena estate. In turn, Don Tadeo by 1803 seems to have succeeded in having these lands taken back from Iturralde's widow and her children by Iturralde.[21]

The long-term, multigenerational conflict with Iturralde was unusual, for Don Tadeo participated in much joint economic activity with all his five sons-in-law, even after the deaths of his daughters. This activity supports the hypothesis that Don Tadeo was using his daughters' marriages as a way to ensure commercial alliances with up-and-coming younger merchants. The fact that the *dotes* were promissory notes rather than full cash settlements meant that the fortunes of these young men became tied to the fortunes of their father-in-law. Clearly here, as Susan Socolow has shown for Buenos Aires merchants in the same period, marriage, dowry, and kinship ties were being used by merchants to form long-lasting and binding commercial partnerships in a society with no recognized *sociedades anonimos* or private joint-stock companies.[22]

However much capital Don Tadeo and his sons-in-law were generating in trade, Don Tadeo also was actively pursuing his career as an economically aggressive landowner. So successful

was he at this that by the late 1780's approximately two-thirds of
the estimated value of his real or fixed assets of 417,836 pesos
was in agriculture.[23] (For a detailed analysis of Don Tadeo's holdings, see Appendix A.) In the early 1780's he possessed some
15 rural estates, three of which were cocales and 12 of which
produced grains and foodstuffs. On these estates worked a minimum of 1,300 *colonos* who produced a total of some 13,000 pesos
of commercial crops in the year 1782. Of this amount 95 percent
was produced by the three cocales (Chicalulo, Incapampa, and
Cedromayo). In the statistics of decennial production for all his
estates that Don Tadeo was forced to provide the Audiencia in
the interminable legal conflict with his son-in-law Iturralde, we
find that the year 1782 was unusual in the very high prices paid
for coca. But taking an average of the ten-year period 1782–92,
the breakdown was still on the order of 90 percent of value coming from the cocales (or about 10,000 pesos per annum from *cestos de coca* and 1,200 from a complex mix of grains, root crops,
and other foodstuffs).[24]

Though he would add several more haciendas in the district
of Larecaja in the 1790's, by the end of the 1780's Don Tadeo was
clearly one of the wealthiest landowners—lay or ecclesiastical—
in Upper Peru. As we have seen, he was the largest landowner
in the district of Chulumani in terms of the number of Indian
laborers he controlled. In 1791, for example, we know that his
two major coca estates produced 2,553 cestos of coca, which in
1796 would have represented 2.3 percent of the total output of
all hacendados in the Yungas. In 1786 his 700 Chulumani colonos accounted for 4 percent of the landless yanaconas in the
district.[25] Aside from coca leaf production, Don Tadeo also had
a minimum of some 6,300 sheep (worth approximately 4,477
pesos) stocked on his Omasuyos and Larecaja estates. Finally, in
his estates in Rio Abajo, on the outskirts of La Paz, he was producing a considerable quantity of fruits and vegetables for consumption in the city.[26]

While Don Tadeo maintained his permanent residence in La
Paz and was a typical absentee landowner, he was not a simple
rentier or a frustrated merchant seeking noble status.[27] He in-

vested heavily in rural estates not to escape from his merchant origins or to luxuriate in the status of a country gentleman, but because agriculture in the province of La Paz was a highly profitable venture. His rural holdings were a major source of income as well as an investment, and just as his profits from commerce had been used to develop these estates, the profits from these productive farms were plowed back into his urban and commercial activities.

All of the available records show Don Tadeo to have been as active in his rural empire as in his urban one. He was constantly investing large sums in developing virgin fields and planting commercial products. Given the long time needed to bring coca bushes into production, as well as the high costs of terracing the steep valleys of Chulumani, a high percentage of the value of the estates was accounted for by the coca plantings themselves and physical improvements. Thus, for example, only 15 percent of the very valuable Pacallo coca hacienda of Chicalulo (estimated total worth of 65,000 pesos) was represented by the original cost of the unimproved lands. Nor did Don Tadeo rent out any of his uncleared or producing lands to others, as was a common practice among other landlords; indeed, there are constant references to his efforts to expand his operations as one of Alto Peru's leading coca producers in the late colonial period.[28]

Despite his position in coca production, Don Tadeo did not abandon either his commercial career or his urban real estate interests. In urban real estate purchases he sought basic family living and maintenance incomes and was less concerned with obtaining property for purely rental purposes or for speculative investments. Though his urban properties were quite valuable, they were largely used to produce income to pay for housing, board, and expenses for himself, his wife, and his unmarried daughter. Only the large tambo in La Paz, the 11 stores that were located on the ground floor of his Calle Commercio home, and the house he owned behind the cathedral were exclusively income-producing properties. As can be seen from his grants to his unmarried daughter María Magdalena (who became a nun) and his second wife, most of the 1,300 pesos he received in annual urban rents went for their daily food and clothing needs. Equally, he used the rent from the store on the ground floor in the house he owned in Coroyco for upkeep of the living quarters above so as to have a place to stay when visiting his coca haciendas.[29]

Along with his farm production, his most important capital-generating activity was in his traditional commercial operations. Both in his will of 1792 and in selected notarial documents after that date, Don Tadeo can be seen to be very actively engaged in traditional local and long-distance trade. In December of 1792, for example, he was arranging a letter of credit with a Cadiz merchant for the purchase of an estimated 20,000 pesos' worth of Castillian manufactured goods for importation to America.[30] In August of 1794 he financed the importation of 24,639 pesos' worth of Spanish textiles (*bayetas de castilla*) for two La Paz merchants, with the repayment scheduled in three parts over an 18-month period, and with the goods themselves serving as collateral.[31] In 1792 he bought a second tambo in the city of La Paz for 20,010 pesos in cash, from which in 1809 his widow was receiving annual rents of 1,000 pesos.[32] Thus Don Tadeo can be seen as operating in a consistently rational manner in all his activities as merchant, urban proprietor, and rural agricultural producer throughout his career. Funds flowed freely from one type of investment to another, and Don Tadeo sought profits on his investments regardless of their urban or rural setting. Also, the sums he was still investing in commerce were very impressive considering the value of his fixed assets and annual income.

To estimate the total wealth of Don Tadeo, and the potential income he could generate in any given year, we have two sources: first, the formal distribution of his property (*hijuela*) that he was required to make in 1789 when he sought to obtain a *mayorazgo* (or entailed estate) for his two sons; and second, the formal will he wrote after a very long illness in May of 1792, which built upon the 1789 division and included more complete details of his current economic activities, including both liabilities and assets. The result is shown in Table 2.1.

As can be seen from the table, Don Tadeo estimated the total

TABLE 2.1
The Joint Estate of Don Tadeo Diez de Medina and Doña Antonia Solis at the Time of Its Liquidation in 1789
(in pesos a 8)

I.	JOINT PATERNAL AND MATERNAL ESTATE: GROSS VALUE	
	A:	
	1. Urban properties	119,154
	2. Rural properties	227,533
	3. Dowries (*dotes*) of three married daughters[a]	86,252
	GROSS VALUE	432,939
	B:	
	1. Mortgages (*censos*) on rural properties	44,000
	2. Mortgages (*censos*) on urban properties	6,500
	TOTAL MORTGAGES	−50,500
	C:	
	1. Expenses for two sons' education in Spain until the mid-1780's (i.e. death of wife)[b]	16,510
	GROSS DEDUCTIONS	−67,010
	GROSS VALUE OF JOINT ESTATE	365,929
II.	MATERNAL ESTATE:	
	1. Gross value of maternal estate (½ joint)	182,965
	2. Wife's funeral expenses, purchase of a special *capellanía* for her masses, and special bequests	− 7,450
	NET VALUE	175,515
III.	PATERNAL ESTATE:	
	1. Gross value of paternal estate (½ joint)	182,965
	2. Subtraction of personal fifth (*quinto*)[c]	−36,593
		146,372
	3. Subtraction of personal third (*tercio*)[d]	−48,791
	NET VALUE	97,581
IV.	JOINT PATERNAL AND MATERNAL ESTATE: NET VALUE	
	1. Net Value of Maternal Estate	175,515
	2. Net Value of Paternal Estate	97,581
	3. Personal third (*tercio*) of paternal estate freely added to joint estate	48,791
	NET VALUE	321,887

(table continues)

fixed assets of his joint estate with his first wife at 432,939 pesos. By any standards this was a great sum. Though the accounting takes into consideration funds that he had already given his sons-in-law and that therefore were no longer totally under his control, even the remaining 346,687 is one-fifth greater than all the royal tax income generated by the Intendencia of La Paz, Alto Peru's second wealthiest province, in the year 1790.[33] Tak-

TABLE 2.1 (*continued*)

V. Post-Estate Liquidations of Don Tadeo:	
A:	
1. Liquidations of some mortgages on rural property	29,200
2. Liquidations of a mortgage on urban property	4,500
3. Special land purchase on the hacienda Incapampa	4,000
4. Dowry (*dote*) for daughter who became a nun	6,000
5. Sons' Spanish education after the mid-1780's	11,912
GROSS ADDITIONS TO ESTATE	55,612
1. Reduction of Don Tadeo's *quinto* & *tercio*	−25,952
NET ADDITIONS TO ESTATE	29,660

source: AGI, Audiencia de Charcas, legajo 556, expediente 10, documento 6 (dated Mar. 21, 1789). All reales have been rounded to the nearest peso.

[a] These dowries broke down as follows: for Maria del Carmen (Iturralde), 26,042; for Maria Francisca (Retina), 26,087; and for Maria Antonia (Eguino), 34,123.

[b] This includes a special charge of 610 pesos for a debt to one Don Matias de Calahumana. There is also a discrepancy of 390 pesos in this listing. I have used the total figure given in the document.

[c] The personal fifth (*quinto*) was the amount of funds that the "testator" could freely dispose of from his own individual estate.

[d] The personal third (*tercio*) was the amount of funds that a "testator" without children could freely dispose of. The implication here is that without children from his new second marriage, Don Tadeo was adding from his own separate estate from his new marriage funds from his so-called legitimate "third" to the inheritance of his children by the previous marriage. From these two sources of funds, which Don Tadeo was free to dispose of as he wished, he granted his new wife 47,715 pesos (the full *quinto* of 36,593 pesos from his Paternal estate and the fifth of the value—11,122 pesos—of the post-liquidation expenses he added to his deceased wife's joint estate with himself).

ing his rural properties alone, Don Tadeo was the largest coca producer in Upper Peru and the second-largest private landowner in terms of yanaconas controlled; his rural holdings were worth one-fourth more than the 34 properties owned by the Jesuit province of Upper Peru. Still, by American standards, Don Tadeo's total wealth, while impressive and important, was at the lower end of the scale of elite wealth. Of the 28 titled families in eighteenth-century Mexico, the richest colony of the Spanish American empire, 17 had estates evaluated at over 1 million pesos, with the spread of all families going from 350,000 pesos to 3.8 million.[34]

Of this gross amount of Don Tadeo's estate (still excluding the dowries) some 66 percent was in rural properties and only 34 percent in urban holdings. It is also evident that Don Tadeo had considerable liquid assets, for he seems to have had little difficulty in generating some 55,000 pesos in the few years after his first wife's death to clear several major accounts by paying off principal on mortgages due on her death as well as general expenses (see Table 2.1, section V).[35]

The source of this liquid capital was his ongoing commercial activities and his agricultural production and urban rents. Unfortunately, given the dispersed nature of his commercial dealings and the lack of his account books, it is almost impossible to reconstruct his income from sales, loans, and other trade activities. However, some estimates can be made of his income from his rural and urban properties. While his production expenses are not known, his gross receipts from his rural properties were on the order of over 30,000 pesos per annum, with another 1,300 pesos in urban rents.[36] (This is not counting several farms for which no data are available.) At a rough guess this would mean a gross income of from 35,000 to 45,000 pesos per annum.[37] Given his frugality, which Don Tadeo admitted to in his will, his expenses must have been relatively low. He noted in this context that all of the expenses for his burial, as well as the settlement of all his outstanding debts and the payment of his outright bequests of cash to friends (which I estimate at approximately 8,000 pesos), could easily be handled by income from two-thirds of a year's production of his coca fields, and the first full year's income from his non-coca estates in the year after his death.[38] At a minimum, then, he was clearing on his agricultural production alone probably on the order of 10,000 pesos per annum above expenses. This still leaves his urban rents, which it is my impression he was using largely for maintenance, as well as the interest he was generating on his trading loans and the profits he was making on his commercial activities.

Furthermore, Don Tadeo appears to have been reasonably prudent by contemporary standards in his borrowing policies on his properties in terms of maintaining high equity and low mortgages. Don Tadeo kept his indebtedness in *censos* and *capellanías* relatively low. Thus for four of his Chulumani coca plantations, worth 143,385 pesos, the mortgage rate (of both *censos* and *capellanías*) was 28 percent of total value. In the case of the six haciendas he listed in his appeal for a *mayorazgo* in 1789,

Don Tadeo's total indebtedness was only 19 percent. When his urban properties are included, the total value of his real properties, as we have noted, reaches 346,687 pesos, with mortgages (*censos* and *capellanías*) equalling 50,500 pesos, or only 15 percent of the total assessed value.[39] This compares with an average of 27 percent on some 37 Yungas haciendas for which information was available from the La Paz notarial records in the period 1787–1803, and to a 41 percent average indebtedness for some 36 haciendas in the Mexican Bajío region in the eighteenth century.[40]

Don Tadeo's frugality appears to have extended to his personal purchases, for he admitted to owning very little silverware in his main house, and appears to have owned only two slaves, both women, and both of whom were employed in domestic chores. He did have a *mayordomo* (or steward) for his city house and he obviously had some reasonably expensive furnishings, since his La Paz home was evaluated at 8,650 pesos. But in his provisions for maintenance of his daughter in the convent, or for his wife after he died, he implied that the rents from the urban properties would be more than sufficient for both to live in a more than adequate style. He estimated that his daughter the nun could live on 6 pesos, 6 reales a week, or 351 pesos per annum, and he seemed to imply that a similar sum would take care of his widow's food and daily expenses.[41] We can assume, then, that almost all of the net income we have conservatively put at some 10,000 pesos was reinvested in Don Tadeo's many economic activities. Thus Don Tadeo seems to have been the model of an economically aggressive merchant and productive landowner.

But what of Don Tadeo's perceptions of the future? For the five daughters and two sons who reached adulthood from his first marriage, what social and economic vision of the future did he possess? Clearly, four of his five daughters were used primarily to cement commercial relations with up-and-coming merchants who became close economic allies of Don Tadeo. (The fifth daughter joined the Convent of La Purissima Concepción in La Paz as a nun in 1787.) His sons-in-law were encouraged to join Don Tadeo both in his commercial trading ventures and, equally, to invest in both urban and rural properties. For his two sons, however, it appears at first glance that Don Tadeo sought to remove them from this commercial-agricultural world, for he sent them to Spain in 1778 to obtain an expensive legal education. The elder, Juan Josef, was only 17 years old when the two boys accompanied the *oidor* (royal judge) Dr. Francisco Tadeo Diez de Medina to Spain. Reaching Madrid safely, they both entered a prestigious secondary school in the city (the Real Seminario de Nobles). It would also appear that Don Tadeo provided Dr. Francisco Tadeo with generous funding for this trip and never asked for an accounting. Both sons continued their training and obtained law degrees, Juan Josef studying at the Colegio del Sacro Monte in Granada and later at the Universidad de Orihuela, where he obtained the titles of *bachiller* and Doctor in Canon Law in 1785.

Though both sons finished their schooling in the mid-1780's, they lived in Madrid for another decade, with their father providing them with generous stipends.[42] To maintain his two sons, Don Tadeo established a trust fund ("fondo perdido y compañía") for them with a merchant in Cadiz for the initial sum of 3,000 *pesos fuertes*. This paid an interest of 10 percent per annum, giving his sons each a yearly income of 150 *pesos fuertes*. Furthermore, he provided them with general spending funds that came to 23,422 pesos a 8 as of 1789.[43] To further strengthen their position in Madrid, Don Tadeo then took advantage of both changes in the *mayorazgo* laws on entailed estates issued by the Crown in 1786 and the death of his first wife (prior to 1787) to petition the Crown, beginning in 1789, for the right to provide a *mayorazgo* for his two sons. Providing the owner with both status and the right to have a part of his inheritance free of mortgage, the *mayorazgo* was a crucial indicator of extreme wealth to the society at large. For the payment of the sum of 15,000 pesos, Don Tadeo was allowed to declare 40,000 pesos of any part of his property as inviolate and part of the entailed estate.[44]

It would appear, then, that Don Tadeo was investing his income in the future in terms of removing his sons from his own class into a higher category. But this was not in fact the case, for as his will repeated over and over again, he had every intention of having his sons return to take over the active management of his estates and commercial activities. This was especially his thought for his elder son, and in fact well before his death Don Juan Josef did return to La Paz (sometime before 1796) and take over active direction of his own affairs. It would also seem that the early death of Juan Josef in 1814 brought the second son, Tadeo Antonio, home from Europe as well to continue his father's activities.[45] To further strengthen the hand of his returned elder son, Don Tadeo in 1796 transferred to him his title of "24" *regidor perpetuo*,[46] and by the census of Chulumani of 1803 both he and his father jointly appeared to be working their own estates.[47] Don Tadeo Antonio took over this role on the deaths of his father and brother.[48] Thus, though his sons obviously enjoyed better and much more costly educations than he had, Don Tadeo did not bankrupt himself on that account, and he had every intention that they should combine both the legal profession and commercial activity, land ownership, and agricultural production. In fact, that was the very model of the career of Don Tadeo's much admired relative, Dr. Francisco Tadeo Diez de Medina, the *oidor*.[49]

Even in his very generous grants to the church and in his heavy commitment to *capellanías* for the saying of masses, Don Tadeo does not seem to have gone to such an extreme that he had to mortgage his estates. At the time he made his will in 1792, the total of the *capellanías* was 13,700 pesos, which along with some outright gifts of annual income (not related to official *capellanías*) came to a total annual rent of 1,235 pesos.[50] To these he seems to have added other *capellanías* before he died sometime in the first decade of the nineteenth century. These bequests were obviously a burden on the estate, but even had they come to 1,500 pesos per annum they would only have represented some 15 percent of the estimated net income Don Tadeo was generating from his rural properties alone.

The purchase of the *mayorazgo*, by contrast, was an expensive and obviously status-related item, and it cost Don Tadeo the significant sum of 15,000 pesos. This, however, was his only real extravagance in relationship to his sons. While he bequeathed them the *mayorazgo* and a considerable amount of land, the laws of partible inheritance meant that he actually established six thriving landed-merchant families out of his wealth. In fact, the two sons in their combined inheritance obtained only 45 percent of the total maternal and paternal estate. All the sums he used to provide them with valuable educations and the purchase of offices and titles (each was a member of the Real Orden de Carlos III) made it possible for them to supplement their merchant-landowner incomes with access to legal and government revenues. Thus, though the expense of their education and maintenance in Spain plus the purchase of their municipal council seats and society memberships probably cost Don Tadeo a minimum of 45,000 to 50,000 pesos,[51] this was meant as an investment that would produce a direct commercial and economic advantage for his sons within the Alto Peruvian economy.

One investment that seems to have had no economic return whatsoever was the dowring of his fifth daughter, María Magdalena, to the Convent of La Purissima Concepción in the city of La Paz.[52] While it appears to have been common practice for fathers who had provided dowries for their daughters entering convents to later receive loans from those convents, Don Tadeo does not appear to have availed himself of this source of capital.[53] Moreover, he assigned his daughter only life rents for her maintenance at the convent, which consisted of some 700 pesos per annum from the rents of his 11 stores in La Paz plus numerous small gifts from his personal "fifth" of the estate, which included the delivery of weekly supplies of mutton and the use of one of his house slaves (a woman named María Antonia valued at 500 pesos, who was provisionally freed on his death provided she worked for his daughter until the daughter's death).[54] In total, these grants of services, supplies, and moneys came to a maximum of 1,000 pesos per annum. Moreover, all of these rents and services terminated with the death of his daughter and did not become a permanent burden on his estate or that of his heirs.

From this rapid examination of the income and expenditures of a very wealthy Alto Peruvian merchant and landowner, it is difficult to see behavior that was not influenced by market conditions, or that inhibited active participation in commerce and commercial agriculture at the same time. Throughout his entire career, Don Tadeo engaged in both rural and urban economic activities and constantly invested his profits to improve his position in both worlds. Moreover, he married off three of his four marrying daughters to merchants, and his sons, though trained in the law, eventually returned to work the estates and carry on the business developed by their father. Don Tadeo's wealth also revealed a high degree of economic specialization: his lands were all located within the Intendencia of La Paz, and his importing activities—manufactured goods from Spain, sugar from Lima, and wheat and animals from Cochabamba—all seem to have been centered on the La Paz market.[55] The fact that this very wealthy merchant did not engage in mining would also seem to suggest a relatively advanced degree of economic specialization among the Creole economic elite of Alto Peru.

Thus the career of Don Tadeo Diez de Medina is suggestive of the economic aggressiveness of the merchant class of La Paz and its active intervention in its rural environs as important members of the landed aristocracy. Given that the lowland coca estates were the wealthiest in all of Alto Peru, but that they required expensive improvements and a long period before the bushes matured and the initial investments could begin to be recouped, it was inevitable that they required the use of capital generated in the urban centers—either in commercial or in government activity—to provide the necessary base for expansion, though obviously capital could also be generated from farming itself. The fact that Don Tadeo looked to merchants rather than landowners for husbands for his daughters would also seem to suggest that title to land per se was no guarantee of wealth and that a landed career without access to urban incomes and commercial resources led only to decline and disappearance. Moreover, the fact that Don Tadeo was extremely reticent about his own parents in all his documents would suggest—given the usual style of elaborate touting of ancestral status—that he was of relatively humble origin and that such a modest beginning did not prevent access to the ranks of the landed class.

Finally, given the rules of partible inheritance and the consequent plethora of contested land cases in the legal and notarial records, transferring a landed empire was not a simple task. If the inheritors could not agree on joint administration (some 10 percent of the estates in the province of La Paz were clearly of such a joint ownership when listed as owned by the *herederos* or inheritors of a long-deceased owner) then the conflicts could and did lead to the deliberate breakup of large and well-functioning units into smaller and often not very viable estates. Clearly Don Tadeo did give his sons unusual wealth and a chance to gain alternative sources of income. Also, the accident of death left only one of them with the major estates by the second decade of the nineteenth century. Nevertheless, the empire itself was much reduced and broken into several independent family units after Don Tadeo's death. By the first complete republican census of 1829, the Diez de Medina family and its two surviving immediate collateral families had lost considerable ground, at least in the district of Chulumani. Of the 10 Yungas coca estates Don Tadeo at one time had held in his portfolio of properties, his descendants owned just four. His only surviving son, Don Tadeo Antonio, held the major estate of Chicalulo with 100 yanaconas. One of his granddaughters, Doña Patricia Guillen, owned Monte with 67 yanaconas and Mutuguaya with another 194 resident Indians. The other grandchild, Doña Vicente Eguino, held Ataguallani and its 64 Indians. Together these three families controlled only 425 Indians on these four estates.[56] Clearly the once mighty empire was now reduced to three medium-sized hacendado families.

From this analysis of the origins, growth, and decline of the landed empire of Don Tadeo Diez de Medina, it can be seen that the La Paz landed elite was a decidedly open one in terms of economic and social mobility. Clearly people who held both Indians and lands did so in order to use them productively and profitably. The costs of tribute and mortgages required a constant ex-

penditure of capital that could only be obtained by profits de-
rived from agricultural sales. Marriage alliances between old
and new wealth and other social devices were used by the elite
to guarantee some stability even for economically incompetent
offspring in the rigors of an open market. But all these attempts
to modify the impact of the market in no way prevented the
changing economic fortunes and unequal distribution of abili-
ties from guaranteeing a relatively open pattern of mobility in
the landed class of the province of La Paz.[57] While the *paceña*
experience may not be universal to all rural highland Andean
areas in the eighteenth and nineteenth centuries, it nevertheless
is important enough to force a revision of the traditional view of
the hacendado class as a closed, immobile, and non-market-
oriented group.

CHAPTER THREE

The Structure of the Indian Communities in the Late Eighteenth Century

IN THE HISTORY of rural society in Latin America, the interplay between the large landed estate, or hacienda, and the free Indian landowning community, known as the *ayllu* or *ejido*, has proven one of the most complex issues to understand. The struggle for land, labor, and markets between these two seemingly competitive rural landholding institutions varied over both time and space, and only in a few limited areas has this interrelationship been fully analyzed. Of the few studies that have so far been undertaken, the majority have concerned themselves with the major areas of Amerindian peasant concentration in Mexico.[1] In the Andean region the limited number of studies have been primarily concerned with coastal Peru and Chile.[2] Until recently, Alto Peru (Bolivia) was largely ignored.[3]

Even in the context of the limited number of rural studies that exist for Latin America, more is known about the haciendas than about the free Indian peasant communities, and more stress has been given to issues concerning land and capital than to labor. Yet the data to redress this imbalance exist, first in the surveys carried out in Peru in the eighteenth century by the more advanced intendants,[4] second in some general accounts given by the viceroys,[5] and third and most importantly in the voluminous and well-preserved accounts of the royal treasury records of the colonial administration. From these sources one can begin to reconstruct the distributions of Amerindian peasant populations, their age and sex structures, their migration and growth patterns, and their response to differing regional economic and ecological systems. From the *alcabala* (or sales tax) books, trade flows and regional economies can be accurately determined, and from the fundamental Indian tribute lists the demographic structure of the rural masses of both colonial and nineteenth-century Peru and Bolivia can be reconstructed with great accuracy.

In this chapter, I turn from my focus on the hacendado elite and examine in more detail the rural Indian populations and their relative distributions and structures within the two basic rural institutions—the hacienda and the *ayllu*. I continue to use the province of La Paz as the basis for my analysis, though in this case I will concentrate on comparing two contrasting districts within this region to more sharply define the unique features of each of the rural institutions as seen from their working-class populations. Using the tribute lists, I will try to determine the comparative demographic structures of both haciendas and free Indian communities in one base year, that of 1786. The two selected zones are the *altiplano* district of Pacajes, located along the southeastern shores of Lake Titicaca and stretching to the border of the province of Oruro, and the eastern escarpment tropical valleys known as the Yungas, which made up the relatively new district of Chulumani. The first zone, that of Pacajes, is an area of traditional agriculture and grazing whose major crops were Amerindian root plants and their derivatives, and alpaca and llama products.[6] Its 42,000 Aymara Indians were primarily concentrated in the free communities, but important grazing and agricultural haciendas were scattered among the *ayllus*. The Spanish, or non-Indian, population of Pacajes was quite small, and individual towns were almost totally Aymara-populated hamlets.

By contrast, the 20,000 Aymara of Chulumani were primarily found in haciendas scattered among at least an equal number of Spaniards. These Spaniards were the major dwellers in the region's many small market towns.[7] Unlike Pacajes, Chulumani was a zone par excellence of commercial agriculture. But, in a rather unusual fashion, the cash crop of Chulumani was coca leaves, a pre-Columbian plant consumed by the Amerindian peasant society of both Alto and Bajo Peru. The sale of coca leaves was, in fact, one of the few examples of the successful commercialization and conversion into an exclusively cash crop of a pre-Columbian product. Except in certain ceremonial uses among all Indian peasants, coca was primarily destined for use as a mild tranquilizer and hunger suppressant among high-altitude Indian working populations. As noted in Chapter 2, Chulumani was a relatively new coca-producing zone in the 1780's, and thus had a thriving, if minority, *ayllu* concentration that also engaged heavily in coca plantings.[8]

Thus the two zones include two out of the basic three ecological regions of Andean society: the highlands and the eastern *montaña* (or eastern escarpment valleys), though not the Pacific coast. They also embrace largely subsistence and barter markets as well as cash-cropping areas. Both also contain an abundance of all the major varieties of commercial and/or subsistence haciendas and *ayllus*. In short, they represent most of the types of rural holdings and ecological zones where the bulk of the Aymara Indians resided in late-colonial Alto Peru.[9]

Before proceeding further, it is essential to define the *ayllu*. Unfortunately, defining the free Indian community in the Andes is a complex task, since there is still much disagreement about its origin, structure, and even purpose.[10] The *ayllu* also changed dramatically over time, and at different rates from region to region, so that it was never universally the same, even in one period. At the most basic level, the *ayllu* is a group of families claiming a common identity through real and fictive kinship and using that claim to hold communal land rights. Originally, neither these communal lands nor the residences of *ayllu* members were necessarily contiguous. The traditional Andean adaptation to sharp ecological variations meant that agricultural holdings would be scattered in an "archipelago" fashion and that colonies of settlers would be maintained at quite long distances from the original "seat" of the *ayllu* to work those holdings. From the Spanish conquest on, however, the *ayllus* were pressured toward a more European definition of community, in terms of nucleated villages with contiguous land areas. This dynamic between dispersion and concentration varied both from region to region and over time, and thus made for important local variations.

The members of the *ayllu* were mostly endogamous, but some anthropologists do not consider the *ayllu* a closed corporate community because there was some movement in and out of *ayllu* membership and descent seems to have been bilateral in many cases—though again this is not fully resolved in the literature.[11] Usually a region—pueblo or canton—had numerous *ayllus*, typically grouped into a system of pairs. North of Potosí, in the region little influenced by hacienda advances or central government control, these *ayllus* finally coalesced into regional confederations that claimed a "national" identity. These confederations are probably the closest remnants to the older nations of the preconquest period, though the historical depths of these north Potosí "naciones" is still in question. In the La Paz region, however, there were few remains of these "national" distinctions at least from the late colonial period on, and the binary *ayllus*, which could reach 20 or 30 per "pueblo," seemed to be grouped into nothing larger than a community confederation.[12]

Each *ayllu* was governed by its own elected elders, who were generally known by the Aymara term *jilakata*. These elders meted out internal justice, determined inheritance rights, controlled communal lands, and decided land distributions among the members of the *ayllu*. They also represented the *ayllu* before inter-*ayllu* organizations (of the town and region) and before the state. In turn the state traditionally acknowledged these elders as local authorities with rights to judge traditional law and land arrangements and held them responsible for tax collection and conscription of workers for various corvée labor obligations, including the *mita*. Below the *jilakata* level there also existed an elaborate and hierarchical system of *cargos* or offices, involving both civil and religious functions, to which individual *ayllu* members were "elected." Success in farming and in performing these lower offices usually led to higher ones through life, until a select few people rose to the position of *jilakata*. These offices required an enormous expenditure of personal savings and thus functioned to level income inequalities in the *ayllu*. They also guaranteed very powerful local governments by the most successful and respected elders of the community.[13]

Groupings of many *ayllus* were usually governed by officials called variously caciques, *kurakas*, or *mallkus* (the Aymara term for this office). Unlike the *jilakata* position, this office tended to be hereditary in leading local families who claimed, in most cases, descent from the local preconquest nobility. They also owned lands independent of *ayllu* control and had traditional claims on the labor time of *ayllu* members. While important in the early colonial period, the kurakas seem to have lost power by the late colonial era due to their progressive economic decline and/or acculturation into the Spanish world. Finally, as a response to the Tupac Amaru rebellion of 1780–82, royal officials became more actively involved in the selection of these officials, breaking the traditional hereditary ties in many cases so that the resulting kurakas could not always claim their legitimacy from previous generations. Given their infrequent appearances in republican documentation, it is unclear how many kurakas survived into the nineteenth century and how the tasks of those who did differed from those of their predecessors.

The individual families within each *ayllu* had access to a group of lands known as their *tierras de origen*. These included communal lands as well as inheritable permanent household plots (*sayañas*), on which a family usually constructed its main house, grazed its domestic animals, and raised some crops. The communal agricultural lands (*aynuqa*) were allocated as plots (called *liwa qallpa*) to the *originarios* on a conditional basis by the *ayllu* and were subject to complex rules of crop rotation and fallowing. The community typically possessed some 10 to 30 such common land areas. The system of fallowing and crop rotation on these lands—the only viable alternative in the face of low use of fertilizers—was a strong bone of contention with colonial and republican officials, who were always charging Indians with having excessive and unused lands, which were in fact lands at rest.

The individual scattered plots in the *aynuqa* fields were small, varying from 200 to 10,000 square meters in modern times, with a typical family holding between 20 and 60 such plots in the different ecological zones of the *ayllu*. Crops are traditionally grown for 3 or 4 years and then the land is left fallow for another 4 to 8 years, at which point the cycle begins again. Both the permanent *sayañas* and the temporarily granted *liwa qallpa* lands were worked individually by each family, though reciprocal labor arrangements were used to help in such tasks as planting and harvesting of crops. Although land ownership was ultimately defined in communal terms, each family disposed of its production from its plots as it saw fit and used the lands as private property until such time as they were again redistributed to other members of the community. *Ayllu* members also had claims to common pasture lands. In return for all these benefits, the *ayllu* members had to perform communal labor obligations and pay their tribute taxes.[14]

This idealized structure only included originario families in the *ayllu*, but the *ayllu* also contained a varying number of families that did not belong to it. These forasteros, or agregados, fit into this scheme by being given *sayaña* plots for their homes by the *jilakatas* and by obtaining access to communal plots through labor service to the originario families of the community. Over several generations, forasteros and their families came to be attached to individual originario families through complex ritual ties. It also appears that the *jilakatas* carefully governed the number of forastero families granted to each originario so as to prevent major inequalities developing. While ritual kinship and gift-giving bound the originario to his dependent forasteros, when severe pressures on land occurred (as they did toward the end of the nineteenth century and afterward) forasteros often lost their land rights and were expelled from the community. There were even subcategories within the forastero group to cover later arrivals who simply provided their labor for food and even more temporary land access. No group of forasteros had any rights to land other than through the originarios they worked for, and they did not participate in the governance of the *ayllu*. In most communities even today such forasteros have no rights to land outside their immediate region (for example, to valley lands for those living on *puna ayllus*). Also given their ultimately rather tenuous land rights, they were less willing to migrate seasonally out of the community for wage labor. Both access to distant lands claimed by the *ayllu* and the ability to enter the Spanish labor market without losing land rights were the exclusive domains of the originarios.[15] It appears that over time, and in some regions, the very sharp distinctions drawn between originario and forastero would be worn down as many generations of forasteros continued to live on the same *ayllu*. Nonetheless, in the second half of the twentieth century investigators still found *ayllu* community members clearly distinguishing between *tierras de origen* and lands belonging to agregados. But there is some disagreement about whether this was still as important a distinction in all regions as it was in the eighteenth and nineteenth centuries.

The sources for this study of the *ayllus* are the Amerindian tribute censuses. While such lists lack territorial measurements associated with cadastral records, they are a mine of information about the demographic structure of these communities. Information is also available from these records on hacienda ownership and the relative economic importance of the *ayllus* as measured by their differing tax assessments. Thus the *visitas de tributo* (also called *revisitas* or *padrones de indios*) are a basic and as yet largely unexplored source for describing the labor input into the *ayllus* and haciendas of late colonial Peru and its distribution over time and space.

My reason for selecting 1786 as my base year for this analysis is related both to the sources themselves and to the general economic and social conditions in Alto Peru. The census of 1786 was the first full census for the newly created district of Chulumani, and throughout the highlands it was the first really complete total population count taken by royal officials in the history of the tribute census (due to the administrative and accounting reforms associated with the introduction of the new intendencia system). It was also the first complete census taken after the 1780–82 rebellion of Tupac Amaru, and it was taken at a time when all contemporary commentators agreed that the social order had finally returned to normal and that the area was once more in a peaceful and prosperous state.

In analyzing the census data, I have used the general summary categories provided by the census takers themselves. The reason for using these grouped age/sex categories has to do with the failure of the government officials to list any ages for women over twelve, which makes it impossible to generate reasonable age data by sex. Also given my desire to test a series of economic and social variables—in this case, those relating to wealth and land tenure—over large populations for large areas and eventually over long periods of time, these summary categories are the most efficient way to analyze these materials in this first full-scale analysis.[16] The census takers aggregated the Indian population into nine age and sex categories, five for men—*niños* (under age 13), *proximos* (13 to 17), *tributarios* (18 to 50), *reservados* (over 50 and no longer subject to tribute), and *ausentes* (tributary-age males who were missing from the community at the time of the census and not accounted for in the parish death books)—and four for women—*niñas* (to 12), *solteras* (unmarried women 12 years and older), *casadas* (married women), and *viudas* (widows).[17]

The royal officials then broke the tributory population down into three categories on the basis of access of the taxed Indian to land. The highest-taxed group consisted of originarios, who had prime access to the lands of the *ayllu*. The next group was the agregados or forasteros, who as we have seen had negotiated access to some community lands through relationships with originarios.[18] The third group, taxed at the same level as the forasteros, were the yanaconas, non-landowning Indians living on the private estates of the Spanish and cholo landowners. While the yanaconas had no legal rights to lands, the traditional form of payment for their labor service on the haciendas was the so-called colonato system, under which they were granted plots to work on the hacienda in exchange for providing free labor (often tools and seeds as well) on those estate lands worked by the

TABLE 3.1

Average Indian Population by Property Type in Chulumani in 1786

	[1] Yanaconas on haciendas		[2] Originarios on *ayllus*		[3] Forasteros on *ayllus*		Total [2] + [3]	
Pueblo	No. of haciendas	Ave. pop. per hacienda	No. of *ayllus*	Ave. pop. per *ayllu*	No. of *ayllus*	Ave. pop. per *ayllu*	No. of *ayllus*	Ave. pop. per *ayllu*
Wealthy zone								
Chulumani	16	52	7	137	7	188	7	325
Irupana	43	15	6	41	6	41	6	81
Laza	13	44	3	39	3	51	3	90
Zuri	20	22	3	65	3	99	3	164
Ocabaya	8	30	5	41	5	47	5	88
Chirca	31	43	4	66	4	106	4	172
Pacallo	27	48	–	–	1 [a]	44	1	44
Coroyco	69	67	1	158	1	272	1	430
Coripata	34	98	–	–	–	–	–	–
Chupe	9	40	3	79	3	159	3	238
Yanacachi	4	78	3	149	4 [a]	116	4	227
SUBTOTAL	274	51	35	81	37	106	37	182
Poorer zone								
Palca	37	67	10	67	10	221	10	287
Collana	–	–	9	35	9	36	9	71
Mecapaca	14	82	–	–	–	–	–	–
Cohoni	18	73	4	60	4	112	4	172
SUBTOTAL	69	72	23	53	23	129	23	182
TOTAL	343	55	58	70	60	115	60	182

SOURCE: AGN, Sección Contaduria, Padrones—La Paz (1786), legajo 24, libro 2 (13-17-6-5).

NOTE: All "ausentes" (males aged 18–50 and unaccounted for) and all Indians listed as liv within the towns were excluded from this and subsequent tables.

[a] In Pacallo and Yanacachi there was one *ayllu* containing only forasteros.

landowner. Thus the yanacona sometimes had access to as much private land as the forastero in the free community—if not more.[19] That this was recognized by the crown is evident in the taxing system, which almost always charged forasteros and yanaconas the same amount.

In the following comparative analysis of Chulumani and Pacajes, I have used the categories set out above in an effort to determine the basic demographic characteristics of these districts in terms of the hacienda and *ayllu*. In comparing the districts, their relative commercial importance seems to weigh more heavily in determining their demographic structures than

TABLE 3.2

Average Indian Population by Property Type in Pacajes in 1786

Pueblo	[1] Yanaconas on haciendas		[2] Originarios on *ayllus*		[3] Forasteros on *ayllus*		Total [2] + [3]	
	No. of haciendas	Ave. pop. per hacienda	No. of *ayllus*	Ave. pop. per *ayllu*	No. of *ayllus*	Ave. pop. per *ayllu*	No. of *ayllus*	Ave. pop. per *ayllu*
Caquiaviri	11	57	12	109	12	97	12	206
Caquingora	1	42	7	187	7	151	7	337
Collapa	1	87	7	194	7	158	7	351
Curaguara	10	61	9	144	9	99	9	243
Ulloma	–	–	4	168	4	76	4	244
Calacoto	–	–	8	427	8	208	8	635
Santiago de Machaca	3	77	2	434	2	544	2	978
San Andres de Machaca	1	95	4	265	4	324	4	589
Jesús de Machaca	1	270	10	192	11[a]	160	11[a]	335
Guaqui	10	121	9	125	9	98	9	223
Tiahuanaco	10	131	7	207	7	190	7	397
Viacha	26	85	9	138	9	124	9	262
Achocalla	16	71	2[b]	367	–[b]	–	2	367
TOTAL	90	87	90	197	89	153	91	345

SOURCE: AGN, Sección Contaduria, Padrones—La Paz (1786), legajo 23, libro 1 (13-17-6-4).
[a] Jesús de Machaca contained one *ayllu* with only forasteros.
[b] Achocalla's two *ayllus* were so poor they had no forasteros.

their internal *ayllu*-hacienda divisions. To begin with, the commercial tropical valleys (or Yungas) of Chulumani contained on average far fewer persons per agricultural unit than in the *ayllu*-dominated subsistence agricultural zone of Pacajes. As can be seen in Tables 3.1 and 3.2, this feature was shared intrazonally by both types of properties. Thus, while the total populations were not too dissimilar, there were far more properties in the Chulumani valleys (403 units), despite their much smaller geographic spread, than in the open lands of Pacajes, which contained only 182 units. This meant that the number of persons per property in Pacajes on average was slightly over double the Chulumani number.

But this difference in average size did not mean that Pacajes

TABLE 3.3
The Economically Active Indian Population in Chulumani in 1786
(Percent)

Pueblo	Yanaconas on haciendas	Originarios on *ayllus*	Forasteros on *ayllus*	Total on *ayllus*	Total population
Wealthy zone					
Chulumani	61%	54%	68%	62%	62%
Irupana	66	65	66	66	66
Laza	63	53	63	58	62
Zuri	63	62	64	63	63
Ocabaya	64	68	62	65	65
Chirca	66	60	69	66	66
Pacallo	56	–	61	61	56
Coroyco	57	63	66	65	58
Coripata	59	–	–	–	59
Chupe	60	59	66	64	62
Yanacachi	56	54	64	59	58
SUBTOTAL	60%	58%	66%	63%	61%
Poorer zone					
Palca	46%	50%	46%	47%	47%
Collana	–	53	41	47	47
Mecapaca	46	–	–	–	46
Cohoni	45	51	47	48	46
SUBTOTAL	46%	51%	46%	47%	47%
TOTAL	56%	56%	57%	57%	56%

SOURCE: Same as for Table 3.1.

NOTE: The economically active population is defined as men in the census categories tributarios plus proximos and women in the categories solteras and casadas.

TABLE 3.4
The Economically Active Indian Population in Pacajes in 1786
(Percent)

Pueblo	Yanaconas on haciendas	Originarios on *ayllus*	Forasteros on *ayllus*	Total on *ayllus*	Total population
Caquiaviri	45%	44%	48%	46%	46%
Caquingora	55	51	49	50	50
Collapa	40	50	49	49	49
Curaguara	55	50	53	51	52
Ulloma	–	54	54	54	54
Calacoto	–	56	53	55	55
Santiago de Machaca	59	53	53	53	54
San Andres de Machaca	43	52	52	52	51
Jesús de Machaca	49	53	49	51	51
Guaqui	53	53	48	51	52
Tiahuanaco	51	49	49	49	50
Viacha	52	53	50	52	52
Achocalla	49	51	–	51	50
TOTAL	51%	52%	50%	51%	51%

SOURCE: Same as for Table 3.2.

NOTE: The economically active population is defined as men in the census categories tributarios plus proximos and women in the categories solteras and casadas.

had a greater percentage of its population in the work force than did the Chulumani properties. In fact, it would appear that the opposite was the case. Using the tributarios as a rough approximation of the male labor force, and tributarios, solteras, and casadas as an approximation for the total labor force, we get a labor force participation figure in Chulumani higher both for males and for total workers than in Pacajes. This would seem to indicate that there was a much lower ratio of workers to nonworkers, or dependents, in the latter zone than in the Yungas. Also labor force participation figures, just as those for average size, transcend differences in access to land or between *ayllu* and hacienda, and stress a commonality of demographic features in one given zone as opposed to pronounced interregional differentiation. Nor is there any correlation between large estates in terms of population and labor force participation rates. In all the townships and through all the properties, the prime factor is region, with large or small units having no significant correlation with greater or lower percentage of adult males from eighteen to fifty years of age.

The greater potential productivity of the population in the Chulumani coca region, because of its higher ratio of economically active persons, is thus an important indication within the demographic structure of the contrast between a relatively rich and a relatively poor zone in Alto Peru. Moreover, the contrast in the sex ratios between these two zones shows a clear response to the relative desirability of these two regions on the part of the laborers themselves. For the higher proportion of adult males in the Chulumani region is matched by their underrepresentation in Pacajes, thus indicating the classic in-and-out migration of working male population. While Pacajes was known to export labor both to the mines and to other Andean valleys besides the Yungas, some of its male population was also a source for the large number of in-migrants coming to the Yungas.[20]

Aside from this permanent and largely voluntary *altiplano* migration to the Yungas, there was also a definite seasonal migration during the time of the harvest of the coca crop. Dependent upon supplementary outside laborers to harvest the crop, the

TABLE 3.5
Sex Ratios of the Indians in Chulumani in 1786
(Men per 100 women)

Pueblo	Yanaconas on haciendas	Originarios on *ayllus*	Forasteros on *ayllus*	Total on *ayllus*	Total population
Wealthy zone					
Chulumani	124	108	137	124	124
Irupana	125	137	164	150	135
Laza	119	100	120	111	117
Zuri	117	107	121	115	116
Ocabaya	122	148	123	134	130
Chirca	118	92	117	107	114
Pacallo	122	–	159	159	123
Coroyco	122	119	147	136	123
Coripata	122	–	–	–	122
Chupe	131	109	134	125	127
Yanacachi	121	104	142	121	121
SUBTOTAL	122	111	134	124	122
Poorer zone					
Palca	102	109	94	98	100
Collana	–	96	71	82	82
Mecapaca	102	–	–	–	102
Cohoni	93	88	90	89	92
SUBTOTAL	100	101	91	94	97
TOTAL	115	108	113	111	114

SOURCE: Same as for Table 3.1.

TABLE 3.6
Sex Ratios of the Indians in Pacajes in 1786
(Men per 100 women)

Pueblo	Yanaconas on haciendas	Originarios on *ayllus*	Forasteros on *ayllus*	Total on *ayllus*	Total population
Caquiaviri	93	82	82	82	84
Caquingora	121	96	79	88	89
Collapa	78	90	77	84	84
Curaguara	98	89	88	89	91
Ulloma	–	96	95	96	96
Calacoto	–	90	96	92	92
Santiago de Machaca	125	101	95	98	100
San Andres de Machaca	90	92	84	87	87
Jesús de Machaca	79	89	77	83	83
Guaqui	80	92	73	83	82
Tiahuanaco	88	89	87	88	88
Viacha	93	105	78	91	92
Achocalla	87	106	–	106	94
TOTAL	90	92	84	88	89

SOURCE: Same as for Table 3.2.

hacendados paid these *altiplano* laborers in coca leaves, which they in turn carried with them to the *altiplano* on their return and converted into cash or other goods. In fact, local officials argued in the 1780's that an important part of the funds used by the *altiplano ayllus* to pay their tribute tax came from seasonal workers engaged in the coca harvest.[21] This temporary migration, much like the mita labor migrations, probably had a strong nonvoluntary element to it, since it was partially initiated to meet royal demands for cash, rather than simply as a response to the economic needs of the *altiplano* populations. But this pattern of using the tribute to force the Indians into the market seems to have been a fundamental factor in the Alto Peruvian economy from the earliest times, and especially since the Toledan reforms of the last quarter of the sixteenth century had shifted tribute from payment in kind into a money payment.[22] A detailed study of three *ayllus* in Chaqui in the province of Potosí in the early seventeenth century found that these relatively rich *puna* and upper-valley agricultural communities could not meet their tax and mita obligations through traditional agricultural production alone—it barely covered the annual food consumption needs of the members of the *ayllu*—but were probably forced into the Spanish market through the sale of animal fodder (barley), use of their llama herds for transport, and other extra-agricultural activities in the nearby Potosí city market.[23]

Another reflection of the relative attractiveness of the two zones to permanent migrants is seem in the ratio of forasteros to originarios on the *ayllus*. Whereas Chulumani had more forasteros than originarios, in a ratio of 1.6 to 1, the reverse was the case with the *ayllus* in Pacajes. Here there were only 0.7 forasteros for every originario. This would seem to imply that the *ayllus* of Pacajes were less attractive to migrating families than the coca-producing *ayllus* of the Yungas. In this respect, in fact, it is worth noting that all the *altiplano* zones of the province of La Paz—except the district of Omasuyos along the shore of Lake Titicaca—had fewer forasteros than originarios.

Finally, though still a small percentage of the total population, the missing, or ausente, tributary male population also shows

TABLE 3.7
The Children-to-Women Ratios of the Indians in Chulumani in 1786
(Children per 100 women)[a]

Pueblo	Yanaconas on haciendas	Originarios on ayllus	Forasteros on ayllus	Total on ayllus	Total population
Wealthy zone					
Chulumani	112	132	89	107	108
Irupana	80	100	100	100	88
Laza	91	150	119	133	103
Zuri	89	115	78	92	90
Ocabaya	84	105	82	92	89
Chirca	93	113	70	85	90
Pacallo	112	–	63	63	111
Coroyco	120	102	92	96	118
Coripata	108	–	–	–	108
Chupe	110	124	89	100	104
Yanacachi	123	147	97	121	121
SUBTOTAL	108	125	88	103	107
Poorer zone					
Palca	147	157	144	147	147
Collana	–	152	88	114	114
Mecapaca	157	–	–	–	157
Cohoni	139	171	120	136	138
SUBTOTAL	147	158	132	139	143
TOTAL	118	134	107	117	118

SOURCE: Same as for Table 3.1.
[a]"Children" = niños + niñas; "women" = solteras + casadas + viudas.

TABLE 3.8
The Children-to-Women Ratios of the Indians in Pacajes in 1786
(Children per 100 women)[a]

Pueblo	Yanaconas on haciendas	Originarios on ayllus	Forasteros on ayllus	Total on ayllus	Total population
Caquiaviri	128	118	114	116	118
Caquingora	59	122	102	113	111
Collapa	97	120	104	113	112
Curaguara	102	123	97	112	110
Ulloma	–	95	98	96	96
Calacoto	–	89	94	91	91
Santiago de Machaca	96	115	108	111	109
San Andres de Machaca	119	122	111	116	116
Jesús de Machaca	118	107	95	101	102
Guaqui	91	121	77	99	96
Tiahuanaco	105	124	105	114	111
Viacha	109	123	87	104	107
Achocalla	105	134	–	134	116
TOTAL	105	112	99	106	106

SOURCE: Same as for Table 3.2.
[a]"Children" = niños + niñas; "women" = solteras + casadas + viudas.

the same zonal differences. Whereas Pacajes was missing 1,209 tributarios as against 7,421 resident ones (or 16 percent), in Chulumani, the ausentes numbered only 75 against the 8,206 accounted Indians, or less than 1 percent.[24]

The last ratio that can be calculated from the aggregated tributary categories is a rough one that stands as a proxy for fertility, here defined as the ratio of all children (girls under 13 and boys under 14) to all women. Whereas the sex ratios, the ratios of the economically active population, and even the ausente ratios clearly defined differences between the districts, the children-to-women ratios show no such clearly defined differences. Like the figures for average number of persons per agricultural unit, these figures seem at first glance to be distributed randomly between the two districts.

Up to this point in the analysis, we have been seeking to determine differences between the districts in terms of their broad demographic characteristics. While this is useful, it does not tell us whether these contrasts are due to factors of relative wealth or are the result of differing migration patterns. To help distinguish these causal factors, we can use the tax records to discriminate between wealthy and poorer zones in the district of Chulumani. As noted earlier, for Chulumani the tax differs sharply from pueblo to pueblo, thus indicating a richer and a poorer zone within the district itself. While the tribute tax in the first eleven pueblos runs from 15 pesos, 3 reales, to 20 pesos, 2 reales—an extraordinarily high head tax by Andean standards—the last four pueblos in the district[25] were all charged a tax below that of any Pacajes *ayllu*, 9 pesos, 1½ reales. This internal differentiation within Chulumani thus enables us to test more accurately which factors reflected recent patterns of migration and which were associated with a successful export commercial crop agriculture.

While no differences can be noted within the two subregions of Chulumani regarding average size of haciendas or *ayllus*, there were important differences in the rates of the economically active population, the sex ratios, and the children-to-women ratios. The poorest pueblos of Chulumani, with their economically active rates of 46 percent for haciendas and 47 percent for *ayllus*, were closer to the economically active population rates for Pacajes (51 percent and 51 percent) than to those of the wealthy Chulumani pueblos (60 and 63 percent, respectively). Equally, the sex ratios shown for this poorer Chulumani zone (100 males per 100 females for haciendas and 94 for *ayllus*) were closer to the *ayllus* and haciendas of Pacajes than to the rest of Chulumani. It might thus be argued that crude rates of the economically active population are directly related to wealth factors—the wealthier the zone, the higher the ratio of the economically active population—and that sex ratios are moderately affected by this variable as well, insofar as they reflect male migration toward the richer area. As with the interdistrict comparisons, the figures for average number of persons per agricultural unit show no clear differentiation when we look at the Chulumani subregions. One factor that does clearly emerge in the subregional analysis, though not at the regional level, is differences in the children-to-women ratios. These ratios for the poorer zone of Chulumani were higher than those not only for the richer zone but for any other district in the province of La Paz except Omasuyos. Why this should be the case is difficult to determine at this point.[26]

But what of the comparative differences in the Indian population owing to their different socioeconomic status? Does analysis of these demographic indices help to determine the relative well-being of these peasant populations? Rates of the economically active population and the sex ratio show no consistent difference among the two categories of *ayllu* members and the yanaconas. There is, however, among the originarios a consistently higher ratio of children to women in both Pacajes and Chulumani, and within the poorer and richer districts within the latter area. It might be argued from this that their greater access to land gave the originarios a better division of the limited resources available in the rural areas and thus promoted higher children-to-women rates. I stress the issue of survival rather than birth rates, since even in modern times it has been shown that *altiplano* birth rates have been consistently high, with the

TABLE 3.9
The Indian Population of Chulumani in 1786, by Sex and Age

	Yanaconas	Originarios	Forasteros	Total
MEN	10,141	2,100	3,663	15,904
Niños (under 14)	3,739	859	1,191	5,789
Proximos (14–17)	540	0[a]	180	720
Tributarios (18–50)	5,020	1,167	2,019	8,206
Reservados (51+)	842	74	273	1,189
WOMEN	8,788	1,949	3,232	13,969
Niñas (under 13)	3,049	751	1,097	4,897
Solteras (13+)	671	134	270	1,075
Casadas (13+)	4,392	963	1,479	6,834
Viudas (13+)	676	101	386	1,163
TOTAL	18,929	4,049	6,895	29,873
Ausentes	55	0	20	75

SOURCE: Same as for Table 3.1.

[a]This is obviously an understatement, since young men 14 to 17 had to exist. Yet this figure is recorded in both the individual *ayllus* and the general summary manuscript tables for all originarios. It would seem that for some reason these males were counted with the tributarios.

TABLE 3.10
The Indian Population of Pacajes in 1786, by Sex and Age

	Yanaconas	Originarios	Forasteros	Total
MEN	3,695	8,517	6,220	18,432
Niños (under 14)	1,561	3,714	2,554	7,829
Proximos (14–17)	289	629	391	1,309
Tributarios (18–50)	1,471	3,239	2,711	7,421
Reservados (51+)	374	935	564	1,873
WOMEN	4,111	9,233	7,430	20,774
Niñas (under 13)	1,348	3,135	2,414	6,897
Solteras (13+)	815	1,924	1,486	4,225
Casadas (13+)	1,413	3,424	2,305	7,142
Viudas (13+)	535	750	1,225	2,510
TOTAL	7,806	17,750	13,650	39,206
Ausentes	195	134	880	1,209

SOURCE: Same as for Table 3.2.

rates of population increase being held down by the extremely high rates of infant mortality.[27] This suggests that through their access to more lands, originario members of the *ayllus* had better access to food and, therefore, could maintain more children alive past infancy than the other types of rural workers.

That originario widows more frequently remarried may also be related to this question of land access and the wealth and security this entailed. It would appear from anthropological studies of other areas that the primary means of entry of male forasteros into the originario class was through marriage to a widow who had originario status. Thus originario families were more likely to have two adult worker heads of households than families of the other Indian classes. In fact, the revisitas do show that among the originarios there were far fewer widows in proportion to the total population than among the yanaconas or forasteros. Since such access to land resources seems to have been less available to either the non-originario widows of the *ayllu* or widows among the yanaconas, it would seem that they remarried far less than originario widows. This difference between ratios of widows by land access categories also shows up cross-regionally. Pacajes Indians in all categories had higher proportions of widows than the Indians of Chulumani, although in both cases the originarios had the smallest percentages.[28] This difference between a poorer and a richer zone in terms of the percentage of widows seems to suggest that this ratio is a reasonable indication of wealth differences among Indians.

But what of the hacendado class in Chulumani? How does it differ from the latifundista class as a whole in the province of La Paz and what role does it play in the production process? From the earlier analysis of the haciendas in the province in the 1780's and 1790's, it was apparent that Chulumani estates were among the smallest in size, averaging some 56 workers, comparable only to the much poorer zone of Larecaja. But this curious result has more to do with the ecology than the wealth of the district. The Chulumani estates were almost all terraced plantations scaling the sides of steep semitropical valleys. In both Chulumani

TABLE 3.11

Characteristics of the Hacendados Who Owned Land in Chulumani in 1786

Social category	Men	Women	Total
Spaniards	141	37	178
Cholos	36	4	40
Licenciados and doctores	32	0	32
TOTAL	209	41	250

SOURCE: Same as for Table 3.1.
NOTE: There were also four religious corporations that owned estates in the district.

and Pacajes the haciendas in turn are clearly distinguished from *ayllus* by their having smaller average populations. Although the haciendas in Pacajes obviously contained more persons per unit than those in Chulumani (and in fact were above the provincial norm of 75 yanaconas per estate), both were much smaller than the combined population per *ayllu* in their respective districts.

As the survey of the hacendado class in Chapter 1 showed, the wealthier multiple hacienda owners were most likely to have an estate in the coca zone of Chulumani. Thus the Chulumani landowners tended to be consistently among the top 10 percent of provincial owners or, to put it another way, it was only the hacendado elite that could afford the high initial costs of commercial coca production.[29]

As a class, the hacendados of Chulumani were overwhelmingly Spanish, male, non-university-educated, and lay. Only 16 percent were women (close to the provincial average—see Table 1.9), only 16 percent were cholos, and just 13 percent were university-trained. Given the relatively recent nature of settlement in this zone and its very rich agricultural potential, it is not too surprising that the church controlled so little property. In all the Yungas, there were only four church-related institutions that owned property. One was the Augustinian order, and three were different convents outside the zone.

That the planters were overwhelmingly male and Spanish was, of course, to be expected. But it is important to stress that females were an important minority, and that they appear even among the cholo landowners. The small percentage of university-educated landowners is not surprising, given that Alto Peruvian society in the eighteenth century was predominantly illiterate. The *paceño* bureaucracy was staffed by university graduates, and it is probably from among them that this segment of landowners comes.

Whether the hacendados as a whole were an absentee or resident class can be determined by a royal survey made in 1796 of the Yungas coca zone. A partial census of landlords in the Chulumani district, the 1796 survey covered 10 pueblos and 308 haciendas. It found that there were 240 hacendados, of whom 105 lived in the city of La Paz, 2 lived in Oruro, and 133 were resident on their estates in the Yungas.[30] Thus absentee landlords accounted for 45 percent of the total, while resident hacendados made up the majority. Interestingly enough, however, 98 percent of the absentee hacendados lived in the major city of the province, which was the key entrepôt for all trade with the Yungas. Nor was Chulumani unique in this respect. In the revisita of 1792 for Omasuyos, the sub-delegado in charge of the census reported that the owners of estates were also "for the most part residents of La Paz." He also pointed out that the absentee landlords ran their estates either with *mayordomos* or with the *jilakatas* of the local resident Indians.[31]

While it is impossible for us to analyze productivity by size of estate—given the current lack of information on output per unit—the demographic evidence would seem to suggest that for the Indian peasants working on the estates of the Spaniards, size of estate was an important factor. Examining the relative importance of tributarios in terms of the total population, the data for Pacajes and Chulumani again exhibit the same patterns that were seen for the entire population of yanaconas in the province of La Paz. The ratio of economically active males to total population (as measured by tributarios) declines as size increases (see Table 3.12). Thus in Chulumani and Pacajes, there was a moderate negative correlation between size of estate and ratio of economically active adult males.[32] This factor suggests the existence of more dependent persons on larger estates, and thus larger

TABLE 3.12

Yanaconas, Tributarios, and the Adult Male Economically Active Population on the Haciendas of Chulumani and Pacajes in 1786

Hacienda size (no. of yanaconas)	No. of estates (n = 426)	Mean population		Adult Male E.A.P.[a]
		Yanaconas (s.d.)	Tributarios (s.d.)	Pct. (s.d.)
1–9	66	5 (2)	2 (1)	39% (21%)
10–19	54	14 (3)	5 (2)	33 (11)
20–49	112	33 (9)	9 (3)	28 (8)
50–99	101	72 (15)	18 (6)	26 (7)
100–199	72	139 (29)	34 (10)	25 (6)
200–299	18	247 (29)	59 (14)	24 (5)
300–499	2	316 (6)	69 (18)	22 (5)
500–999	1	594	151	25
MEAN		65 (69)	17 (17)	29% (12%)

SOURCES: Same as for Tables 1.1 and 1.2.

NOTE: The total yanacona population of the two districts was 27,661, and the total tributario population 7,049.

[a]The adult male economically active population is defined here as the ratio of tributarios to total yanaconas.

family size. This may be due to the capacity of the larger haciendas to provide more usufruct lands for their workers, who were in turn able to maintain larger families on the basis of the lands they worked.

The hacienda listings also show that the free Indian communities of Pacajes were aggressive landowners. Of the 12 haciendas owned by communities in the province of La Paz in the 1786–97 sample discussed in Chapter 1, ten were owned by the *comunidades* of this province. Nor were these necessarily small haciendas. The *ayllu* of the comunidad of Viacha held two of the largest estates in the province with a total of 589 yanaconas. Moreover, some of these Pacajes comunidades held their haciendas far from their own regions, usually in the semitropical valleys. Thus Jesus de Machaca owned two haciendas with 267 yanaconas in the maize-producing lands of Timusi in the district of Larecaja.[33] Nor were such arrangements unique to Pacajes. Even as late as 1881, *ayllus* in Oruro and Potosí held large haciendas in the distant Chuquisaca province of Yamparez.[34]

One last area that can be partly explored on the basis of the 1786 census is the relationship between coca production, popu-

TABLE 3.13
Coca Production in the Yungas in 1796

Pueblo	No. of tributarios		Total coca production (in cestos)[a]	Pct. of coca produced by			Avg. cestos per tributario produced			Index of relative hacienda/ayllu output per worker[a]
	On haciendas	On ayllus		Hacendados on their own lands	Yanaconas on their lands on haciendas	Indians on their ayllus	On land of hacendados	On land of yanaconas	On ayllus	
Chulumani	301	779	26,939	25%	9%	66%	22	8	23	132
Irupana	229	183	22,445	44	30	26	43	29	32	224
Zuri	130	63	2,183	35	1	64	6	0	22	27
Ocabaya	73	165	8,443	35	15	50	40	17	26	227
Chirca	464	232	18,499	57	29	14	23	11	11	299
Pacallo	331	0	11,824	68	32	0	24	11	–	–
Coroyco	1,237	147	59,888	69	26	5	33	13	21	217
Coripata	954	0	37,645	65	35	–	26	14	–	–
Chupe	115	247	6,019	54	17	29	28	9	7	532
Yanacachi	81	296	5,539	40	18	42	28	12	8	511
TOTAL	3,915	2,112	199,424	55%	25%	20%	28	13	19	221

SOURCE: AGI, Audiencia de Buenos Aires, Legajo 513, "Estado que manifiesta el numero de Haciendas . . . en el Partido de Yungas . . . ," 17 mayo 1796.

NOTE: Since the 1796 census did not count tributarios, I have used the 1786 census figures for tributarios, which closely approximate the 1796 materials. However, it is probable that yanaconas were underestimated and that actual output per worker on the haciendas was somewhat lower than indicated here.

[a]Cestos were woven baskets in which coca was shipped. It was estimated by the President of the Audiencia of Charcas in 1782 that one cesto weighed 22 libras (pounds). AGN, Seccion Gobierno, Guerra y Marina, leg. 6, expediente 26 (9-23-10-6).

[b]This index takes ayllu output as 100 and includes total hacienda output (that produced on the lands of the hacendado as well as that produced by the yanaconas on their usufruct estate lands).

lation, and property type. While not equivalent to the 1786 census data, the 1796 survey of Chulumani does provide some information on coca production for ten of the 15 towns in the region. These data give an approximate ratio of production to agricultural unit and type of property. What is abundantly clear from these data is that the haciendas produced the bulk of the coca. Thus, of an estimated 199,424 *cestos* of coca produced in these ten townships, 80 percent came from the haciendas. But not all this hacienda production was controlled by the hacendados themselves. Yanaconas working on their own usufruct parcels produced 50,183 *cestos* out of the total of 160,247 harvested on the haciendas. Thus yanaconas and members of the *ayllus* together accounted for some 45 percent of the district's production. But, as might be expected, the core lands used by the hacendados for their own production on the haciendas were the best. If the 1786 numbers of yanaconas and tributarios can be accepted as approximately the 1796 population, then it is evident that with 28 *cestos* per worker output per annum on their demesne, the hacendados were far ahead of both the yanaconas on the usufruct estate lands, with their 13 *cestos* per worker, and the *ayllus*, with their 19 *cestos* figure. Combining the output of the yanaconas on their own and the lands of the hacendados, production per worker on the haciendas was double the output per worker on the *ayllu*. This suggests a higher productivity of the hacienda as compared to the *ayllu*. This seeming productivity difference, however, could be due to a number of factors. We can assume that the haciendas had access to better virgin lands than the *ayllus*. But they also had access to capital, which allowed them to hire the labor for the expensive terracing of their estates and to plant a large number of new and initially nonproducing stands of coca bushes, which took several years to mature. The *ayllus*, on the other hand, were unable to acquire capital through the usual mechanism of church loans. It is also probable that the *ayllus* concentrated more on food production and thus had a more mixed crop potential than is indicated in the export figures either of coca or of other products for the Yungas. Probably much of the food produced by the *ayllus* went

TABLE 3.14

Demographic Characteristics of the Hacienda and Ayllu Populations of the Major Districts of the Province of La Paz in 1786

Districts	Sex ratio		Children-to-women ratio		Pct. of economically active pop.		Average pop. size		Pct. of pop. on hac.	Pct. of forasteros on ayllu	Total Indian pop.
	Hac.	Ayllu	Hac.	Ayllu	Hac.	Ayllu	Hac.	Ayllu			
Pacajes	90	88	105	106	51%	51%	87	345	20%	43%	39,206
Larecaja	99	103	91	106	53	53	54	178	37	71	39,979
Omasuyos	93	100	153	147	46	48	127	211	53	93	42,750
Sicasica	101	97	128	126	50	49	79	274	37	26	30,789
Chulumani	115	111	118	117	56	57	55	182	63	63	29,873
TOTAL	100	98	122	118	51%	51%	74	234	42%	58%	182,597

SOURCE: Same as for Tables 3.1 and 3.2 for Pacajes and Chulumani; and AGN, 13-17-6-2 (legajo 26, libros 1–3) for Larecaja; AGN, 13-17-5-4 (leg. 19, libro 3) for Omasuyos; and AGN, 13-17-6-5 (leg. 24, libro 3) for Sicasica.

NOTE: Omitted from this table are the three rural parishes of the city of La Paz plus the isolated eastern lowland frontier of Caupolican, with its 4,000 or so missionized Indians.

to feed the local, more specialized haciendas, and thus did not enter the accounts of local exports. For these reasons, it is difficult to fully compare these two institutions on more than just the coca production aspects of their labor.

The 1796 coca survey also confirms the general impression of the wealth of the pueblos in the district of Chulumani. Coroyco, with 30 percent of the total production, was also the leader in practically all other exports from the region.[35] It was, as we have seen, the leading center of haciendas, one of the major townships for large haciendas, and it had all the other indices indicating it to be a leading hacienda area. Surprisingly, however, its productivity per worker for the local haciendas was only slightly above average for the entire province.[36]

While Coroyco was the township par excellence of hacienda coca production, Chulumani pueblo reveals itself as the most thriving center for the coca production coming from the *ayllu* lands. Its *ayllus* produced 46 percent of the total coca shipped by the *ayllus* from the Yungas, and it was the township with the highest percentage of the pueblo's crop being produced by the local *ayllus*. Although the productivity of Chulumani's free communities was considerably higher than average, it still was not the highest in the district.

Having analyzed Pacajes and Chulumani districts on the basis of the demographic characteristics of their Indian populations, their wealth, and even the structure and productivity of their haciendas, I will try at this point to place them in the larger context of Alto Peruvian economy and society. For this purpose, a rapid survey of the three other major districts of the province of La Paz will be useful. Once this is done (see Table 3.14), the unique qualities of Pacajes and Chulumani will stand out in sharper contrast.

Chulumani was an area of heavy recent immigration newly integrated into the market economy, and its sex ratio seems to reflect this fact of recent settlement more than the zone's advanced economic standing. Obviously male workers were attracted to the ever-expanding Yungas haciendas, and this is reflected in those haciendas having the highest ratio of men to women of any haciendas or *ayllus* in the five principal districts of La Paz province. In several of their essential statistics, the districts of Sicasica, Omasuyos, and Larecaja fall between the two contrasting districts of Chulumani and Pacajes. This is seen in their male to female ratios, and in their economically active population percentages (with the exception of Omasuyos). In terms of average size of estate, with the exception again of Omasuyos, they seem to define the outer limits in terms of average hacienda population, and also *ayllu* size (with Larecaja falling just below the low Chulumani figure). Thus in most respects Pacajes can be said to be the most backward settled area in the province of La Paz while Chulumani was the province's most economically prosperous region for both haciendas and *ayllus*. Given the fact that Sicasica, Omasuyos, and Larecaja were all traditional pre-Columbian settlement areas, the loss of male population by Pacajes was in this case reflective not of its nature as an old settled region, but of its relative poverty, possibly associated with its more specialized activity in grazing.[37]

TABLE 3.15
The Tribute Tax Rate Charged Against Originarios in the Major Districts of the Province of La Paz, Late Eighteenth and Early Nineteenth Centuries

District and year		No. of pueblos	No. of origi-narios	Average tax per originario (pesos)	Tax range (pesos/reales)	Modal rate (pesos/ reales)
Pacajes	(1802)	12	3,602	9.67	9/3–10/1	9/5
Omasuyos	(1786)	16	713	9.60	8/2–10/3	10/0
Sicasica	(1792)	12	2,716	9.49	9/1½–10/0	9/1½
Chulumani	(1803)	13	1,210	13.66	9/1½–20/2	15/3
Larecaja	(1786)	22	1,545	5.99	5/0–15/5	5/0
		75	9,786	9.53	5/0–20/2	

SOURCES: AGN, 13-17-9-4 (legajo 36, libro 1, unnumbered insert page) for Pacajes, 1802; AGN, 13-17-5-4 (leg. 19, libro 3, folio 520) for Omasuyos, 1786; AGN, 13-17-7-2 (libros 1 & 2), for Sicasica, 1792; AGN, 13-17-9-4 (leg. 36, libro 4) for Chulumani, 1803; AGN, 13-17-6-3 (libro 1), for Larecaja, 1786.

NOTE: Full tax listings were not available in the 1786 revisitas, so it was necessary to look at later years. But given the inflexibility of these rates (often established in the 1740's and lasting to 1825), these alternative years differ little from 1786.

These two districts do not define the outer limits. Omasuyos had much the highest children-to-women ratios (thus explaining its relatively low rate of economically active population), and Larecaja defined the lowest limit. Thus in and of itself the children-to-women ratio is not as precise a correlate of wealth as one would wish, though the generally poor quality of estates in Larecaja seems to find reflection in its very low children-to-women ratios. The percentage of forasteros on the *ayllus*, which will be seen later to have been an important index of economic change over time, does not well reflect wealth indices when used in a comparative synchronic analysis as applied here.

One final index of relative wealth of the differing districts of the province is the tax evaluations made by the royal officials in terms of the value of *ayllu* properties held by the originarios. Just as in the data on overall demographic ratios and comparative hacienda production, the value of *ayllu* lands reveals sharp contrasts between Chulumani and all the other districts in the province (see Table 3.15). The modal tax rate, for example, shows the *ayllus* of Pacajes just slightly ahead of the *ayllus* in Sicasica and slightly behind those of Omasuyos, but these three districts were considerably behind the unusually rich Chulumani *ayllus*, which were probably among the most wealthy free communities in all of Alto Peru.

The analysis of these two districts in the best census taken during the colonial period provides a base point from which we will be able to examine the changes that took place in the first century of republican life. From this survey of the peasant populations, and the previous analysis of the hacendado class, we have now elaborated a series of basic indices that can give us a means of comprehending the demographic changes that resulted from the profound economic changes of the nineteenth century.

CHAPTER FOUR

The Mining Crisis and the Peasant Populations of Chulumani and Pacajes, 1786–1838

IN THIS AND the following chapter, I will examine the impact of market forces—both in times of crisis and in times of growth—on the evolution of the structure of rural society. The nature of the hacendado class and of the labor force both on the haciendas and on the *ayllus* at the prosperous end of the colonial period has already been established as a baseline. In this chapter, as in the previous one, I concentrate on the geographical mobility and demographic structure of the three land-related categories of Indians we have already encountered: yanaconas, forasteros, and originarios. Again, the focus is on the premier hacienda zone in the Department of La Paz, the district of Chulumani, and the quintessential center of free community activity, the Lake Titicaca district of Pacajes.

The half century covered by this study includes not only an era of marked prosperity but also the most catastrophic depression in Bolivian history. Beginning in the late 1790's the Bolivian economy went into an economic decline from which it would emerge only slowly in the 1830's. This era began with the severe disruption in international trade caused by the European wars associated with the French Revolution and the Napoleonic era, and it was then reinforced by the massive epidemics in 1804 and 1805, and finally by the ruinous wars of independence which started in 1809 and lasted until 1825.[1]

Because coca leaves were a basic consumption item for the workers in the mining centers of Oruro and Potosí, and because the Yungas valleys of Chulumani were the primary center of coca production in all the region east and south of Lake Titicaca, the decline in the mining industry that began in the first years of the nineteenth century had a great impact on the hacendado class. Coca was important in the diet of all *altiplano* Indians, but it was of utmost importance as a hunger suppressant and stimulant in the high-altitude mines and was often used in partial payment for labor by the owners of the mines and smelters.[2] From various sources it can be estimated that as much as one third of the Yungas coca production overall was absorbed in the mining centers of Oruro and Potosí. Analysis of the coca exports from the pueblo of Chulumani and a few surrounding pueblos for the year 1790 shows that almost half (or 49 percent) was destined for the *altiplano* mining centers.[3] In turn coca leaves made up a substantial amount of Potosí's own imports. Of the total taxable imports into the city of Potosí in the period 1777–78, for example, coca accounted for 17 percent and was the second most valuable American-made item imported after *aguardiente* (cane alcohol). All of this coca came from within the confines of Alto Peru (Bolivia) and most of it originated in the Yungas.[4] Finally, even coca that was not consumed in the mining districts was still consumed in Alto Peru (or later, within the borders of the Bolivian republic): an estimate of Yungas production in 1846 suggested that less than 2 percent of the coca leaf exports from the Yungas entered international trade.[5]

The censuses that best cover this period of crisis for the Yungas are the *padrones* of 1786, 1803, 1829, and 1838.[6] They capture the late colonial mining boom of the 1780's, which brought silver production to new peaks and stimulated the full development of Yungas coca production. But having reached peak levels of production by the 1780's, the mining economy of the *altiplano* faltered in the following decades, a crisis that turned into a long-term secular trend of decline by the first decade of the nineteenth century (see Figure 4.1).[7] This secular downward trend

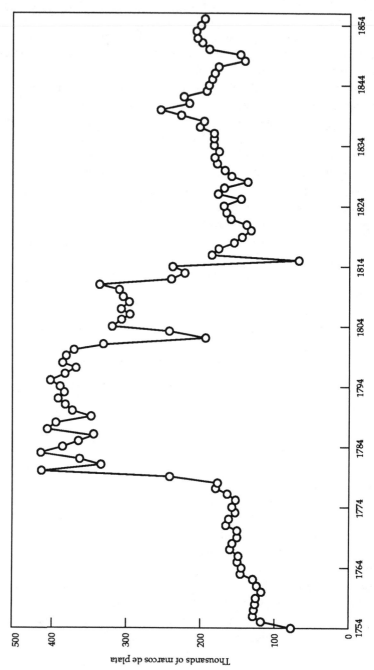

Figure 4.1. Bolivian Silver Production, 1754–1854. Based on data in Rück, *Guía general de Bolivia*, pp. 169–73.

TABLE 4.1
Estimated Capital Outflows of the Bolivian Economy, 1825–45
(In millions of pesos)

Quinquenium	Total monetary emissions	Deficit in balance of trade	Capital outflows	Accumulated capital outflows
1826–30	9.05	13.60	4.55	4.55
1831–35	9.52	14.78	5.26	9.81
1836–40	9.78	12.78	3.00	12.81
1841–45	9.79	11.39	1.60	14.41

SOURCE: Prado Robles, "Política monetaria," p. 118. Based on data provided in Dalence, *Bosquejo estadístico de Bolivia*.

reached its lowest point in the 1830's, when production, as measured by government mineral purchases (a state monopoly), was just half of what it had been in the 1780's.

This secular decline in mineral purchases by the Potosí mint (which until the early 1850's received the overwhelming majority of actual production) was matched by a long-term negative balance in international trade that marked the initiation of republican life and lasted until the 1860's. In 1825, official Bolivian exports of goods and non-precious metals were estimated by the British observer George Pentland to be some 349,000 pesos, while imports were 4 million pesos. As of 1846, this negative trade situation had only modestly improved, with goods and non-precious metals exports valued at 563,000 pesos and imports at 3.7 million pesos—signifying that such exports in the first years of republican life paid for only 9 percent of imports and that in 1846 the situation had improved to only the extent that 15 percent of imports were paid for with non-precious metals exports.[8] The amount of legally mined and minted gold and silver was insufficient to make up the trade deficit (see Table 4.1). Though non-minted (and therefore contraband) precious metal production was of some importance, estimates suggest this smuggled metal was only a fraction of legal output prior to 1850. Thus legal and contraband precious metal output was insufficient to meet the trade deficit and Bolivians were being forced to expend the accumulated savings generated from previous eras of growth to pay this ever increasing debt.[9]

One response to this liquidity crisis was the resort of the hard-pressed government to producing a debased coinage known as "moneda feble"—a silver coin with a high content of copper—largely to maintain a circulating medium in the local Andean economy.[10] Beginning in the 1830's, the government began to mint this debased coinage, which moved from being a modest portion of minted silver (some 19 percent of the total in 1835–39) to become the dominant coinage minted by the early 1840's.[11] As will be seen later, this debased currency has become a major theme of debate concerning the nature of the peasant economy in the early nineteenth century and its ability to survive an open economy. But for now, this production of debased coinage—whether it had unintended protectionist effects or not—was one more fundamental indication of economic decline, capital loss, and the inability of the mining industry to recover its colonial splendor.

To analyze how the Indian population responded to these changed economic conditions, there exist detailed periodic republican tribute censuses as well as the traditional royal ones of the late colonial period. Fortunately for comparative purposes, all the republican censuses were based on the late-eighteenth-century model of a *padron de indios*, and are identical in the types of information generated.[12] They provide a detailed listing of all taxable male Indians and their families by type of landholding upon which they resided. Both in the colonial period and in the republican era, all Indians aged 18 to 50 years were required to pay a tax in specie to the central government (called a *tributo* in the colonial period and a *contribución indigena* after 1825—and eventually named *contribución territorial* after the 1880's).[13] The rate of the tax differed among Indians and was based on the economic and legal conditions of the particular Indian community to which the Indian male belonged, and on his status in the community. If the land was rich and the taxpayer had direct access to it, he paid one rate. If he was a member of a free community but had less direct access to land ownership or use, he paid a lesser rate. Finally, if he lived on a hacienda of a non-Indian as a landless laborer, he paid a standard, lowest-rate tax. The crown and republican governments thus divided the Indians into three relatively homogeneous groups of originarios, forasteros, and yanaconas that we have established as our analytical categories in previous chapters. There were, however, some moderate changes in these categories in the republican period, which from time to time appeared in the manuscript censuses, and seemed to reflect attempts to define groups crossing between categories.[14]

The republican censuses used the same summary age and sex categories as the colonial ones, which for convenience I will repeat here. Men were divided into the four traditional rankings of *niños* (to age 13), *proximos* (14–17), *tributarios* (18–49), and *reservados* (50 years and older). The last category was that of *ausentes*, for any male tributary missing from the community at the time of the census and not accounted for in the parish death registers (*libros de difuntos*).[15] Women were divided into *niñas* (to 12), *solteras* (single over 12), *casadas* (married women), and *viudas* (widows of legal marriages). Finally all migrating Indians were to be counted as *forasteros sin tierra*, unless they married a woman with a claim to originario status. These were to be counted as members of their new communities after a year of residence.[16]

For consistency of analysis where Chulumani is concerned, I have confined myself in this chapter to the 11 principal coca-producing pueblos. While the republican governments redrew Chulumani's boundaries, this involved only the marginal towns that were not significant producers of coca or major centers of either *ayllu* or hacienda populations. And though in the censuses of 1829 and 1838 the pueblo of Yanacachi was formally divided into two subdistricts, I have counted it as one in all the following tables. Also, I have eliminated from all calculations the small number of taxable Indians listed as resident in the urban centers of the pueblos (*abecinado en el pueblo*), or the even smaller number exempted from taxation because they were working on parish church lands that maintained the religious institution in the local towns.

To place these population changes in context, it is essential first to note that the best estimates of the growth of the Bolivian population in this period suggest a positive growth rate of minimally 1 to 1.5 percent per annum for the period to mid-century. This is then thought to have slowed to .5 percent per annum in the mid-century decades due primarily to the impact of a series of poor harvests and the outbreak of cholera epidemics in the 1850's, after which it is estimated to have returned to over 1 percent per annum by the last quarter of the century.[17] The total population was estimated at 1,088,898 in the census of 1831, and 1,378,896 persons in the next major estimate of 1846.[18] Of this population, just over half (or 51 percent) were estimated to be Indians in 1846, and a very high proportion of these were found in the Department of La Paz. La Paz was the largest department and contained 30 percent of the total population in 1846, but its 295,442 Indians represented 42 percent of Bolivia's indigenous population in that year.[19] It also contained the largest city, that of La Paz, with some 43,000 persons.[20] Of the two districts I will be considering, Chulumani contained some 6,000 male tributary Indians in the general *padron de indios* of 1838 and Pacajes another 14,000. Together, these two districts accounted for some 16 percent of the total Indian tributary population of Bolivia in this year.[21] (For complete population statistics on Chulumani and Pacajes for the 1786–1838 period, see Appendix B.)

In the context of this overall population growth, the most striking factor revealed by these four Indian censuses for Chulumani during the period 1786–1838 is the severe population decline the coca valleys suffered. The sharp decline in silver output beginning in the years 1799 and 1800 was immediately reflected by a population loss in the census of 1803: in every community total Indian population fell relative to 1786 (see Table 4.2). Some communities began to grow again between 1803 and 1829, but most continued to decline. Even for the few that somewhat recouped their losses, all but Yanacachi ended up with a negative growth rate between 1786 and 1829. The populations are broken down by land and residence categories in Tables 4.3 and 4.4. The census of 1829, taken during the worst decade for mine output since the 1770's and the worst decade of nineteenth-century production, shows the continued link between silver production

TABLE 4.2
Total Indian Population in the Pueblos of Chulumani, 1786–1838

Pueblo	1786	1803	1829	1838
Chulumani	3,105	2,535	1,637	1,644
Irupana	1,124	731	762	810
Laza	845	660	401	483
Zuri	940	635	409	632
Ocabaya	684	578	582	644
Chirca	2,030	1,501	1,110	1,165
Pacallo	1,336	905	898	968
Coroyco	5,039	4,526	4,794	4,985
Coripata	3,337	2,748	2,850	3,233
Chupe	1,073	908	790	914
Yanacachi	1,219	1,138	1,272	1,320
TOTAL[a]	20,732	16,865	15,505	16,798

SOURCES: The four censuses are found in the following archives: 1786 in AGN, 13-17-6-5, legajo 24, libro 2; 1803 in AGN, 13-17-9-4, legajo 36, libro 4; 1829 in ANB, Archivos del Tribunal Nacional de Cuentas, no. 166; and 1838 in ANB, ATNC, no. 177.

[a] In this and subsequent tables, total population encompasses men, women, and children.

TABLE 4.3
Population Change by Category of Indians in Chulumani, 1786–1838

Category	1786	1803	1829	1838
Yanaconas	13,985	10,713	10,235	11,076
Originarios	2,825	2,935	2,556	2,602
Forasteros	3,922	3,144	2,795	3,120
TOTAL AYLLU	6,747	6,079	5,351	5,722
TOTAL INDIANS	20,732	16,792	15,586	16,798

SOURCES: Same as for Table 4.2.

TABLE 4.4
Population Growth Rates by Category of Indians in Chulumani, 1786–1838

Category	1786 to 1803	1803 to 1829	1829 to 1838	1786 to 1829	1786 to 1838
Yanaconas	−1.56%	−0.16%	0.84%	−0.71%	−0.45%
Originarios	0.22	−0.53	0.20	−0.23	−0.16
Forasteros	−1.29	−0.45	1.23	−0.78	−0.44
TOTAL AYLLU	−0.61%	−0.49%	0.75%	−0.54%	−0.32%
TOTAL INDIANS	−1.23%	−0.28%	0.81%	−0.66%	−0.40%

SOURCES: Same as for Table 4.2.

and population in the Yungas. The revival in silver production in the 1830's resulted in increases in the population figures in the 1838 census.

Between 1786 and 1829 the Indian peasant population in Chulumani declined at the brisk rate of −.66 percent (annualized over the period; see Tables 4.3 and 4.4). Moreover, the most mobile of the peasant populations were the most affected: the forasteros on the *ayllus* (at −.78 percent) and the yanaconas on the haciendas (at −.71 percent). Even the most stable group, the original landholding members of the *ayllus*, also experienced a decline (−.23 percent) in this period. While there was a modest recovery by the time of the census of 1838, still the overall result was a loss of population in the 52 years between the first and the last census. Over the entire period from 1786 to 1838, the same patterns revealed in the 1786–1829 period held true. The most mobile groups were those most affected, and the originarios were those least affected by the overall crisis.

Although the general trends in the three population groups were similar, a closer examination of various indices shows somewhat differing responses among each. Turning to the most important sector of coca production, the haciendas and their yanacona populations, it is apparent that there was a decline in both population and the number of operating haciendas as well. All haciendas systematically lost population, and thus average size of estates went down as well as total population, as can be seen in Table 4.5.

If just the more economically viable producers had remained and only the marginal ones had been eliminated, then the average size of populations should have risen on the remaining estates. But in fact the opposite occurred, which suggests that all estates, not just the marginal ones, were losing workers during this period of crisis. Aside from the overall decline in the figures for average workers per estate, there is also supporting evidence showing that the hacendados themselves, a minority of whom owned more than one estate, also saw their average total yanacona population declining quite considerably from a height of 64

TABLE 4.5
Changes in the Haciendas of Chulumani, 1786–1838

Indices	1786	1803	1829	1838
Number of haciendas[a]	270	236	230	229
Average population per hacienda	52	45	42	48
(s.d.)	(66)	(53)	(53)	(59)
Median population per hacienda	28	26	24	24
Average tributarios per hacienda	15	12	13	15
(s.d.)	(18)	(13)	(15)	(18)
Average yanacona population per hacendado	64	51	48	55
GINI coefficient of distribution of yanaconas among hacendados	.612	.583	.593	.596

SOURCE: Same as for Table 4.2.
[a]Excludes haciendas without yanaconas, so totals differ slightly from those in Table 4.7.

yanaconas per hacendado in 1786 to a low of 48 in 1829, with only a modest recovery by 1838 (see Table 4.5). Given the generalized loss of population from all sizes of estates, it is evident that the relative distribution of yanacona workers among estate owners changed little over the period, with the most unequal distribution occurring in 1786, and with stabilization thereafter in the next three censuses. Finally the dispersions around the mean (as measured by the standard deviation) show relatively little change over the three censuses, thus reinforcing the idea that the decline as indicated by the mean population figures was a reliable index of the changes that were occurring.

There were also some changes in ownership patterns, which were obviously a response to the increasing crisis affecting Chulumani's coca markets. In view of the high costs of maintaining the estates, opening new *cocales*, and replacing aged plants so as to guarantee continued output, the declining market forced many to abandon their estates. Not only did the total number of estates decline, but the number of owners possessing more than one estate also declined. Single estate owners, who made up 83 percent of the owners in 1786, controlled just over half of the yanacona workers in that boom year, but their share of that population increased with every ensuing census, until the trend

TABLE 4.6
Multiple Ownership Among Hacendados of Chulumani, 1786–1838

No. of haciendas owned	No. of owners	Yanacona population	Percentage of		
			Owners	Estates	Yanaconas
I. 1786					
1	182	7,267	82.7%	75.8%	52.0%
2	27	4,205	12.3	22.5	30.1
3+	11	2,493	5.0	1.7	17.9
	220	13,965	100.0%	100.0%	100.0%
II. 1803					
1	190	7,984	90.9%	80.5%	74.6%
2	15	1,344	7.2	12.7	12.6
3+	4	1,368	1.9	6.8	12.8
	209	10,696	100.0%	100.0%	100.0%
III. 1829					
1	193	8,188	91.9%	82.5%	80.8%
2	14	1,051	6.7	12.0	10.4
3+	3	896	1.4	5.6	8.8
	210	10,135	100.0%	100.0%	100.0%
IV. 1838					
1	180	7,683	89.1%	78.9%	69.8%
2	19	2,339	9.4	16.7	21.2
3+	3	993	1.5	4.4	9.0
	202	11,015	100.0%	100.0%	100.0%

SOURCE: Same as for Table 4.2.

began to reverse itself again in the moderate recovery year of 1838 (see Table 4.6).

This phenomenon of general declining populations on all estates raises some interesting questions about the little-known relationship between hacendado and yanaconas. It has traditionally been assumed that the standard means of payment for Indian laborers on the haciendas was the granting to them of usufruct lands for their own use. In examining numerous land sales of Yungas coca haciendas, I have never found any listing of yanaconas in the sales, nor any monetary evaluation given to them. It would appear that, initially, yanaconas were attracted to the haciendas by wages in order to carry out the very time-consuming task of terracing, which was required for almost all the coca haciendas. During this period no land was available for use by either the hacendado or the Indians. But once fields were terraced and cleared, all sources seem to agree that neither food, seeds, tools, nor wages were provided by the landowner. Thus there appears to be no incentive for a hacendado to expel workers from his cleared fields during times of crisis. Given this fact, the resulting mobility of the yanaconas in times of crisis would seem to suggest that these workers were not as tied down to the haciendas by nonmarket mechanisms as has traditionally been assumed. It was primarily the availability of the land and the possibility of selling their production in the coca markets (yanaconas in the 1796 survey of Yungas coca production produced 25 percent of the region's output) that provided the key incentives and constraints for workers living on the haciendas. Once retrenchment in the coca market occurred, these haciendas no longer became such attractive places for work, and voluntary out-migration occurred.

Although the mean number of workers per estate declined in most estates and in most regions, the pace of that decline was not identical, and in fact there occurred some changes in the relative importance of production among the various pueblos. It is clear that in the crisis years of 1803 and 1829, there was a systematic drop in the relative number of yanaconas in all districts of the Yungas except for the two leading centers of production—Coroyco and Coripata—and the small zones of Chupe and Yanacachi (see Table 4.7). With the revival of 1838, some of this trend toward increasing concentration of yanacona population was reversed, though the patterns of distribution did not return to precrisis levels. Such areas as Chulumani, Laza, Zuri, Ocabaya, and even the formerly third-ranked Pacallo all continued to decline in relative importance and were unable to recover their former significance. On the other hand Coripata and Coroyco, the two leading population zones for yanaconas, increased their relative importance census after census and went from 57 percent of the total yanacona population in 1786 to 74 percent in 1838.

Just as there was a decline in the number of haciendas and

TABLE 4.7

Number of Haciendas and Average Yanacona Population per Hacienda by Pueblo, Chulumani, 1786–1838

Pueblo	1786		1803		1829		1838	
	No. of haciendas	Avg. yanacona pop.	No. of haciendas	Avg. yanacona pop.	No. of haciendas	Avg. yanacona pop.	No. of haciendas	Avg. yanac pop
Chulumani	18	46	11	38	12	18	12	23
Irupana	43	15	31	12	31	14	25	17
Laza	13	44	11	36	8	23	12	16
Zuri	20	22	21	14	12	10	12	13
Ocabaya	8	30	9	16	5	25	5	19
Chirca	31	43	22	42	28	24	27	26
Pacallo	27	48	22	38	21	40	21	44
Coroyco	69	67	56	72	63	68	58	75
Coripata	34	98	41	67	37	77	35	92
Chupe	9	40	9	32	14	20	17	22
Yanacachi	4	78	4	66	4	64	7	52
TOTAL	276	51	237	45	235	44	231	48

SOURCES: Same as for Table 4.2.

their overall populations, there seems to have occurred a corresponding phenomenon on the free community lands. The overall *ayllu* populations responded in the same manner as the yanaconas on the haciendas, declining in the census of 1803, suffering further loses in 1829, and recovering in 1838. Thus their percentage importance within the Yungas changed little from census to census.

There were, however, some important internal differences— as might be expected—between the two major groupings on the *ayllus*. While the originarios differed from the other two categories of peasants in their ability to retain their population in the 1803 census, they too would show the effects of the crisis in the census of 1829. But as in the case of the other peasants, they were able to recover their numbers somewhat by the time of the 1838 census (see Tables 4.3 and 4.4 above). The originarios thus showed a greater ability to survive the impact of a declining market, just as they were to suffer the smallest losses. In effect, in times of crisis their share of the *ayllu* population increased, just as returning prosperity involved a return of the more migratory forastero population and thus a fall in their relative importance.

TABLE 4.8
Total Forastero Population by Pueblo, Chulumani, 1786–1838

Pueblo	1786	1803	1829	1838
Chulumani	1,315	1,113	686	714
Irupana	243	173	161	199
Laza	152	145	142	204
Zuri	296	159	149	265
Ocabaya	236	118	166	219
Chirca	425	279	245	277
Pacallo	44	61	67	48
Coroyco	272	287	350	430
Coripata	0	0	0	0
Chupe	477	397	293	336
Yanacachi	462	412	536	428
TOTAL	3,922	3,144	2,795	3,120

SOURCES: Same as for Table 4.2.

The more migratory forasteros responded in a manner quite similar to the yanaconas, losing almost an equal ratio of persons, on average, in the two censuses of 1803 and 1829, and recovering somewhat in 1838 (see Tables 4.3 and 4.4). As will be seen when examining the patterns in Pacajes, this was the obverse of what would occur in a region with an expanding population. This loss occurred for the majority of communities (see Table 4.8) and thus reflected a regional phenomenon. Nevertheless, there were some differences, the most important being the very severe decline of the forastero population in the pueblo of Chulumani, which in turn paralleled the pattern of loss among the yanaconas. Here, as elsewhere, it was the forasteros who were most similar to the yanaconas, and both responded in a common manner to general market as well as local production problems.

Within this relatively common picture of change in the *ayllus*, there was, as in the case of the haciendas, some relative change in regional importance. In examining the two largest pueblos (Chulumani and Yanacachi) in terms of total *ayllu* population, it is obvious that some structural changes were also occurring (see Table 4.9). Thus Chulumani, while maintaining its position as the leading zone of *ayllu* population, progressively lost population. Containing 34 pecent of the province's combined originario

TABLE 4.9
Total Ayllu Population by Pueblo, Chulumani, 1786–1838

Pueblo	1786	1803	1829	1838
Chulumani	2,274	2,091	1,421	1,365
Irupana	487	368	341	374
Laza	270	267	216	295
Zuri	491	349	287	474
Ocabaya	442	438	455	548
Chirca	688	580	510	472
Pacallo	44	61	67	48
Coroyco	430	436	529	654
Coripata	0	0	0	0
Chupe	713	616	509	539
Yanacachi	908	873	1,016	953
TOTAL	6,747	6,079	5,351	5,722

SOURCES: Same as for Table 4.2.

NOTE: Total originario population can easily be obtained for any pueblo in a given year by subtracting the forastero population in Table 4.8 from the total *ayllu* figure here.

and forastero population in 1786, it held only 24 percent by 1838. Equally, the second place Yanacachi progressively increased its share to 17 percent. Thus trends in terms of regional change were also present in the free communities as well as the haciendas.

In one area, however, the *ayllus* were sharply different from the haciendas, and that is in the number of units in operation throughout the four censuses. Up to 1829 all *ayllus* remained intact. In that year, however, the *ayllu* of San Roque in Irupana was turned into a hacienda, and for unexplained reasons the *ayllu* of Siripaya in Yanacachi was omitted (it was again registered as such in 1838). Another two *ayllus*—those of Choclla in Yanacachi and Guancapampa in Chirca—became haciendas in 1838, but in the meantime two new *ayllus* were registered in Zuri (Charapacci and Toriri). These changes meant that overall, the number of units changed little in the period of the four censuses. Clearly the *ayllus*, with their more mixed economies and poorer-quality coca leaf production, did not simply go out of business, as did the haciendas, but found alternative opportunities for their populations either in shifting to more subsistence agriculture or concentrating on valley food products desired in barter or for sale to the highland peasant communities. Their access to rich semitropical lands producing citrus crops, bananas, and other products not available to the majority of *altiplano* communities meant that these communities still were important poles of attraction for free but landless Indian peasants. Although coca income might decline, other goods were available for barter in the *altiplano*. Equally, their production of lesser-quality coca leaf, compared to the supposedly higher-quality product grown on the haciendas, probably meant that they were less affected by the mining decline than the haciendas. The miners could afford to buy the best-quality leaf, while the poorer-quality *ayllu* production probably went primarily to traditional agricultural peasants on the *altiplano*, a market that seems to have held steady during the mining crisis. This retention of market may explain why the *ayllus* both kept their number of units of production and ownership intact, and continued to maintained their share of the laboring population of these valleys at a relatively stable one-third of the total Indian population.

While the crisis of mine production and mining-related coca consumption had an impact on the coca plantations of Chulumani, it is clear that this shock was not catastrophic. Evidently the Yungas coca producers, both haciendas and *ayllus*, were able to find markets for the majority of the coca that was formerly consumed by the *altiplano* miners. The most obvious alternative was the expanding rural populations of the highlands, which seem to have been less affected by the decline of mining and to have developed a complex local and regional marketing system that permitted them to save more and consequently to increase their coca purchases.

However much these new and altered markets may have compensated local producers, it was evident that the miners were still the most desirable market. The increase in population, and presumably of coca output, by 1838 was clearly a reflection of the returning prosperity of the mines of the *altiplano*. The fact that the region could respond so positively and quickly to the increasing mine production meant that unused capacity existed in the Yungas despite the existence of alternative markets, and that even though these alternative markets may have been reasonably developed, they could not fully compensate for the older but more remunerative mining markets for coca.

An analysis of these four censuses provides an opportunity to reexamine the demographic variables I previously used in my synchronic analysis of the census of 1786. From the perspective of these fifty years, what were the significant continuities and changes in these gross demographic and economic indices?

The forasteros in these nineteenth-century censuses still exhibited demographic indices most closely associated with a migrant population (see Table 4.10). By and large they had the highest ratio of males to females of all three land-related groups. Equally, their economically active population was consistently higher than that of the other two categories of workers. The forasteros also had fewer children than any other group, as measured by the child-to-women ratio. This ratio consisted of niños and niñas per 100 women over 12 years of age (solteras, casadas, and viudas). This supports the earlier findings about the forasteros. The major difference here, however, is that the yanaconas, who should also have had lower rates than the more stable originario population, in the censuses after 1786 show a surprisingly high child-to-women ratio. In fact, they surpass the originarios in the censuses of 1803 and 1829, only to fall back again in 1838. Between 1829 and 1838 growth returned to these Chulumani pueblos (see Tables 4.3 and 4.4 above), so that by 1838 the relative positions on this index were again what they were in 1786—that is the originario had far and away the largest ratio of children to potential mothers and the other two were considerably below the originario standard. Nevertheless, it is quite clear that in the period of rapid decline the level of this ratio in all three groups had changed, so that they all had higher ratios in 1838 than in 1786.

For all groups there must have been a major leaving of younger adults, with if anything more females going than males. This pattern is suggested by the rising ratio of males and the increasing number of children to women (see Table 4.10). All three

TABLE 4.10

Basic Indicators of Population Structure in Chulumani,
by Tributary Category, 1786–1838

	Sex ratio	Pct. of EAP[b]	Pct. of tributary pop.	Children-to-women ratio[c]
I. Total[a]				
1786	122.3	60.7%	30.6%	106.6
1803	123.8	58.8	29.0	125.7
1829	124.0	59.7	31.9	137.3
1838	131.2	60.6	32.6	131.0
II. Originarios				
1786	110.7	58.0	30.7	124.7
1803	118.2	59.7	30.9	124.0
1829	134.9	61.2	34.3	141.1
1838	132.7	59.2	32.2	146.8
III. Forasteros				
1786	134.3	66.0	36.6	87.5
1803	133.2	63.6	36.0	119.0
1829	131.6	64.4	37.0	119.2
1838	152.0	64.5	39.7	134.6
IV. Yanaconas				
1786	121.5	59.7	29.0	108.4
1803	122.7	57.1	26.4	128.1
1829	119.5	58.0	29.9	141.3
1838	125.6	59.8	30.7	126.7

SOURCES: Same as for Table 4.2.

[a]Excludes ausentes.

[b]Economically active population is defined as the four categories of solteras + casadas + tributarios + proximos.

[c]Niños+niñas divided by viudas+solteras+casadas.

land-related groups felt the impact of this out-migration, including the most favored, the original members of the communities with direct access to land.

The slow return to growth between the censuses of 1829 and 1838 seems to indicate a return toward the patterns evident in 1786, at least with some of the indices. But it would appear that this growth was still recent enough so that no coherent trends are seen to be emerging. Moreover, the levels attained are now somewhat different than before. Although the ratio of economically active population has changed little, the ratio of tributarios and the sex ratio indicate a systematically higher proportion of males than before. Does this mean that fewer females were returning to the coca fields? Unfortunately, these indices alone are insufficient to clarify this issue.

What can be determined with precision, however, is the pattern of loss and how it affected the three categories of peasant workers in the pueblos of Chulumani. The tributary population of the Yungas, whether working on the haciendas or living on the free communities, all responded in some fashion to the restriction of coca markets as a result of the severe and relatively sustained early-nineteenth-century crisis of *altiplano* silver mining. All three categories of peasant—yanaconas, originarios, and forasteros—lost population in the crisis years of 1803 and 1829, and all recovered somewhat in the moderate boom period of 1838. Thus their relative positions within the province changed little despite impressive population losses. Moreover, that population loss spread evenly among the largest and smallest coca plantations—whether haciendas or *ayllus*—which also meant that the population responded to market incentives, no matter what its relationship was to the land. Though all groups experienced changes, it was in fact the originarios, with most direct access to land, who were least influenced by the general economic crisis. But the landless, whether on the estates or the communities, migrated out of the zone during times of crisis and only returned in significant numbers during times of improved market growth.

It was only in the area of regional production that the crisis engendered some long-term changes, more sharply developed among the hacienda populations than among the *ayllu* ones, though evident in both. Local zones such as the pueblo of Chulumani lost importance in both hacienda and *ayllu* populations, while the two traditionally wealthiest coca-producing zones, Coripata and to a lesser extent Coroyco, were the big gainers.

If a rich agricultural zone dominated by commercially based haciendas such as Chulumani was experiencing sharp fluctuations in its labor force in response to changes in its external markets for coca, what was occurring in the poorer traditional agricultural communities of the *altiplano* such as those of the district (or, in republican usage, the province) of Pacajes? Though involved to a greater extent in subsistence agriculture than the coca production zones, even these highland communities and landed estates were integrated into the market economy. These Lake Titicaca farms produced traditional high altitude grains and root crops and Andean animal products that fed into the local urban and regional markets as well as the Potosí mining communities. It has also been suggested by several authors, though with little supporting data, that the decline in the mining economy and its exports was somewhat compensated for by a relative growth in nontraditional exports in these first republican decades of crisis, especially locally produced Andean food crops to Peruvian markets.[22]

This difference in markets, together with the continued growth of the Pacajes population, may account for the basic difference in the district's response to the crisis. The tributary population of Pacajes grew from some 37,000 to some 42,000 between 1786 and 1838, although this growth occurred in only 6 out of the 12 pueblos (see Table 4.11). Nor was this growth uniform throughout the entire period. Total Indian population in Pacajes grew rapidly in the late eighteenth century (at over 0.5 percent per an-

TABLE 4.11
The Indian Tributary Population in Pacajes, by Pueblo, 1786–1838

Pueblo	1786	1792	1803	1838
Caquiaviri	3,089	3,122	3,476	4,601
Caquingora	2,404	2,471	2,639	2,794
Collapa	2,547	2,508	2,623	2,585
Curaguara	2,802	3,035	3,151	4,512
Ulloma	975	1,047	1,140	775
Calacoto	5,078	5,163	5,439	2,907
Santiago de Machaca	2,185	2,613	2,684	1,602
San Andres de Machaca	2,449	2,361	2,622	2,692
Jesús de Machaca	3,953	4,381	4,669	5,939
Guaqui	3,215	3,353	3,144	2,723
Tiahuanaco	4,087	3,967	4,500	3,745
Viacha	4,558	4,588	5,204	7,577
TOTAL	37,342	38,609	41,291	42,452

SOURCES: AGN, 13-17-6-4, libro 1 (for 1786); AGN, 13-17-9-4, libro 1, and 13-17-10-2, libro 3 (for 1803); ANB, Archivos del Tribunal Nacional de Cuentas, no. 163 (for 1838).

TABLE 4.12
Population Change by Category of Indians in Pacajes, 1786–1838

Category	1786	1792	1803	1838
Yanaconas	6,676	6,836	7,209	8,928
Originarios	17,016	13,912	16,014	9,568
Forasteros	13,650	17,861	18,068	23,956
TOTAL AYLLU	30,666	31,773	34,082	33,524
TOTAL INDIANS	37,342	38,609	41,291	42,452

SOURCES: Same as for Table 4.11.

TABLE 4.13
Population Growth Rates by Category of Indians in Pacajes, 1786–1838

Category	1786 to 1792	1792 to 1803	1803 to 1838	1786 to 1838
Yanaconas	0.40%	0.48%	0.61%	0.56%
Originarios	−3.30	1.29	−1.46	−1.10
Forasteros	4.58	0.10	0.81	1.09
TOTAL AYLLU	0.59%	0.64%	−0.05%	0.17%
TOTAL INDIANS	0.56%	0.61%	0.08%	0.25%

SOURCES: Same as for Table 4.11.

num), but slowed considerably between 1803 and 1838, the crisis period in the early-nineteenth-century republican economy (see Tables 4.12 and 4.13). Even among the three categories of Indian peasants, growth was not equal. The forasteros grew most rapidly, followed by the yanaconas, with the originarios surprisingly losing almost half of their total numbers from 1786 to 1838. Although the growth of the forasteros on the *ayllus* more than offset the decline of the originarios until 1803, by the census of 1838 the decline of the latter was so dramatic that for the first time the relative share of total population found on the community lands began to fall (to 79 percent of the total population compared to a high of 83 percent in 1803).

In the context of this slow but steady population growth, there was also a change in the average size of units. Among the haciendas, there was a decline in total numbers, and thus a substantial rise in the average size of populations per farm (see Table 4.14). At 135 persons per hacienda in 1838, these estates were some three times larger than the average coca hacienda in the Yungas valleys, just as the *ayllus* were three times the size of their counterparts in Chulumani. For their part, the *ayllus* in Pacajes also grew in this half century, not only in terms of average size, but also in the number of operating units.[23]

Did this growth relate to changes in the local economy? This is a difficult question to answer from the given data. In general, the Amerindian population of the highlands had been growing at a relatively steady pace from the early part of the eighteenth century, and would continue to grow throughout the nineteenth and twentieth centuries. Birth rates were sufficiently high to overcome high death rates at most times of peace and relative agricultural prosperity. Only the cholera epidemics in the middle decade of the nineteenth century and local harvest crises and labor drafts would slow or stop this growth. At the same time, it has been suggested that the relative decline of international trade led to an increase in local and regional economies.[24] Although the urban and highland populations serviced by the Pacajes villages were on the increase and evidently importing more foods, the data on international exports contained in the contemporaneous nineteenth-century studies of Pentland and Dalence suggest that exports to Peru and other neighboring states actually fell between 1825 and 1846, which would challenge the model of an increase in Andean trade.[25] If growth of

TABLE 4.14
Average Tributario and Average Total Population per Unit in Pacajes,
1786–1838

Year	No. of *ayllus*[a]	Originarios		Forasteros		No. of haciendas	Yanaconas	
		Ave. trib. pop.	Ave. total pop.	Ave. trib. pop.	Ave. total pop.		Ave. trib. pop.	Ave. total pop.
1786	88	35	193	30	153	74	17	90
1792	88	36	158	38	192	74	20	92
1803	94	38	170	44	188	76	23	95
1838	91	26	105	72	263	66	32	135

SOURCES: Same as for Table 4.11.
[a]With both originarios and forasteros. Several *ayllus* containing only forasteros have not been included.

the internal economy surely expanded Pacajes markets, there is some question about the growth of its Peruvian, Chilean, or Argentine exports.

Whichever market was expanding, there is no question that these Pacajes villages experienced both overall growth and a subtle but profound change in the distribution of categories of Indians within the *ayllus*. This change involved a shift in numerical importance between the originarios and the agregados or forasteros, and profoundly influenced the relative importance of each group within the communities. Whereas the landless community members made up less than half the *ayllu* population in 1786, as in previous censuses, by 1792 they had surpassed the originarios. The census of 1803 showed a decline in their importance, though they were still the dominant group, but by 1838 there was a very significant change and over two-thirds of the community now belonged to the landless category (see Table 4.14). While the cause for this change will be analyzed in more detail in the following chapter, when the entire departmental and national populations are examined, this trend replicates those found everywhere in Bolivia's free communities in the second half of the nineteenth century.

The steady growth of the Pacajes Indian population is reflected in the basic demographic indices (see Table 4.15). From census to census, the child-to-women ratio figures increase, just as do the percentage of the economically active population and of the male tributary population. This growth in the number of children to women is a correlate of the natural growth of the population and the increasing role that younger persons were coming to play in these villages. But it would also appear that the ratio of males was increasing as well in all groups, which would suggest that some in-migration was adding to the population as well. This could well represent the impact of dismissed miners who were returning to the land as agriculturalists, or harvesters and workers returning from the Yungas. This hypothesis of migration as a factor in the growth of the Pacajes Indian population is supported when we examine these indices by category of peasant worker. Thus, as would be predicted by this

TABLE 4.15
Basic Indicators of Population Structure in Pacajes, by Tributary Category,
1786–1838

	Sex ratio	Pct. of EAP[b]	Pct. of tributary pop.	Children-to-women ratio[c]
I. Total[a]				
1786	88.5	51.3%	19.0%	105.7
1792	99.4	52.7	21.0	117.0
1803	109.8	58.2	23.2	108.7
1838	116.8	56.9	26.1	128.4
II. Originarios				
1786	91.7	52.0	18.2	111.4
1792	108.0	54.8	22.7	146.3
1803	107.8	58.3	22.5	118.0
1838	111.0	57.7	25.1	140.1
III. Forasteros				
1786	83.7	50.5	19.9	99.0
1792	93.2	51.3	19.5	97.8
1803	110.8	57.4	23.5	104.0
1838	120.4	57.9	27.3	118.8
IV. Yanaconas				
1786	90.3	51.4	19.1	105.3
1792	99.1	52.3	21.6	119.2
1803	112.0	59.6	23.8	100.9
1838	113.8	53.6	23.7	142.4

SOURCES: Same as for Table 4.11.
[a] Excludes ausentes.
[b] Economically active population is defined as the four categories of solteras+casadas+tributarios+proximos.
[c] Niños+niñas divided by viudas+solteras+casadas.

hypothesis, the two categories of landless workers, yanaconas and forasteros, had the highest ratio of males, and this ratio increased most rapidly among them compared to that of the originarios. It was the originarios who showed the least growth in the male population figures, though even here the ratio of males increased considerably from the low figure registered in 1786, though it remained relatively stable thereafter.

The question remains of whether these transformations led to changes in the distribution of estates, *ayllus*, and populations. It is evident that growth was not constant in all regions (see Table 4.11). Calacoto, the largest of the pueblos in terms of total population in 1786, dropped to sixth place a half century later, while

TABLE 4.16
Yanaconas as a Percentage of Total Population by Pueblo, Pacajes,
1786–1838

Pueblo	1786	1792	1803	1838
Caquiaviri	20.1%	17.5%	16.9%	13.1%
Caquingora	1.7	2.2	1.3	0.0
Collapa	3.4	2.9	2.2	0.0
Curaguara	21.9	21.0	22.6	25.9
Ulloma	0.0	0.0	0.0	0.0
Calacoto	0.0	0.0	0.0	0.0
Santiago de Machaca	10.5	10.8	18.8	22.0
San Andres de Machaca	3.9	2.1	3.7	0.0
Jesús de Machaca	6.8	6.4	6.9	7.1
Guaqui	37.6	39.2	35.2	45.9
Tiahuanaco	32.1	34.5	34.5	48.4
Viacha	48.2	48.6	43.0	43.9
TOTAL	17.9%	17.7%	17.5%	21.0%

SOURCES: Same as for Table 4.11.

Viacha grew at an impressive 0.98 percent per annum during this period and emerged as the district's most populous center. Moreover, that quintessential community zone Jesus de Machaca also grew rapidly, becoming the second most populous region, largely through the increase of its forastero population, which now made up 65 percent of *ayllu* members.

Although population growth was not evenly spread among the pueblos, it did not affect the relative importance of different types of agricultural units in them. Not only did the number of such units remain relatively constant over time (see Table 4.14), but population growth did not change the relative domination of free Indian communities in the district. This is well reflected in the share of yanaconas, for example, in the total population in each pueblo (see Table 4.16). Only in Tiahuanaco and in lakeside Guaqui was there a modest increase in the relative importance of these landless peasants.

Finally, the internal changes noted in the *ayllu* populations were consistent across all villages. Except for the very poor zone of San Andres de Machaca, every community-dominated zone saw a steady increase of the forastero populations until they represented the dominant labor force on the local *ayllus* (see Table

TABLE 4.17
Forasteros as a Percentage of Total Ayllu Population by Pueblo, Pacajes,
1786–1838

Pueblo	1786	1792	1803	1838
Caquiaviri	47.0%	63.6%	60.1%	76.0%
Caquingora	44.6	58.6	58.1	85.0
Collapa	44.9	54.3	52.0	80.2
Curaguara	40.7	56.7	54.6	76.5
Ulloma	31.1	50.2	44.1	66.5
Calacoto	32.8	46.5	44.8	66.6
Santiago de Machaca	55.7	67.6	64.8	81.9
San Andres de Machaca	55.0	60.5	56.0	56.6
Jesús de Machaca	47.8	60.7	54.5	65.4
Guaqui	44.1	49.7	44.7	68.4
Tiahuanaco	47.8	57.1	51.0	72.1
Viacha	47.4	52.5	53.9	68.2
TOTAL	44.5%	56.2%	53.0%	71.5%

SOURCES: Same as for Table 4.11.

4.17). In some communities the forastero growth was more rapid than in others, but in the end ten communities saw these landless Indians become the dominant labor group on the *ayllus*.

From this diachronic analysis of over fifty years of change in these two districts of Chulumani and Pacajes, what conclusions can be drawn with regard to the initial set of hypotheses posed earlier? To begin with, despite the differing reactions of the districts to the crisis in the export economy, and differing levels of in- and out-migration, both maintained their basic character. The *ayllus* as well as the haciendas in the coca valleys of Chulumani were consistently smaller than those in Pacajes. This size factor had much to do with the ecological limits to production in the capital-intensive agriculture of the Yungas valleys, as compared to the less capital-intensive and more extensive production on the flatter but poorer lands of the *altiplano*. If anything, the relative differences in size grew even greater due to the temporary decline in the average size of units in Chulumani and their steady expansion in Pacajes.

Equally evident, though not with absolute agreement in every census, were the differences between the originarios and the other two categories of peasant workers. The forasteros on the free communities and the yanaconas on the estates of the non-Indians were the first to migrate, had higher ratios of males, and usually lower children-to-women ratios. All this again suggests that the originarios, with their direct land ownership, were both less prone to migrate and more likely to have a more balanced demographic structure, and probably more stable family lives.[26]

Finally, two long-term developments are evident in the Pacajes census, though not at all a factor in the evolution of the Chulumani economy. The first was the dramatic rise to dominance of the forastero population in the free communities. The second was the steady expansion of the hacienda populations. The slow but steady growth of the population of the city of La Paz was beginning to make the traditional *altiplano* foodstuff haciendas, with their low capital requirements, an attractive investment and one that would result in steady hacienda expansion at the expense of the free communities. The trend of increasing forastero and yanacona populations would become even more pronounced in later decades. In the Yungas, forasteros already represented over half the free community population even in the 1780's and did not increase their share into the late 1830's. Moreover, there seemed to be a limit to hacienda expansion in these coca-growing valleys, at least so long as the export economy did not expand.

While the above demographic evidence is only one part of the picture, its relative availability, as opposed to production and price data, makes it the prime source for the history and evolution of the peasant populations of late colonial and republican Bolivia. Thus, despite the limitations of the sources and the indices, an analysis of these demographic responses to economic change suggests that traditional perceptions of a relatively stable peasantry unresponsive to market demands must be seriously revised—at least for Bolivia. These responses suggest that both the free Indian communities and the haciendas were far from being either "feudal" or "passive" traditional institutions incapable of responding to changing market conditions. These data also suggest that the yanaconas were more independent of hacendado control than has been previously assumed. Moreover, the supposedly "feudal" haciendas themselves fully responded to changing market conditions, expanding or contracting in response to changes in their prime markets. Equally, the supposedly "traditional" and "closed corporate communities" were themselves quite responsive to market change and evolution. As the market expanded at an ever more rapid rate in the middle and later decades of the nineteenth century, many of the trends in this first half of the century would become stronger and dominate the pattern of change.

CHAPTER FIVE

Peasant Response to the Market and the Land Question in the Nineteenth Century

RECENT STUDIES OF nineteenth-century Indian peasant societies in the Andes have stressed the enormous resilience of the free Indian communities and their surprising ability to maintain their lands and their economic independence until late in the century.[1] It has usually been assumed that this ability to survive had more to do with the backwardness of the respective republican governments and their continued dependence on income from Indian tribute tax than it did with any positive activity on the part of the communities themselves. But this position, as I will argue in this chapter, is an unnecessarily negative one and implies that the Indians were passive and exploited peasants incapable of defending their interests, especially in the face of a systematic penetration of the market economy. But just as the model of an unchanging rural society dominated by the hacienda has given way to the knowledge that the free communities were powerful in Andean society until the most recent past, the same holds true as well for the model of the helpless peasantry. What becomes clear from an examination of the evidence, especially for the middle decades of the nineteenth century when the Bolivian export economy achieved a new level of growth, is that the communities survived and prospered against the ever-increasing penetration of the market.

In this chapter I will try to determine the mechanisms by which the Indian communities adapted to the growing penetration of the market after the middle of the nineteenth century, and to evaluate their relative degree of success in meeting market demands for their labor and their agricultural output. Once again, I take as my prime area of analysis the region of La Paz, here defined by the republican departmental boundaries.

Unfortunately for this analysis of the *ayllus* and their resident populations, systematic data on production and prices for the national or even regional markets are not yet available for the nineteenth century. For lack of such evidence, it is necessary once more to use the unpublished tribute censuses for examining the problem of markets and peasant response. These will be examined here in order to determine the size and distribution of the various categories of rural Indian labor during the rapid growth of the market in the post-1840's period.

Until well into the nineteenth century, the Bolivian government relied on the Indian tribute because of the crucial economic importance it played in terms of government income. Whereas the tribute in the region of Bolivia had been an important but only secondary source of income after mining and commerce in the colonial period, it was the largest and the most important source of government revenues in the republic of Bolivia until the late 1850's, when mining and commerce taxes again became dominant in the national accounts (see Table 5.1).

The cause for this importance of tribute income is not hard to find. The wars of independence had been long and destructive. International trade had been upset for Bolivia even prior to the war, and finally most of the mines were flooded and could only be reopened at enormous expense. With little national capital and no foreign capital available, Bolivian silver production continued its long decline, reaching an extraordinarily low point in the 1820's and 1830's. The Bolivian government therefore decided to reinstitute the colonial tribute and continue with the *revisitas* based on the colonial model. By this act the new republican regime continued the discriminatory tax on the Indians, but it also guaranteed the communities in their corporate possession of land. Thus not only did the new republican governments ignore Bolívar's suggestion of terminating the tribute on Indians,

TABLE 5.1
Estimates of Tribute as a Percent of Total Government Revenues, 1827–80
(In pesos)

	Estimate A		Estimate B	
Year	Tribute income	Pct. of total revenues	Tribute income	Pct. of total revenues
1827	–	–	618,115	41%
1828	–	–	717,920	48
1829	–	–	717,920	48
1830	–	–	717,920	47
1831	716,543	43%	717,920	37
1832	600,453	34	600,453	39
1833	650,208	39	650,208	45
1834	–	–	700,000	40
1835	677,694	39	677,694	39
1836	685,695	43	635,695	41
1838	759,695	53	759,695	–
1839	745,287	36	759,695	53
1840	–	–	745,237	45
1841	670,115	31	752,275	43
1842	–	–	743,536	30
1843	756,740	40	756,740	38
1844	766,939	32	766,939	35
1845	–	–	823,481	36
1846	864,239	36	864,239	38
1847	877,904	35	877,836	35
1848	655,635	27	665,635	33
1849	637,474	28	637,474	33
1850	–	–	919,006	–
1851	–	–	–	–
1852	664,156	28	664,156	30
1853	572,222	24	765,886	36
1854	498,438	20	874,821	37
1855	–	–	882,562	38
1856	–	–	836,606	32
1860	–	–	650,000	37
1861	–	–	–	–
1862	699,636	26	859,205	31
1863	790,057	35	708,446	–
1864	–	–	835,658	38
1865	–	–	693,779	41
1866	–	–	–	–
1867	531,946	17	425,557	17
1868	459,994	13	367,995	13
1869	381,805	8	305,444	8
1871	424,723	14	339,779	20
1880	764,152[a]	23	723,994[a]	25

SOURCE: Estimate A is from Sánchez-Albornoz, *Indios y tributos*, p. 198. Estimate B is from Ovando Sanz, *El tributo indígena*, pp. 483–88.

NOTE: After 1880 tribute income went to departmental treasuries and no longer formed part of the national accounts.

[a] *Bolivianos.*

but they also abandoned the liberal model of private property in the rural area for all classes and races that had also been part of the liberal ideology of the independence movement.[2]

This period of support for the traditional patterns of dual landownership in the rural areas, with communal property rights coexisting with private individual ownership, remained the norm of rural life in Bolivia, and above all in the Department of La Paz, until the 1860's. Just as the maintenance of the traditional system can be explained by the harsh economic necessities of local government, despite the verbal acceptance of liberalism, the final acceptance of the liberal model can equally be explained by the end of the fiscal importance of the tribute tax. While the income from tribute continued to grow with the growth of the Indian population throughout the nineteenth century, its relative importance began to decline after the 1850's (see Table 5.1).

The cause for this relative decline in tribute revenues was the growth of the national economy and government revenues as a result of both major new investments in the *altiplano* silver mines and the beginnings of commercial mining activities on the Pacific Coast. By the time of the Melgarejo government in the 1860's, Bolivia was generating more income from mining and commercial activities than from tribute taxes. The new mining elite tied to silver was also making a major attack on all the remnants of the mercantilist policies that had been dominant in Bolivian policies from the late 1820's until this period. They demanded free trade in silver and an end to all government monopolies.[3] In this context of liberal economic thought, it was inevitable that the "anti-modern" and supposedly nonproductive land-ownership patterns represented by the corporate communities would be challenged. The result was the decision of the government in 1866 to destroy the previously recognized property rights of the Indians in their community lands, and to declare that the tribute tax was simply a rent for lands which were owned by the State and which were now declared vacated. In the several land decrees of that year, the government went out of its way to prevent Indians from purchasing their former community lands by requiring that all purchases be of a substantial minimum size and a high minimum cost. To favor the government speculators it permitted the payment for these lands to be made with government debt obligations.

From 1866 until late 1869 the government disposed of some 356 *comunidades* throughout the republic for a total value of 865,550 bolivianos (or over 1 million pesos a 8), only some 30 percent of which was paid in cash. Massive fraud and economic dislocation was the immediate result of the decree. The reaction from the peasants was slow, but in 1869 and 1870 three major uprisings occurred at Tliquina, Guaycho, and Ancoryames. Over a thousand Indians were killed by Melgarejo's troops and this, along with the wild speculations generally, finally elicited widespread elite opposition. Several white legislators even wrote pamphlets protesting the land laws and demanding justice for the Indians. With the overthrow of Melgarejo in January of 1870, the land confiscations were revoked.[4]

It quickly became apparent, however, that general elite opinion disagreed not so much with Melgarejo and his land ideas as with his timing and execution. Access to Indian lands under the Melgarejo decrees had really been limited to people with political influence. Moreover, the boom in the mining sector was still absorbing most of the available capital within the republic. Thus it was not until the maturation of the silver industry in the late 1870's that enough capital was finally made available for alternative investments. Concurrently, the growth in the urban centers now created enough of a national market and enough capital for the elite to begin to invest seriously in rural lands. By the late 1870's such investment began in earnest and enough pressure was finally built up among the elite that the government repented of its abolition of the Melgarejo decree and in 1874 issued a new and definitive law abolishing corporate ownership in land and forcing all Indians to purchase their holdings.

But the rulers of 1874 had profited by the experience of the previous decade. The new act declared that only the supposedly "excess" lands of the *ayllu* belonged to the state and guaranteed that the communal and individual plots belonged to the Indians in "absolute ownership," which of course included the right to alienate that land. The language of the decree also spoke of "*exvinculación*," meaning that the end of communal ownership and the assumption of individual property rights would supposedly free the Indians from discriminatory labor obligations and also the retrograde hand of their own communal governments.[5] Finally, the enabling decrees were not issued until 1880, thus permitting time for adjustment.

The result of this more cautious approach was that Indian response was initially confused and quite legalistic. No Indian mass movements took place initially, and only in the next decade did the tempo of revolts intensify as the Indians began to realize the fraudulent nature of the law. In 1895 and 1896 rebellion spread throughout the highlands, affecting most of the *altiplano* provinces of La Paz. Then in 1899 a major peasant army was organized by the Aymara *kurakas* in alliance with the Liberals in the Federal Revolution of that year, with the Indians demanding an end to the sale of their lands. The result, in fact, was a temporary halt to the sales in 1900–1901. But the Liberals quickly rejected this compromise, and not only were sales intensified, but the leaders of the Indian forces were executed by the government.[6]

Thus despite violent protest and the supposedly "liberal" nature of the law, in fact, the post-1880 period saw a fundamental attack on the free community lands. Allowing sale of "unused" lands permitted the alienation of core lands of the corporate *ayllu*, and it took little effort to challenge the land titles of the remaining *comunarios*. Moreover, in contrast to the limited number of interested persons in the 1860's confiscations, in the 1880's there now existed a class of entrepreneurs ready to take an active role in agricultural production. A new class of wealthy elite now existed in the urban centers, especially La Paz, who wanted to invest in rural lands. Denied access to the increasingly industrialized and monopolized mining sector, which relied mainly on foreign capital, they found *altiplano* haciendas an ideal outlet for their new wealth.[7] In 1881, Augustín Aspiazu, the Bolivian Director of the 1880 Cadastral Survey (which replaced the tithes with a land tax for whites and cholos), claimed that the value and production of *puna* haciendas had doubled between 1860 and 1880. The reasons for this growth, he felt, were to be found in the increase in national population and the incredible "security for capital employed in this type of investment." Buying a highland estate, one did not have to add any investments in animals, buildings, or machinery, since the work-for-usufruct-land arrangements on traditional haciendas guaranteed that the *peones* (or *pongo-colonos*) supplied all basic necessities including the seed and farm implements. Moreover, he noted, urban demand was so strong for highland food products that prices continued to rise and demand seemed inelastic. For this reason, went on the Director, banks were delighted to lend money on land titles to *puna* estates and there was no problem in mortgaging these estates to a quite high percentage of their value.[8] Given these conditions, the incentive to reduce the initial cost factor even further by using government troops to seize lands from "rebellious" Indians was an irresistible temptation that led to a massive assault on Indian land ownership.

The resulting process of purchase or theft of title from a few Indian originarios resulted in the ejection of entire communities or in the partial dismemberment of the land stock of the surviving *ayllus*, greatly weakening their ability to survive as viable units into the twentieth century. The process was crude, fraudulent, and filled with bloodshed, and took some thirty years to accomplish. It was carried out against many Indian rebellions and with the liberal use of the army in all rural regions as a police force to enforce the change in landownership. The results of this campaign can be seen in the dramatic decline in communities and corresponding growth of haciendas in all regions, but especially the *altiplano* (see Table 5.2).

This in bare outline is the history of the process of rural land ownership in Bolivia in the eighteenth, nineteenth, and early twentieth centuries. In a schematic way it outlines the history from the perspective of the elite. But it is evident that the role of the peasant in these various changes was not a passive one in this period. The sixteenth- and seventeenth-century reforms

TABLE 5.2

The Change in the Number of Ayllus and Haciendas in the Department of La Paz, 1846 and 1941

Region	1846		1941		Annualized percentage change	
	Ayllus	Hacdas.	*Ayllus*	Hacdas.	*Ayllus*	Hacdas.
Puna	716	500	161	3,193	−1.6%	2.0%
Middle Valley	106	795	62	4,538	−0.6	1.9
Valley	14	28	22	101	0.5	1.4
Yungas	43	302	36	675	−0.2	0.9
TOTAL	879	1,625	281	8,507	−1.2%	1.8%

SOURCE: Demelas, *Nationalisme sans nation?*, p. 163.

NOTE: Demelas based her geographic divisions on Dalence's 1846 census. The Puna region consists of most of the provinces of Omasuyos and Pacajes, and small sections of Larecaja and Sicasica. The Yungas consists of Chulumani and a small part of Sicasica. The Middle Valley and Valley regions consist essentially of the provinces of Sicasica and Larecaja, with a few sections of Omasuyos.

had created a multiclass system in the rural areas. From all types of records it is clear that the communities entered the market and obtained cash either for their products or from their members who sold their labor. Each community had its own *caja* or treasury which contained such income. Sufficient surplus was generated beyond the needs of royal taxation for the Crown to use this surplus to provide mortgage funds (or *censos*) to Spaniards wishing to invest in rural lands or improve their haciendas. These funds were invested at interest, and while defaulting on Indian-community loans was not uncommon, enough judicial evidence exists to show that income was reasonably guaranteed for the communities.[9]

Equally, evidence exists that government officials were also able to extract considerable cash from the Indians in the colonial period. In lieu of reasonable salaries, the Crown permitted its local rural officials, the *corregidores*, to forcibly sell to the Indians imported merchandise and mules at high cost. It has been estimated that some 563,000 pesos were generated in the Viceroyalty of the Rio de la Plata from this source alone, of which 36 percent—the largest share—came from La Paz. Equally, the region of La Paz had been the largest single contributor of tribute income when it was part of the Viceroyalty of Peru prior to 1776.[10] Thus in just these three ways, rather large sums of money were extracted from the free communities, clearly indicating that they in turn had the ability to generate such sums from the market.

A less direct indication of this ability is the unusual activity that occurred within the rural communities of the *altiplano* when the external pressures extracting this surplus were reduced. Thus in the century-long crisis in silver mining from 1650 to 1750, the *revisitas* note a decline in the number of haciendas, many listing themselves with no yanaconas whatsoever. This was clearly the result of the precipitous collapse of the urban markets and the decline in urban population during the depression, which in turn forced a stagnation, if not an actual retrenchment, in the growth of haciendas in the rural area. At this same period the free communities were heavily investing in community churches throughout the highlands of the province of La Paz. This in fact was the most extraordinary period of major and very expensive church construction in rural Bolivia, and the Indian and cholo artisans employed even produced their own unique and original mestizo art style employing many preconquest and rural Indian motifs.[11]

To accept a theme in the dependency literature, it might be suggested that the decline of the central government and its ability to tax efficiently leads to a decline in exploitation from the center, which permits the rural periphery to save more of the income it generates and invest it in projects that it deems important. While the Indian communities must have also suffered from a decline in the urban markets, the continued vitality of the exchange markets and their increasing importance may have compensated them sufficiently to guarantee the funds necessary to undertake this costly church construction.

But what was occurring in the period of national economic growth in the nineteenth century that permitted the peasants to continue to respond to the market as both hacienda pressures increased and demands on their resources escalated? How did the internal organization of the *ayllus* change so that the communities survived? To answer these questions in even the most preliminary way, it is essential to analyze the changing role of the various groups among the peasants in eighteenth- and nine-teenth-century Bolivia as seen from the perspective of the re-visitas of the department of La Paz from 1786 to 1877.[12]

A detailed analysis of these censuses shows that the Indian peasant population subject to taxation was increasing through-out the late eighteenth and nineteenth centuries. Thus, despite the pestilence and famine of the first decade of the nineteenth century and the virulent cholera epidemics in the mid-1850's, In-dian male tributary-age population in all categories was growing throughout this period. While it would be useful to compare age and sex ratios and total populations, it turns out that any serious demographic analysis can only be based on the male tributarios. Only from the 1780's until the censuses of the 1830's do the government officials systematically record women and children. Though numbers are still given for women and children after that date, these categories tended to be underrecorded in many regions. Thus while the *tributario* population continues to in-crease, the non-tributary population begins to decline in the censuses of the 1850's through to the last ones of the late 1870's. When we check sex ratios and child-to-women ratios in this pe-riod, it is obvious that women and children were often not re-corded properly, a pattern of underregistration that had also been the norm in the pre-1780's period. But it appears as if this underreporting is random, so the use of these categories for sev-eral demographic indices is still viable. But this problem with the post-1830's censuses renders difficult attempts to estimate general population growth using the total population estimates.

Analyzing the available censuses for male tributary popula-tion—that is, landowners and/or heads of households aged 18–50 (see Table 5.3)—reveals that the fastest-growing segment of the rural population throughout this 90-year period was the fo-rasteros living on the *ayllus*. The forastero population of the major highland and valley regions experienced very rapid rates of growth in excess of all other groups.

Though forasteros were only second in importance and repre-sented just one-third of the total rural labor force in the late colo-

TABLE 5.3

Tributary Population of the Department of La Paz by Category, 1786–1877

Category	1780's		1830's		1850's		1870's	
	No.	Pct.	No.	Pct.	No.	Pct.	No.	Pct.
Originarios	10,259	26%	11,599	20%	12,941	19%	13,123	19
Forasteros	13,105	33	25,805	44	31,108	46	33,441	48
Yanaconas	16,300	41	21,277	36	23,305	35	22,899	33
TOTAL	39,664	100%	58,681	100%	67,354	100%	69,463	100

SOURCES: Colonial censuses, AGN, Sala XIII; republican censuses, AHLP and ANB.

NOTE: The provinces treated were Chulumani, Larecaja, Pacajes, Omasuyos, Sicasica, and the ou skirts of the city of La Paz known as the Cercado. All of these provinces were reorganized by the state the nineteenth century, and I have therefore regrouped all the towns of each province as they existed the census of 1786. Thus the new province of Inquisivi and Muñecas were reassigned to their origir provinces, Pacajes and Larecaja, respectively. Also I eliminated several Yungas pueblos that were co stantly shifting between the Departments of La Paz and of Cochabamba. The extreme reorganization the Cercado district from census to census has made it very difficult to make coherent with the 17 definitions, and I have not used the later figures for comparative purposes. All of these recalculatio on my part mean that my total figures are somewhat under the official government figures publish for this period in 1901 (see Appendix Tables C2–C4); also my exclusion of "pueblo" Indians and the u of different revisitas means that my total tributario figures will not agree completely with those Greishaber (see Appendix Tables C2–C4).

nial period, by the 1870's they were the predominant group and accounted for just under half of all peasants. Though both the originario and the yanacona populations also grew at this time, their rates of increase were not as rapid. The originarios over the entire period, however, grew more rapidly than the landless yanaconas, which meant that the *ayllu* population experienced even faster growth than the hacienda populations. Given the fact that the number of *ayllus* remained stable or even declined somewhat in most regions, average population size on the majority of *ayllus* was increasing throughout the period under study (see Table 5.4).

The one exception to this overall pattern is the coca-growing region of the Yungas or Chulumani. This was a region with a long history of powerful haciendas and wealthy but reduced *ayllus*. Much of this region in fact was virgin territory until late in the colonial period.[13] In the nineteenth century, Chulumani was especially affected by the decline in mining production because miner consumption of its coca decreased accordingly. Also, the very restricted availability of land in the narrow ter-raced valleys led to a local pattern of *ayllu* growth different from

TABLE 5.4

Average Number of Male Tributarios (Originarios and Forasteros) per Ayllu, Department of La Paz, 1786–1877

Province	1780's	1830's	1850's	1870's
Chulumani	62	56	61	44
Pacajes	64	91	116	119
Omasuyos	56	83	106	114
Sicasica	52	99	105	n.a.
Larecaja[a]	38	52	51	n.a.
Cercado	50	n.a.	65	122
PROVINCIAL AVG.	52	(83)	88	(171)
No. of *Ayllus*	451	(450)	503	(273)

SOURCES: Same as for Table 5.3.
NOTE: Numbers in parentheses indicate incomplete totals; "n.a." means that the relevant censuses of those years did not provide numbers of *ayllus*.
[a]The Larecaja total for 1838 is combined with the earliest extant revisita for Muñecas, which is 1848.

the departmental norm. This explains why little significant change occurred in the *ayllu* population of the region over this period.

If the departmental *ayllu* population was expanding and the average size of each *ayllu* was increasing, what was happening on the haciendas? Though not quite as rapidly as the *ayllu* peasants, the hacienda peasant population was also on the increase for most of the nineteenth century. Total numbers of yanaconas were greater in the 1870's than in the late colonial period. But given the number of abandoned haciendas left from periods of extreme depression and retrenchment—or haciendas "without workers" (*sin gente*) as the local census officials eloquently put it—the increase in yanaconas did not lead to an increase in average size (see Table 5.5). Abandoned units were simply brought back into production as the market opportunities increased. Thus average size in all areas but Omasuyos remained remarkably stable.[14]

These findings unquestionably point to the growing importance of the forasteros as the single most significant change in the rural life of Bolivia in the nineteenth century. At the time of increasing market penetration, the peasant labor force became progressively more dominated by the forastero category of

TABLE 5.5

Average Number of Male Yanaconas per Hacienda, Department of La Paz,
1786–1877

Province	1780's	1830's	1850's	1870's
Chulumani	15	15	16	17
Pacajes	17	33	37	33
Omasuyos	29	32	41	41
Sicasica	16	19	19	n.a.
Larecaja	10	15	10	n.a.
Cercado	54	n.a.	24	44
PROVINCIAL AVG.	17	(24)	22	(45)
No. of Haciendas	976	(871)	1,073	(508)

SOURCES: Same as for Table 5.3.

NOTE: Numbers in parentheses indicate incomplete totals; "n.a." means that the relevant censuses of those years did not provide numbers of haciendas.

workers. Their share of population in the *ayllus* went from 56 percent at the beginning of the period to 72 percent by the end, and their share of total population grew from one-third of the peasantry in the 1780's to some 48 percent in the late 1870's. If increasing production for the market was being met by the forasteros, then it would appear that they were even more successful at this than the yanacona class, which in fact steadily lost ground to them in this period. Whereas yanaconas represented 41 percent of the rural population at the beginning of the period, they dropped to just one-third of the total by the end. Thus there were 2.5 forasteros for every originario by the 1870's, or double what the ratio had been in the earliest censuses, and one-and-a-half forasteros for every yanacona, again just about doubling in the ratio since the 1780's (see Table 5.6).

Although the general long-term trends are quite evident, the detailed short-term growth patterns from census to census are not quite as easily explained. What is revealed from a detailed inter-census study is that the growth of each of the Indian categories was not uniform over the entire 90-year period. An analysis of the compound annual growth rates shows that the entire rural Indian population grew more quickly in the earlier depression periods than in the later periods of the expansion of the domestic and international market (see Table 5.7). If the model of

TABLE 5.6
Ratio of Forasteros to Originarios in the Department of La Paz, 1786–1877

Province	1780's	1830's	1850's	1870's
Chulumani	1.7	1.5	1.2	1.7
Pacajes	0.8	2.2	2.2	2.2
Omasuyos	2.3	4.6	6.2	6.1
Sicasica	0.5	2.0	2.1	2.3
Larecaja	2.2	1.2	1.2	1.3
Cercado	2.3	3.8	2.7	3.6
TOTALS	1.3	2.2	2.4	2.5
Forastero-to-yanacona ratio	0.8	1.2	1.3	1.5

SOURCES: Same as for Table 5.3.

TABLE 5.7
*Annual Growth Rates of the Tributary Population in
the Department of La Paz, 1786–1877*

Category	1780–1830	1830–50	1850–70	1780–1870
Yanaconas	0.53%	0.46%	−0.09%	0.38%
Originarios	0.25	0.55	0.07	0.27
Forasteros	1.36	0.94	0.36	1.05
ALL AYLLUS	0.95%	0.82%	0.28%	0.77%
ALL TRIBUTARIOS	0.79%	0.69%	0.15%	0.62%

SOURCES: Same as for Table 5.3.

lessened exploitation during periods of market retrenchment can be accepted, it might be argued that these earlier spurts of growth were proof—as in the analogous seventeenth-century crisis period—that the communities prospered in an inverse relationship to the growth of the white- and mestizo-dominated commercial market. The increasing penetration of that market therefore helps to explain the decline in the growth rates of all groups from the 1830's to the 1870's.

While rural population expansion slowed the more the market economy expanded, the forastero growth rate dropped less than that of the other groups and thus the relative importance of the forasteros consistently increased from census to census throughout most regions. This seems to support the belief that they played a positive role in aiding the communities to meet market penetration. Nevertheless, it does not quite explain why their growth in the earlier period (1780's–1830's) should be so extraordinarily rapid—a very respectable 1.4 percent per annum rate—which was impressive even by contemporary European standards, and why at the same time the originario class grew at less than a quarter of a percent per annum. Equally, why the originarios should then double their growth rate in the next period of increasing market pressure is also unclear.

The relatively precipitous decline of the landless *peones* on the haciendas in the last period of most intense market growth (1850's–1870's), though perplexing, may have two possible explanations. Either the *ayllus* proved to be more productive and competitive than the haciendas in meeting the expanding needs of the market with commercial agricultural production; or the market penetration first put pressure on labor demands—most easily met by the *ayllus*—and only secondarily resulted in increased demand for foodstuffs. Given the lesser mobility of the yanaconas on the haciendas, it might be argued that the flow of labor to the mines, to the railroads, and to the transportation and urban occupational sectors could only be met by the *ayllus* exporting labor.[15] Late colonial Yungas coca production data suggest that the *ayllus* were less efficient market producers than the haciendas, at least in terms of coca production.[16] But this might not have held true for foodstuff haciendas of the *altiplano*. Contemporaries remarked on how much less capital intensive these estates were compared to those of the Yungas.[17] *Altiplano* haciendas thus may not have been as competitive as their *ayllu* neighbors. Unfortunately, given the current level of economic data, the precise pattern of market penetration and the comparative efficiency and productivity of the two types of farming units cannot be determined at this point.

What can be stated with some certitude, however, is that the causes for these shifts in importance among the laboring groups cannot be easily explained by the usual demographic factors. It is evident from all accounts that these peasants represented a relatively closed demographic group. There was no significant urbanization in the region during the entire period under consideration, nor was there significant international migration.

Thus the city of La Paz was estimated to have held some 40,000 persons in 1825, some 43,000 persons in 1846, and only some 57,000 persons by the census of 1900.[18] This resulted in a growth rate comparable to that which was occurring in the city's hinterland in the same 75-year period. Moreover, if the labor demands in the mining camps of the departments of La Paz, Oruro, and Potosí were heavily and permanently drawing off rural *paceña* workers, this would, if anything, have distorted the growth of only the forastero class, and would not have affected all groups. If these demands were seasonal, and permanent residence was maintained in the original communities, which appears to be the case from all later studies, then it could be that the declining growth rate of the forastero class might easily be modified with better data. But this still does not explain the fall in the other two classes.

Peasant migration off the *altiplano* could have affected all classes, but no such migrations are recorded for the nineteenth century. No new regions on the eastern frontier were developed in this period, and none of Bolivia's neighbors imported foreign workers to any significant degree at this time. Finally, the mid-1850's epidemics, which caused serious loss of life among the rural populations of the department, may explain the declines in the post-1850's period but do not explain the post-1830 secular rates of decline, of which the post-1850's trends form a part. Given the lack of systematic censuses or historical reconstructions of family structures for any area of Bolivia, it is difficult to determine more precisely the weight of the various causal factors in slowing growth rates after the 1830's or of fully explaining the very sharp increase in the earliest period.

That the growing importance of the community Indians was not a phenomenon unique to the Department of La Paz can be seen from the scattered evidence from many of the other regions of Bolivia, and from the alternative estimates and calculations published by government sources (see the tables in Appendix C, pp. 183-85). In those reports it is clear that the *ayllu* population throughout the nineteenth century was increasing at a far more rapid rate than the hacienda yanacona populations, not only in the Department of La Paz, but throughout the republic.[19] The only exception to this trend was the Cochabamba valley, which was then undergoing a profound transformation of its Indian population into a cholo grouping (see especially the second through fourth tables in Appendix B).[20]

How does the exceptional growth of the forastero tributary population in the nineteenth century help to explain the ability of the Indian communities to survive the increasing pressures of the national market, especially after 1850? Working from the analogy of the experience of the *ayllus* in the sixteenth and seventeenth centuries, it could be argued that the increasing pressures on the originarios and their communities created more complex internal stratification among the *ayllu* members. Whereas in the colonial period it was external governmental taxation and policies of forced sales and forced labor that were most influential, in the nineteenth century it was more in the nature of demands from the urban markets, the mines, and the communications infrastructure for labor, and the urban and mining centers for foodstuffs, that were putting tremendous stress on the *ayllus*. To respond to these incessant demands for labor and to meet the ongoing costs of tribute payments (which were increased by 20 percent in the Melgarejo monetary reforms of the 1860's), the communities encouraged the creation of a more marginal class of peasants who had less land and were more mobile than the originarios in terms of labor recruitment for work both on the originario lands and outside the community. The elders of the community and the wealthier originarios were thus relieved of increasing demands from the growing community population for lands and at the same time were able to generate new sources of income for the community.

It is worth noting in this regard that commercial agricultural production on the free community lands was important from the earliest colonial period. Thus increasing pressures from the market and ongoing pressures from the state would have led to greater output of commercial agricultural production in the communities and a progressive shift away from traditional foodstuffs and production for exchange. To meet both exchange

and market demands and commercial market needs, increased
output of goods through the efforts of the dependent forasteros
relieved pressures on the communities and allowed them to pur-
sue consumption, exchange, and market output without a serious decline in living standards. With land apparently still relatively abundant—at least compared to post-1880 conditions—
originarios could bring more of their lands into cultivation
through the use of the forasteros, and themselves also engage in
more specialized market activities.[21] Thus both the *ayllus* and the
haciendas were competing for landless free laborers, which in
turn may explain the relatively slower growth of the hacienda.

The final issue remaining in the analysis of the forasteros has
to do with the mechanisms involved in their expansion. The limited evidence presently available suggests that the forasteros in
most districts had higher ratios of economically active males
than did the originarios. This implies that the growth of the forastero population was occurring primarily through migration
rather than through natural increase. It also suggests that the
forastero population was more productive than the originarios
since they had more economically active males and fewer dependent nonproductive members.

The origins of this migrating forastero group and the cause for
forastero migration are still difficult to determine. It would seem
evident that these forasteros, just like the yanaconas, came partially out of the older forastero populations, but also must have
come from the originario class as well. This latter group consistently had the highest child-to-women ratios of the three classes
and therefore must have lost population to the other categories
since their own natural growth rate was so low. Why and how
these originarios gave up their status to move to new areas as
forasteros or yanaconas is another question. Elements of both
compulsion or attraction were clearly at work. It might be argued that in a time of increasing market pressures, the originarios closed off access to their status in an attempt to keep themselves competitive and to increase their supply of cheap labor.
Thus males born to the status, or younger sons, were forced to
seek work and lands elsewhere than in their original commu-

nities, thereby creating for other originarios of the region a cheaper labor pool. Or alternatively, the market demands for goods and labor led the local originarios to increase their offers of idle lands and other rewards for incoming forasteros, thus in fact raising the benefits for these workers. This in turn attracted the sons of originarios from the poorer zones who voluntarily migrated to the richer areas in order to obtain more wealth and lands than were available to them in their home communities. While I would tend to support the second model as the more likely explanation, without more detailed studies of originario inheritance patterns, local land practices, and relative wage rates, it is hard to choose between them.

In either case, however, these primarily market-response explanations for the unusual increase of the forasteros in the nineteenth century might be questioned by those who see scarcity of prime lands under increasing population pressure as the basic explanatory factor. In his study of the province of Chayanta in the northern part of the Department of Potosí, Tristan Platt argues that the rapid growth of the forasteros in this period was simply the response to demographic pressures on limited land resources. Postulating that there was no increase in available *tierras de origen*, he believes that many descendants of originarios were forced to accept marginal lands and lesser status as forasteros.[22] But given the extremely low density of Amerindian peasant population in most zones a century ago, such land pressure could not have been so intense.[23] The Department of La Paz, the region that today contains some 770,000 peasants, held only some 350,000 persons as late as the 1870's.[24] The densities for the department were something on the order of 2.1 Indian peasants per kilometer in all the rural provinces of the department in 1900, and doubled to 4.8 persons per square kilometer in 1950. In 1900 the densest rural zone of La Paz (Muñecas) contained 10.5 persons, while in 1950 Omasuyos was the highest in the region at 31.4 persons.[25] Land pressure in the *ayllus* should also have affected the yanaconas equally, if not more so. Yet it was seen from the censuses that the yanaconas were not increasing as rapidly even as the originarios, let alone the forasteros.

Surely a land squeeze on the *ayllus* would have in fact favored the movement of workers toward the haciendas.

Even more crucially, evidence from contemporary ethnographers has been in agreement in stressing the very recent existence of real land pressure on the *altiplano* communities. In the last thirty years the combined effects of Agrarian Reform and a natural growth rate of 2.7 percent per annum have forced the communities to parcel out the common lands and to give up fallow-field farming altogether. Informants speak of a more open land situation of the communities prior to these changes.

Although the desire of originarios to maintain their domination over land in the face of growing population pressure cannot be denied as a factor influencing the growth of the forasteros, it obviously was not the only or the primary factor. Given the internal stratification in the *ayllus* and the control of the local government by the originarios, it is obvious that their interest predominated. But the fact that the less landed and more marginal peasants remained on the *ayllus* rather than going to the haciendas makes a total land and population pressure model very doubtful. Also the timing of this process during a period of intense national growth with a corresponding increase in *ayllu* size also militates against such an explanation. Just as the origins of the forastero class in the sixteenth century can be attributed to external market pressures and exploitation, so did the forastero class dynamically grow in a new period of increasing external pressures.

Nor does it appear that the government of the republic was loath to support such a development—at least until 1866—for the very tribute censuses were a formal government registration and legitimization of internal community status. Status as originario or forastero was defined by the community but was legitimated by the state. All the revisitas (or tribute censuses) are nominal lists, and the naming of individuals and families from census to census was the state's way of guaranteeing status and enforcing it. Even to this day, the nineteenth-century revisitas are legal documents that can be used to justify land titles, and that are so used by peasants.

The success of what appears to be a conscious policy of the originarios to encourage forastero growth is made evident by the surprising results of my analysis of the eighteenth- and nineteenth-century revisitas. Despite the important growth of the national market in the second half of the nineteenth century, the demographic strength of the communities continued to grow steadily until 1880. The free communities appeared able to use the forasteros to overcome the potentially destructive impacts of a growing commercial foodstuffs market, increasing demands for seasonal non-farm labor, and even the reemergence of a dynamic hacienda system.

This adaptability to a more modern economy was brought to an end only when the government decided to destroy the legality of the communities, invalidate their land claims, and finally encourage seizure of their lands. But even in the post-1880 period, the Indian communities retained enough wealth to attempt a massive purchase of their own lands, only to be denied ultimate control by the government use of fraud and force to prevent them from maintaining their corporate lands intact. Once sales were introduced and individual peasant alienability was allowed, then it became a long, losing, and often bloody battle for the communities to contain the onslaught of the haciendas.

CHAPTER SIX

The Hacendado Class in the Late Nineteenth Century

THE ABILITY OF the *ayllus* to respond to market change and capitalist penetration during the major shifts that were occurring in the national economy in the first three-quarters of the nineteenth century, and the expectation that they would continue to thrive into the twentieth century, convinced the mining and landed elite to respond with extra-market attacks. To destroy the ability of the *ayllus* to respond with an economic defense of their landownership, the government removed the legality of their land titles and allowed whites and cholos to seize the lands which the Indians were so jealously protecting. Already in 1842 the government had declared that all community lands belonged to the state. Then in 1866 had come the forced sales of these lands by Melgarejo. In the opposition to these sales, which were eventually canceled in the early 1870's, both opponents and defenders began to adopt an anticorporatist position in terms of the land rights of the communities. To this white Spanish-speaking and literate elite, the communities were a retrograde economic institution that had to be destroyed. For the liberals, the alternative proposed was to make the Indians landowners with individual title, the idea being to convert them into yeoman-farmers very much on the Bolivarian model. For the conservatives, the answer was a total alienation of the lands and the "education" of the Indians under the tutelage of the hacendados who would absorb their lands.[1]

This ideology now matched a changed economy. The urban elite now could generate the funds necessary to enter into rural production on a large scale, especially in relation to the new rail and road infrastructure that was being created. The revival of the silver-mining industry in the districts of Oruro and Potosí in the middle decades of the century finally brought a new vitality to the national economy. From the decade of the 1850's, Bolivia began exporting more than it was importing and the national government started to enjoy enough surplus funds to engage in infrastructural investments. All this expansion led to the growth of La Paz as the nation's most dynamic commercial center as well as its leading city in terms of population. While the city had always been the center of Bolivia's most important Amerindian population and agricultural production zone, it was only in the late nineteenth century that it became the nation's financial and commercial capital as well. With new urban classes emerging, and new capital to spend, there was both increased demands for foodstuffs production and an aggressive class of urban-based capitalists willing to engage in agricultural production.

Though the region of La Paz had always had a strong hacendado class, this class had mostly concentrated in coca production in the Yungas valleys. It was here that the haciendas were most dominant by the end of the colonial period, and it was here that absentee landlords, the majority of whom lived in the city of La Paz, were most concentrated. There were, of course, haciendas producing everything from corn to potatoes, and from cattle to sheep in all the districts of the Department of La Paz, but in no zone did they totally dominate production as they did in the Yungas.

But the availability of new bank credits, the willingness of the richer and less dependent post-1850 governments to attack Indian land rights, and the growing demand for urban foodstuffs all led to a favorable climate to begin to attack Indian land tenure in the non-coca-producing areas.[2] In the 1860's Melgarejo had attempted to destroy the legality of communal Indian land rights, but massive protest had stopped the land seizures. In 1874 a more subtle attempt was organized under a new law, which in effect turned all communal property into individual holdings. This time the conjunction of economic and political forces was propitious, and a massive attack on Indian properties was begun.[3] While the ferocity of the communities' opposition and their tenacity eventually forced the government to concede the right of Indians to purchase their plots as members of communities "proindiviso" (and thus extra-legally once again recognizing the so-called "excomunidades"), many did purchase their so-called *sayañas* as individual purchasers.[4] Thus while many communities survived in the interior departments, the erosion of community control was such that by the second decade of the twentieth century, most of the richer soil on the *altiplano* was dominated by hacendados, and the landowning communities that survived were pushed back into the more marginal lands.[5]

Along with this legal and very much extra-legal attack on the right of Indian communities to hold land, the government also progressively abandoned its dependence on the Indian tribute, which had previously been such a stable and important part of its income. The importance of the Indian head tax shrank to a relatively minor element in government revenues as taxes on exports now became the crucial basis for government finances.[6] The new conservative party government also decided to revise its entire internal taxing structure in the context of both its major needs for financing the war with Chile and its interests in modernizing government revenues in terms of creating a more complete tax base. Thus in August 1880 it abolished the old colonial tithes (the *diezmos*, *primicias*, and *ventenilias*) used to finance the church and replaced them with a straight 8 percent tax on the annual return (either in profit or rents) on both rural and urban properties. The tax on urban properties, it was promised, would fund municipal government after the war, while the rural one was to become the basis for the government's taxation of agriculture—the majority employer of labor and one of the key sources of wealth in the country.[7] For the first time in republican history, a registration of the ownership, production, and value of rural estates was undertaken on a systematic basis.[8] Though the actual cadastral survey took some two years longer than expected

(being completed only in late 1882), it was in general a well executed undertaking that would become the basis for rural taxation
and later quinquenial surveys until well into the twentieth century.[9] The summary results of this survey were published at the
time,[10] but fortunately as well, many of the original manuscript
registration books have also survived in the archives of La Paz.[11]

The cadastral survey of 1881–82 exists for seven of the eight
principal cantons which made up the Department of La Paz in
this period: those on the northern shore of Lake Titicaca (Omasuyos, Larecaja, and Muñecas) and the three more central and
southern provinces of Sicasica, Yungas, Inquisivi, together with
the district of the Cercado surrounding the city of La Paz.[12] Together these haciendas accounted for almost two-thirds of the
landless workers in Bolivia at this time, and thus the trends evident in this analysis were the dominant trends for rural Bolivian
society as a whole.[13]

In the following analysis of the 1881–82 cadastre of rural
properties, it is my concern to show the size and structure of the
landowning class and the distribution of property and wealth by
zone. But before undertaking this detailed analysis, some pre-
cautionary comments are worth noting. To begin with, the published results of the survey and subsequent taxes collected do
not always correlate with the original manuscript record.[14] Second, though the director of the survey, Augustín Aspiazu, felt
that the results for all the provinces, except the Yungas, were
fairly accurate, it would seem reasonable to suppose that there
was underreporting of values in general. Finally, the survey
completely excludes the lands of the *ayllus* (except when they in
turn owned haciendas) that were exempt from the new tax on
"predios rusticos" (rural properties), which was imposed only
on privately held estates.

The 1881–82 survey occurred early in the process of fraudulent and often violent hacienda construction that lasted from
1881 to 1920 and that was most intense for the Department of La
Paz in the period 1881–85 and again in 1905–15.[15] This attack
would cost the *ayllus* of the Department of La Paz a quarter of
their lands when it was all over (see Table 6.10 below). Thus the

1881–82 survey captures the haciendas on the eve of their most dramatic republican attack on *ayllu* power, and especially before they had made massive inroads on the Cercado, Omasuyos, and Pacajes *ayllus*, which were to suffer the most in the post-1881 period. Nevertheless, it is evident that the survey does partake of some of this new activity as well as the maturation of almost a century of slower but steady expansion of haciendas at the expense of the Indian landholdings under more traditional patterns of expansion into unused or abandoned lands. It therefore can be assumed that the patterns evident from this first cadastre fairly define the system as it would fully mature in the twentieth century.

Without question, the richest zones of the Department were traditional coca-growing areas of the Yungas in the province of Chulumani (even in the undervalued estimate of the 1881–82 cadastre) and the rich lake bottomlands of Omasuyos, the new zone of hacienda expansion, which contained some of the best properties on the shores of Lake Titicaca. The average estate in the coca zones was worth five times the Departmental average and double the average in Omasuyos (see Table 6.1). Moreover in both zones—along with Sicasica—less than 3 percent of the

TABLE 6.1

Value of Haciendas in the Department of La Paz by Province, 1881–82
(In bolivianos)

Province	No. of haciendas	Total value	Mean value	Standard deviation	Minimum value	Maximum value
Chulumani	348	3,946,985	11,342	17,702	40	120,000
Sicasica	290	2,064,115	7,118	15,477	64	150,000
Cercado	453	2,047,776	4,520	8,333	4	120,000
Omasuyos	255	1,937,921	7,600	7,622	80	60,000
Larecaja	938	875,048	933	1,722	10	14,400
Inquisivi	350	678,004	1,937	4,225	10	52,000
Muñecas	492	708,150	1,439	3,058	16	30,000
TOTAL	3,126	12,257,999	3,921	9,402	4	150,000

SOURCES: AHLP/PR, Yungas, libro 11 (1882) for Chulumani; Sicasica, libro 10 (1881); Cercado, libro 26 (1881); Omasuyos, libro 24 (1882); Larecaja, libro 14 (1881); Inquisivi, libro 10 (1881); Muñecas, libro 15 (1881).

NOTE: Two haciendas were listed without values given. Absent from this table are the 94 haciendas of the province of Pacajes, worth a total of 932,440 Bs., for which no manuscript cadastre survives.

TABLE 6.2

Distribution of Estate Values in the Department of La Paz by Province, 1881–82

Estate Value (in bs.)	Chulu-mani	Sicasica	Cercado	Oma-suyos	Larecaja	Inquisivi	Muñecas	Total
1–49	2	–	10	–	103	19	19	153
50–99	1	3	18	1	110	35	34	202
100–199	4	4	60	2	136	28	67	301
200–499	32	26	65	7	248	83	144	605
500–999	35	30	52	6	106	50	73	352
1000–2999	62	71	60	34	149	67	87	530
3000–4999	44	51	52	73	48	33	33	334
5000–9999	47	44	64	67	29	22	25	298
10000–14999	41	33	43	33	9	6	5	170
15,000+	80	28	29	32	–	7	5	181
TOTAL	348	290	453	255	350	492	938	3,126

SOURCES: Same as for Table 6.1.

estates were worth 100 bolivianos or less—compared to one-fifth of the estates falling in this category in the other zones (see Table 6.2). In Omasuyos and Chulumani the median estate value was over 5,000 bolivianos, and both zones had an impressive ratio of very rich estates of over 10,000 bolivianos (19 percent and 34 percent, respectively).

Given the usual wide variation in estate values (as indicated both by the standard deviation and the distributional groupings shown in Table 6.2) the uniformity of land values in Omasuyos and to a lesser extent in Chulumani suggests in both cases a relatively homogeneous environment. In the province of Omasuyos, the agriculture was essentially high-altitude farming and ranching at its best. The value of the estates was most determined by the 150,000 or so sheep,[16] which were raised on 65 percent of the estates, and by such traditional crops as potatoes (*papas amargas*), beans (*habas*), and above all barley (*cebada*). In fact, it was the almost 19,000 cargos of barley (plus another 1,800 fanegas of this product) produced on three-quarters of the estates which, along with the sheep, most influenced the variation in the value of the estates.[17]

The wealth of the Yungas was unquestionably determined by the traditional production of coca on the *cocales* (or coca planta-

tions), and to a lesser extent by coffee.[18] But despite all the transformations that had occurred in the nineteenth century, productivity per worker had changed little since the 1790's (see Table
3.13). Average annual output per worker on the estate of the hacendados was 24 cestos in the 1880's (for 150 estates which had
complete information) versus 28 cestos per annum a century before. The two most productive zones continued to be the cantons of Ocabaya (40 cestos per worker in 1796 and 42 cestos per
worker in 1881–82) and Iruapana (43 and 38).[19]

The eastern province of Larecaja and the two southeastern
provinces of Sicasica and Inquisivi, as well as the eastern frontier zone of Muñecas, all shared the same complex characteristics of varied-quality lands on the *altiplano* and in the eastern escarpment valleys, which made for higher variation around the
mean estate values. These four provinces held over 85 percent of
all privately held estates in this Department of La Paz sample
and had the Department's highest variation around the mean
values (the values of their respective standard deviations being
twice their mean estate values). Of the three, Sicasica, with its
access to some of the best valley lands, had the third-highest
average estate value for the Department with a mixed crop production of traditional *altiplano* and more temperate valley crops,
none of which alone was highly correlated with estate values.
Like Omasuyos and Chulumani, Sicasica had a more even
spread of estate values, though at a lower range—its median estate being in the 1,000–3,000 grouping (see Table 6.2).

Muñecas, a newer zone of hacienda expansion, showed its
geographical diversity with a concentration on corn and potatoes—two ecologically different crops.[20] Inquisivi, like the other
transitional provinces, had a mix of highland and valley crops,
including even some coca estates (given its location along the
southern edge of the Yungas valleys), but sweet potatoes (*papas
dulce*) were the single most important crop.[21]

The Cercado zone consisted mostly of deep valley lands in the
altiplano heartland very close to the city of La Paz. Here the predominant form of agriculture was fruit orchards, though chuño

and potatoes could be found in the higher-altitude estates.[22] It
was this zone that contained estates that could even be used as
suburban and/or weekend residences of the city elite, and would
therefore be especially vulnerable to fraudulent sales of Indian
lands.

In contrast, the poorest hacendados and the least valued haciendas were located in Larecaja, often isolated from easy access
to the urban markets of La Paz. This province had both the
lowest mean value of estates by far, and also the highest percentage of estates under 500 bolivianos (64 percent of the provincial total). In this province estate values were determined to
some extent by wheat production (primarily in the town of Larecaja), while in the more humid and lower-altitude intramoun-
tain valleys corn production was the most important product influencing the total value of an estate.[23]

Finally these same patterns can be observed even more clearly
when examining the very wealthiest estates (worth 10,000 bolivianos or more) and their relative importance in each zone (see
Table 6.3). Chulumani, despite its numerous small estates, was
dominated by the large haciendas to such an extent that they accounted for over 85 percent of the estimated value of all estates.
Equally, Omasuyos, Sicasica, and the Cercado district were all

TABLE 6.3

*The Relative Importance of the Wealthiest Estates ($\geq$ 10,000 Bs.) in the
Department of La Paz, by Province, 1881–82*

Province	Wealthiest estates		Total value of all estates	Relative importance of wealthiest estates	
	Value	No.		Value	Estates
Omasuyos	1,132,243	65	1,937,921	58%	25%
Larecaja	102,380	9	875,048	12	1
Cercado	1,253,697	72	2,047,776	61	16
Sicasica	1,423,918	61	2,064,115	69	21
Inquisivi	236,200	13	678,004	35	4
Muñecas	178,360	10	708,150	25	2
Chulumani	3,335,900	121	3,946,985	85	35
TOTAL	7,662,698	351	12,257,999	63%	11%

SOURCES: Same as for Table 6.1.

influenced by these large haciendas, which accounted for over half the total value of all estates. These clearly were the predominant producers of market crops and suggested the importance of these zones as potential areas for future hacienda expansion.

In examining these larger estates in more detail, some important variations can be noted. Not all such latifundias were worked as individual holdings. In fact, most corporate owners (most especially the church) customarily rented out their properties on an annual basis, and the cadastral surveyors traditionally listed this rental as the annual product of the estate.[24] Thus, for example, the Hospital of La Paz, which owned the estate Macamaca in Sicasica in the Canton of Caracoto, rented out its wine- and temperate-grain-producing hacienda for 13,200 bolivianos per annum (which was both the highest rent paid for any hacienda in the Department and the highest annual income figure as well).[25] A few families also rented their estates. This was the case with the Rivero family, which owned the Sicasica hacienda Chuisivi (in Sapahaqui) and rented this 120,000 boliviano estate out for an annual fee of 6,400 bolivianos.

But even estates run directly by their owners were accustomed to have renters on their properties. Thus Pastro Vidal, who owned Anchocara in Luribay, also in the province of Sicasica, gained 400 bolivianos out of his total annual 4,492 income from *arrenderos* (renters) who worked part of his estate, which like Macamaca concentrated on vineyards and wheat production.[26] Individual renters appeared throughout the Department working on parcels of the large haciendas, usually producing the same products as the principal owner. Such, for example, was the case of hacienda Palomar in the Cercado canton of Mecapaca, whose owner rented out both alfalfa fields and four orchards for 800 bolivianos per year. Bishop Calixto Clavijo not only produced abundant grains and root crops on his Cercado estate of Yrpavi (Obrajes), but he also gained 800 bolivianos for renting some alfalfa fields, and also another 320 bolivianos per annum for renting bare land parcels.[27]

So common was this practice of rentals that the public notaries

TABLE 6.4
Rural Land Sales and Rentals in the Department of La Paz, 1888 and 1889
(Values to nearest boliviano)

| | 1888 | | | | 1889 | | | |
| | Sales | | Rentals | | Sales | | Rentals | |
Province	No.	Value	No.	Value	No.	Value	No.	Val.
Cercado	97	845,983	134	91,180	156	706,690	15	7,41
Omasuyos	16	16,564	4	640	14	9,268	0	
Yungas	75	45,188	25	25,188	4	61,194	1	2:
Pacajes	0		1	450	3	4,860	0	
Sicasica	2	5,583	4	736	0		0	
Larecaja	1	40	2	640	0		0	
Muñecas	0		0		1	6,187	0	
Inquisivi	13	22,030	2	180	6	11,465	1	2:
Caupolican	2	240	0		3	4,232	0	
TOTAL	206	935,628	172	119,014	187	803,896	17	7,8;

SOURCES: Prefecto de La Paz, "Informes que presentan al Supremo Gobierno [1889]" (La Paz, 18c, unnumbered anexo table; and "Informes que presentan al Supremo Gobierno [1888]" (La Paz, 188 anexo table, p.iii.
NOTE: Sales of "sayaña" plots of the comunidades have been excluded.

in the Department in 1888 recorded almost as many rural rental contracts as sale contracts of estates (see Table 6.4). While this was probably a year when many multiyear contracts came due—as contrasted with years when few were rented out—it suggests that rental was a rather standard practice. It also would appear that the Cercado district and the Yungas were prime zones of rental and had the highest average rental figures (977 bolivianos per contract in the Yungas and 662 bolivianos in the Cercado district). While rental of pasturage, marginal lands for food crop production, and even orchards was common, there is no evidence from the notarial and *revisita* materials to suggest that the property owners of the Department of La Paz engaged in share-cropping and small-plot cash tenancies for entire estates, as was common in the more depressed economy of the Department of Cochabamba in the eighteenth and nineteenth centuries.[28]

The 1888–89 contract figures also suggest the dimensions of the land market. Sales were reasonably consistent over both years (in contrast to rental contracts), which suggest that these years are close to the average annual market. Moreover, these sales involve a significant share of the total stock of farms existing in the Department of La Paz at this time. If we take the sales for only the seven selected provinces from the 1881–82 cadastral survey, it would appear that in 1888 some 7 percent of the haciendas were sold, and their sale accounted for an estimated 8 percent of the total value of all estates registered in the 1881–82 survey. The figures for 1889 are 6 percent for both units sold and total values. At that rate of sales, some two-thirds of the haciendas of the Department would have changed hands within a decade.[29] Clearly this was an active land market not that different in terms of entry and exit from what could be expected within even the advanced capitalist economies in nineteenth-century America.[30]

The cadastral survey also provides some idea of the gross income of these haciendas. Since the survey was carried out as a first step in instituting a land tax (to replace the old tithes and first-fruits taxes) and proposed a tax based on a percentage of annual rent of the estate, all estates were evaluated both for their total value and for their annual "rent"—here meaning estimated gross income. In about two-thirds of the cases, the recording officials gave detailed information that justified their assigning both a total value and an annual rental figure. The rent, or income, produced in these estates averaged 8.3 percent per annum (with a standard deviation of 11.7 percent for the 3,126 estates that had complete information). This income, because of its extreme randomness, did not significantly correlate with the value of the estate, or with the province.[31]

Actual labor arrangements on the estates were fairly standardized throughout the department. The lands of the owner—usually a small section of the entire property—were worked by the peon or yanacona families or single adults for usually three to four days per week, in return for varying amounts of usufruct estate lands for their own use. One of the few extant lists of estate worker obligations comes from a coca hacienda in Coripata in 1851 called Anguia. This estate had 25 men and 21 women who worked a total of 145 days per week on the cocales of the owner. The average commitment was three days per week, but there were 11 workers who were obliged to provide four days of labor per week and four who gave only two days (all these being single persons). There were 18 couples, and 10 single adults who were functioning as heads of their own households. Interestingly enough, five of the 18 couples did not have equal labor obligations for husband and wife. Nor was it always the husband who worked the greater time. In three cases the wife gave four days and the husband three, and in the other two the order was reversed.[32] While no explanation is given for these different obligations, they were probably due to the varying quantity of land to which each household had access. Nor was payment a systematic weekly occurrence on all estates. There is even the case of an early-nineteenth-century coca hacienda, Yalaca (in Chirca), where yanaconas worked a rotation of one full week on the lands of the hacendado and the alternate week on their own lands.[33]

Though the documents of the time consistently use the expression "customary law" to describe these work arrangements, there do seem to have existed standard rights that the resident estate Indians could legally protect. One of the few extant sources on the tenure rights of yanaconas comes from a Yungas land dispute case in the 1790's. It was noted that by custom and municipal law the colonos who planted coca fields on the usufruct lands of the estate had the right to pass those lands to their children. If the inheritors did not wish to remain, or if the original peasant owner was expelled or voluntarily left, the hacendado had to pay them a settlement for any improvements on the lands. In the case of these two coca estates, San José and San Pablo of Coroyco, there were official rulings by the corregidor of Sicasica in 1730 and 1751 (to which province Coroyco then pertained) forcing the owners to pay expelled Indians for their land and crop improvements.[34]

That the labor obligations imposed for land rights were limited is suggested by the fact that hacendados paid their estate Indians for any unusual work obligations required, just as if they were nonresident day laborers. One of the few extant hacienda account books comes from the previously discussed wheat farm (called Sayani) and sheep ranch (named Tahana) in the village of Caracato of the province of Sicasica from the period 1794 to 1800. The administrator of this church-owned estate reported that in 1799 work on a variety of special projects required that he pay a total of 24 reales "to the peones" of the estate, plus a rental fee for the use of their axes. In 1800, when the river that crossed the estate needed cleaning, he had to pay 80 reales to the estate "peones" for this special work. All this was aside from the wages he paid to outside nonresident laborers who helped during the harvest.[35]

In the coca regions of the Yungas, a very large body of migratory wage workers—known as *mingas*—was also used to supplement the yanacona labor force. Thus the hacienda of Pacallo (in Pacallo) in the eighteenth century employed 16 yanacona families, one arrendero family, and 59 mingas to clear, plant, clean, and harvest the coca crop.[36] This temporary migrant labor could come either from the *puna* free community zones or from neighboring haciendas, when resident yanaconas decided to work as temporary workers on other estates. This usually involved short periods of labor from a few days to several months. One of the few extant records for minga laborers comes from the canton of Chulumani in the harvest of 1803–4. The coca hacienda of Chimasi, which had a yanacona population of 21 tributarios and a total of 90 resident Indians, employed ten male nonresident wage workers in the three mitas or harvests of November 1803 and March and June 1804 (see Table 6.5).[37] The workers were paid 2½ reales per day for cleaning and weeding (*masi*), and 2 reales per day for harvesting (*quichi*). They averaged 118 days of labor in the former, and 109 days in the latter, for a total average of 227 days of labor. The average worker grossed 64 pesos, 4 reales.

Most mingas appear to have been single men under the age of thirty. In some cases they were paid immediately in cash, with the sums expended in their food rations discounted from their final pay, so that they either owed a little to or were owed a little by the hacendado at the end of the harvest. Although two-thirds of the yanaconas at Pacallo had outstanding debts to the owner (ranging from 1 real, or less than a day's labor, to 11 pesos, 5

TABLE 6.5
TABLE 6.5
Minga Wages for Coca Production on the Hacienda of Chimasi, 1803–4

Worker	Quichi[a]	Masi[b]	Total days worked	Wages earned[c]	Food charges[c]	Gross money wages paid[c]	Owner debts to workers
Ignacio Mamani	137	138	275	77/4	45/4	25/7	6/3
Mariano Carrasco	122	148	270	76/6	14/2	0/0	62/4
Silvestre Menga	136	122	258	72/1	36/6	32/5	3/0
Andres Mamani	102	143	245	70/1	38/2	7/3	24/6
Andres Tapia	112	125	237	69/0	49/6	15/4	4/0
Esteban Choque	117	117	234	66/7	47/6	9/0	10/1
Basilio Aguilar	109	119	228	64/3	37/0	39/0	−11/7
Gaspar Velarde	105	116	221	62/4	46/1	9/4	6/9
Pasqual Quispe	98	81	179	49/6	–	–	–
Velasco Cardenas	56	80	136	39/0	19	15/0	5/0
TOTAL	1,094	1,189	2,283	645/1	333/7	153/3	110/6
Avg. per worker	109	119	228	64/5	37/1	17/0	12/3
No. of workers	10			67/6			

SOURCE: APTS, "Cuenta liquida que yo Juan Andres Martinez instruio al Sr. Don. Antonio del Po tillo, pertenientes a las mitas de Santos, Marzo, y San Juan del año de 1803 . . .," dated March 2, 180
NOTE: There is no information on the food costs or payment to Pasqual Quispe, and therefore calculations of averages of debts, costs, and net income is based on a total of 9 workers and 595 pes and 3 reales of total wages.
[a]Number of days at 2 reales per day.
[b]Number of days at 2½ reales per day.
[c]In pesos/reales.

reales, representing between 31 days and 46½ days of work, depending on the daily wage, which varied from 2 to 3 reales per day depending on tasks performed) and another third were owed sums by the hacendado, only 20 percent of the minga workers had any claims or obligations with the hacendado, suggesting a much more immediate payment arrangement.[38] In the case of Chimasi, however, the accounts for the minga workers were more complex. By the end of the three harvests, of the nine workers who had complete account records, all but one had received some silver for their wages due. These paid wages, however, only averaged 17 pesos, or just over half of what was due to them.[39] After allowing for their food costs—which averaged 56 percent of their gross wages—eight were still owed an average of 12 pesos. However, only one worker, Basilio Aguilar, was left at the end of the three harvests of the year with a debt to the hacendado, in this case some 11 pesos, 7 reales. Surprisingly, there is no correlation between the number of days worked and the amount of food costs charged to each worker (see Table 6.5). This would seem to suggest that workers were feeding larger nonworking families and were thus purchasing more food than for their own individual needs.[40]

Although all accounts were kept by hacendados in pesos and reales (in the colonial period) and bolivianos in the nineteenth century, in fact accounts were sometimes settled in goods. The minga laborers often collected their pay in coca leaves, which could then be sold for cash, and many of the resident workers received their pay in foodstuffs as well as coca leaves. Aside from wages, all workers were provided with daily food rations (called *jallpay* or *guajaya*) when working on the lands of the hacendado. For the resident yanaconas these provisions seemed to have been provided free of charge, unless they were working for wages. For the migratory wage labor mingas, however, the owner charged a rather high price for the food provided, which he deducted from their final pay. Thus in 1818, the administrator of Santiago el Grande in Coripata paid to 36 peones a total of 715 pesos, 3 reales in wages for a total of 2,371 man days (or 63 days per worker) for harvesting the coca (in this case for the mita, or harvest, of November) of that year, plus 527 pesos in food costs to feed the workers a standard daily ration while at their tasks, a sum he probably discounted from their wages.[41] That hacendados in the Yungas coca zones also paid the tribute tax for their yanaconas suggests that aside from land, special tasks wages, and food rations, the hacendados also had to offer to pay their 5-peso-per-year tribute tax to the government as an incentive to attract Indians as resident workers on their estates.[42]

If this evidence suggests a fairly complex and reasonably fluid labor market, it should be recalled that the resident peones were also required to perform the much-hated *pongueaje* free personal service obligation in return for their land usage rights. This involved transport of the owner's crops to the city and periodic duty on the domestic staff in both the household of the local mayordomo (estate overseer or steward) and the owner's urban residence. These duties were all performed free of charge by the peones.

The internal organization of the resident estate workers also tended to differ by regions. In the highland areas of the Department of La Paz, if the old community Indians were still on the estate, the tendency was for the owner and the workers to preserve the old communal structure with elected or chosen elders (the jilakatas) representing the workers before the owners and managers and even before the state authorities. There were even cases recorded of jilakatas who acted as administrators of private haciendas in the absence of mayordomos.[43] In some cases the owners were known to interfere in the appointment of the jilakatas on their estates, and sometimes there were accusations of overly intimate relations between the jilakatas and the mayordomos or owners, which resulted in complaints or exploitation of the regular peasant families. But whether this was a theme of "divide and rule" ideology by the elite or a common practice is difficult to determine. It would probably be the case that jilakatas forcibly appointed by the owner or mayordomo were more likely to be exploiters than those chosen by the peasants themselves.

When we examine the estate owners, we find evidence from the 1881–82 cadastral survey that there had been changes over time in the hacendado class, especially when compared with the results from the comparable regionwide survey done in 1786/1797. Their numbers had increased, since the number of private landed estates had more than doubled over the century.[44] Equally, the distribution of this landed wealth was far more skewed in the late nineteenth than in the late eighteenth century. Though there are difficulties in comparing the two samples (one based on number of workers per estate and the other on estimated wealth), there is little question that the late nineteenth century witnessed a much higher concentration of wealth among the landed class. The GINI coefficients in the two samples were significantly different—0.570 in the late colonial period and a very high 0.767 for the modern period. Unfortunately, only three of the seven provinces had even partial data on estate peones, but what is impressive from these three provinces (Yungas, Muñecas, and Larecaja) is that peones could be found in some numbers even on estates worth less than 100 bolivianos. But even eliminating all estates under 100 bolivianos, as those least likely to have dependent workers (and therefore falling under the category of small farms and not "true" haciendas), still gives a GINI coefficient of wealth concentration as measured by control over peones for 1881–82 of 0.751—again a very significant difference from the earlier period.

As might be expected, multiple property owners did better than single property owners, as a whole. Though single property owners were among the wealthiest in La Paz (see Table 6.6), in fact, multiple owners (21 percent of all owners) held double their ratio of estates (41 percent) and even more (47 percent) of the total value of all rural property (see Table 6.7). When compared with their colonial hacendado counterparts, these multiple property owners were now relatively more numerous and had more financial control. In the 1786/97 survey, multiple estate owners represented just 9 percent of all owners and held only 31 percent of the wealth.[45] It would seem that in this, as in other major indicators, the landed class of the late nineteenth century was a more limited elite than in the colonial era.

Nevertheless, the very extensive interprovincial patterns of ownership exhibited in the colonial period were not quite as evident in this second period. Some 117 of the estate owners (or 5 percent of the total) held lands in two or more provinces and only 18 held them in three or more provinces, while none held lands in all seven provinces of the region (see Table 6.8). Moreover, the relative share of total wealth held by these multiprovincial owners (or 22 percent), while considerably greater than their relative importance among the number of hacendados, was not as impressive as in the late eighteenth century. In the earlier survey multiprovincial owners were 9 percent of all hacendados, held 26 percent of the haciendas, and controlled 31 percent of the total yanacona population. This change in distribution may be related to the more specialized nature of farming,

TABLE 6.6

The Richest Five Percent of Hacendados in the Department of La Paz, 1881–82

(In terms of estate value)

Name	No. of haci-endas	Province of estates[a]	Sex	Total value	Total rent
Alava de Ybarguen, Romana	5	3,5,7	F	207,400	18,065
Clavijo, Benigno	8	1,3,7	M	198,000	11,692
Convento de Carmelitas	13	3	–	179,800	13,680
San Juan de Dios, Hospital de la Paz	3	4,7	–	164,000	14,560
Monasterio de Concebidas	14	1,2,3,6,7	–	147,940	9,513
Indaburo y Juana Pia, Maria	1	7	F	120,000	7,934
Rivero, Los	1	4	M	120,000	6,400
Vidal, Pastor	1	4	M	120,000	4,492
Perez, Carlos	2	4	M	101,200	3,494
Zuazo, Juan	9	1,3	M	99,200	4,900
Mendoza, Anselmo	4	1,2,7	M	94,400	7,958
Eduardo, Graciano	3	3,7	M	93,040	2,885
Clavijo, Calixto	3	3	–	82,000	4,720
Gaena, Piscaro	1	7	M	80,000	3,687
Huiri, Manuela A. de	1	7	F	80,000	7,120
Iturralde, Tenor y Luis	1	7	M	80,000	4,764
Monasterios, Lino	4	1,4,7	M	77,000	3,740
Ballivian, Vicente	2	3,7	M	75,000	6,477
Cipriano Klaye, José	1	7	M	70,000	4,120
Unknown	1	7	–	70,000	1,634
Ballivian, Nicanor	2	3,7	M	68,000	5,633
Villegas, Miguel	5	4,5	M	65,400	5,380
Guerra, Josefa	2	3,7	F	65,000	3,872
Bocangel, Apolinar	1	1	M	60,000	804
Mendez, Julio	1	7	M	60,000	3,058
Veliz, Manuel Antonio	1	7	M	60,000	2,466
Solanos, Francisca	3	3	F	59,000	2,500
Alborta, Hilarion	2	7	M	57,600	3,182
Ascarrunz, Vicente	2	1,7	M	57,000	300
Telles, Melchor	3	7	M	56,600	5,808
Peñaranda, Juan José	2	4,7	M	56,000	855
Sanchez, Cafereno	1	7	M	56,000	148
Pena, José	3	4,7	M	55,600	2,610
Cipriano, Manuel	2	1,7	M	54,000	1,822
Garcia, Pedro	3	1,7	M	54,000	3,016
Criales, Melchor	4	2,5,7	M	51,400	2,398
Mendoza, Fabian	10	1,2	M	50,360	3,011
Andrade, Saturnino	1	4	M	50,000	2,000
Canizares, Juana	4	1,7	F	48,900	2,839
Santa Cruz, Andres	4	1	M	47,600	2,140
Zalles, Cesario	2	3	M	47,600	3,084
Romero, Josefa	3	3,5,7	F	46,050	2,529
Zuazo, Federico	3	3,7	M	45,200	2,440
Ayoroa, Saturnina	3	1,7	F	45,000	2,936
Rivero, José	1	4	M	45,000	1,600
Latorre, Miguel	3	3,4	M	42,000	3,283

TABLE 6.6 (*continued*)

Name	No. of haciendas	Province of estates[a]	Sex	Total value	Total rent
Riva, Claudia	1	3	F	41,600	2,496
Several owners	1	4	–	40,800	1,300
Granier, Rosa	2	1,3	F	40,400	2,032
Belmonte y Norberto, Juana	1	7	F	40,000	4,251
Pavon, Pedro	1	7	M	40,000	3,297
Rodriguez, Patricia	2	3,7	F	40,000	3,825
Villamil, Mercedes	5	1,3,7	F	40,000	1,620
Vinolas y Ramontes, José Luis	1	7	M	40,000	4,256
Convento Mercedarios-Puna	3	–		39,300	1,940
Sanjines, Bernardin	2	1,3	M	38,600	1,240
Asin, Ricardo	2	3	M	38,000	2,160
Convento de la Purissima Concepción	2	6	–	38,000	2,460
Santa Cruz, Oscar	1	7	M	38,000	2,020
Peñaloza, Camilo	4	7	M	37,970	1,837
De Guerra, Pedro José	3	3	M	36,600	2,392
Ballivian, Ricardo	2	3	M	36,000	1,840
Gonzalez, Manuel	3	3,7	M	36,000	1,756
Molina, Lorensa	1	7	F	36,000	2,127
Solares, Clara	1	4	F	35,000	2,101
Cernadas, Prudencio	4	4	M	34,800	1,250
Medina, José	2	1	M	33,600	1,474
Sanjines Uriate, Modesta	2	1	F	33,512	1,570
Machicado, Filiberto	2	1,7	M	33,400	614
Yanguas, Andrea	1	1	F	32,000	1,250
Burgoa, Benancio	1	1	M	31,200	1,000
Yanguas, Wenceslao	1	3	M	31,000	1,900
Seco, Gregoria	5	1,2	F	30,850	1,864
Eduardo, Petrona	2	1,3	F	30,400	1,500
Diez de Medina, Federico	2	1,7	M	30,000	2,156
Rocabado, Mariano	3	7	M	30,000	3,081
Roni, Ignacio	1	7	M	30,000	600
Yriondo, Diego	1	7	M	30,000	3,235
Vidal, Policarpo	1	7	M	30,000	1,640
Cordero, Felipa	3	1,7	F	28,000	1,958
Herrera, José	2	3,7	M	28,000	1,720
Salazar, Narcira	1	6	F	28,000	1,600
Burgoa, Venancio	4	6	M	27,900	1,640
Solares, Mariano	3	4	M	27,760	1,103
Solares de Salinas, Benita	1	4	F	27,660	1,280
Comunidad Sicasica	3	5	–	27,500	1,850
Mejia, Rosalia	4	1,3,6	F	27,400	1,879
Bustos, Vicolasa	1	4	F	26,000	460
Pinedo, Tomás	2	4	M	26,000	1,094
?, Feliciana	1	1	F	25,600	1,000
Torres, Miguel	5	2,7	M	25,190	1,127
Goitia, Benedicto	5	1	M	25,100	1,020
Torres, Marcelina	2	2,7	F	25,080	1,717

TABLE 6.6 (continued)

Name	No. of haci- endas	Province of estates[a]	Sex	Total value	Total rent
Alvarez, Enrique	1	7	M	25,000	1,720
Cordova, Edelmira	1	3	F	25,000	1,000
Hospitales	3	1	–	25,000	1,300
Montenegro, Federico	3	7	M	25,000	770
Monge, Juan	1	3	M	25,000	1,000
Suarez, Josefa	3	4	F	25,000	756
Serruto, Micaela	2	3,7	F	25,000	887
Iturralde, Zenon	2	7	M	24,800	834
Revollo, Manuel	5	4,7	M	24,400	1,950
Flores, Manuel	4	1,2,3,4	M	24,020	1,215
Gamarra, Juan	1	7	M	24,000	1,174
Argale de Maidana, Claudina	1	1	F	24,000	1,582
Castillo, Savala	2	3	M	24,000	40
Luna, Nicasio	2	1,3	M	24,000	1,900
Hernandez, José Maria	1	7	M	24,000	1,881
Peñaranda, Josefina	1	7	F	24,000	3,294
Postigo y Hermanos, Juan	1	7	M	24,000	186
Mbuje, Cefrino	1	7	M	24,000	802
Porcel, Margarita	1	7	F	24,000	1,414
Lizon, Bartolome	1	7	M	24,000	1,517
Monje, Joaquin Rafael	1	7	M	24,000	2,549
Samillan, Rafael	1	7	M	24,000	1,792
Perez, Francisco	1	1	M	23,000	1,000

SOURCES: Same as for Table 6.1.

[a]Provinces are coded as follows: 1, Omasuyos; 2, Larecaja; 3, Cercado; 4, Sicasica; 5, Inquisivi; ◖ Muñecas; 7, Chulumani.

TABLE 6.7

Value and Number of Estates Owned by Each Hacendado in the Seven Provinces of the Department of La Paz Combined

No. of estates per owner	No. of owners	Total value of estates (in bs.)	Pct. of owners	Pct. of estates	Pct. of values
1	1,826	6,451,417	79.3%	58.4%	52.6%
2	286	2,342,286	12.4	18.3	19.1
3	128	1,632,423	5.6	12.3	13.3
4	33	583,990	1.4	4.2	4.8
5	18	529,545	0.8	2.9	4.3
6	3	12,833	0.1	0.6	0.1
8	2	198,450	0.1	0.5	1.6
9	4	126,300	0.2	1.2	1.0
10	1	50,360	0.0	0.3	0.4
13	1	179,800	0.0	0.4	1.5
14	1	147,940	0.0	0.4	1.2
15	1	2,655	0.0	0.5	0.0
TOTAL	2,304	12,257,999	100.0%	100.0%	100.0%

SOURCES: Same as for Table 6.1.

TABLE 6.8

*Number of Provinces in Which Multiple Estate Owners Held Estates,
Department of La Paz, 1881–82*

	No. of owners	No. of estates	Total value (in bs.)	Pct. of owners	Pct. of estates	Pct. of value
Owner in only one	348	904	2,531,072	73.0%	69.7%	43.9%
Owner in two	110	306	2,342,935	23.1	23.6	40.6
Owner in three	17	69	720,295	3.6	5.3	12.5
Owner in four	1	4	24,020	0.2	0.3	0.4
Owner in five	1	14	147,940	0.2	1.1	2.6
TOTAL	477	1,297	5,766,262	100.0%	100.0%	100.0%

SOURCES: Same as for Table 6.1.

or changes in the tight-knit family arrangements of an earlier period. It also will be seen that the church, the biggest of the multi-provincial owners, was no longer a major landowner in rural Bolivia in this later period.

Surprisingly, despite all the liberal reforms of the nineteenth century and the confiscation of church wealth by Sucre early in the republican period, the relative importance of the church was only reduced by half over the century between the *padrones* of the 1780's and the cadastre of 1881–82. Since Bolivia was never a church-dominated society even in the colonial period, the church was always of relatively limited importance in terms of direct land ownership, though it was quite important in providing agricultural credit in the pre-banking period. Excluding the local parish churches that owned haciendas for their maintenance, there were six convents or monasteries that owned haciendas, and they held less than 4 percent of the total hacienda wealth (see Table 6.9), as compared to almost 9 percent in the earlier period. The leading institution was the Monasterio de las Concebidas de La Paz with fourteen estates (see Table 6.6). In the colonial period the Monasterio de la Purissima Concepción de La Paz had been the leading landowner with 22 estates; now it was reduced to only two. If one includes the hospitals and the *Beneficencia* (a government agency created to administer confiscated church estates for social welfare and educational purposes)—all possessing haciendas probably seized earlier from

TABLE 6.9
Estate Ownership by Sex and Institution

	No. of owners	No. of estates	Total value (in bs.)	Pct. of owners	Pct. of estates	Pct. of value
Men	1,650	2,277	8,302,520	72.4%	73.4%	68.3
Women	562	717	2,896,739	24.6%	23.1%	23.8
Corporations	68	110	955,000	3.0%	3.5%	7.9
Convents	6	36	420,140	0.3	1.2	3.5
Comunidades	12	16	75,510	0.5	0.5	0.6
Hospitals	4	10	275,000	0.2	0.3	2.3
Beneficencia	1	3	12,000	0.0	0.1	0.1
Local churches	23	23	28,670	1.0	0.7	0.2
Local municipality	3	3	3,700	0.1	0.1	0.0
Gas company	1	1	22,000	0.0	0.0	0.2
Multiple owners	18	18	117,980	0.8	0.6	1.0
TOTAL	2,280	3,104	12,154,259	100.0%	100.0%	100.0

SOURCES: Same as for Table 6.1.

NOTE: There were 26 hacendados who were unknown as to sex, institution, or value, and 24 haciendas with no information on either owners, sex, or institution.

the Church—and the lands of the local churches, the relative share of landed wealth for the church goes to only 6 percent, which is still less than in the colonial period. In the 1790's, the Church as landowner controlled about 10 percent of the labor force.

An even more significant change was found among women landowners. In the former period they were 17 percent of the hacendado class and controlled 27 percent of the estates and only 15 percent of the workers. But now (see Table 6.9) they represented 25 percent of the hacendados and accounted for the same percentage of the wealth of all landed estates. Clearly the situation of women, even of the upper class, had improved in the nineteenth century.

Surprisingly, despite all the aggression committed against the *comunidades* in their own lands, *paceño* comunidades which possessed their own private haciendas continued to exist in the late nineteenth century. Whereas in the late colonial period 11 *comunidades* were listed as possessing 16 estates and 2 percent of the yanaconas, in the late nineteenth century they had added one estate for a total of 17, but their relative share of wealth was now reduced to less than 1 percent.

What can be concluded from this analysis of the 1881–82 cadastre is that the expansion of the hacienda system clearly varied from district to district. In those with generally better lands
there was a more uniform wealth created, while in the districts
with wide variation of land quality estates would vary more in
wealth. Larecaja, Muñecas, and Inquisivi were particularly filled
with numerous poor estates, most probably owned by locally
resident hacendados, who were of a mestizo or Indian back-
ground. By contrast, the bigger estates in these districts and
most of the estates in Omasuyos and Chulumani (note as well
the numerous multiprovincial landowners who held estates in
these two provinces) were more likely to be owned by persons of
"white" or European extraction who were usually absentee landlords resident in the city of La Paz, and whose principal occupa-
tion was not farming. It was these urban landowners who had
access to the capital and political power necessary to create these
extremely profitable haciendas, which, in turn, required little
long-term investment to maintain their worth. Given the free labor of the Indian colonos and pongos and the fact that the Indians had already cleared the fields and that little new building
or cultivation was engaged in by the new owners, these new estates proved to be excellent investments. As Aspiazu reported
in 1880:

Another of the advantages which the owners of the estates of the highlands [*fincas del puna*] have over those of other rural properties is the
security which is given to the capital employed in these types of ac-
quisitions and the expectation of its increase, without the need to invest
new sums. . . . All the value of these *puna* estates consists in the land.
There are no buildings needing continuous repairs; there are no plantings needing continuous care, and added to these advantages is the important free service given by the *colonos* as domestics and day laborers.
Certainly these estates give a rent proportionally less than those of the
[coca] estates of the Yungas, but on the other hand there is no risk of
loss, their capital is secure.[46]

This intimate relationship between the expansion of the banking system and the haciendas occurred throughout Bolivia. Time
and again, urban whites and cholos forced Indian land sales, ac-
quired estates, and then used those estates as collateral to obtain

bank loans. All this occurred with no major new investments in equipment and with the employment of the ex-owners of the tierras de origenes being employed as landless workers.[47]

From 1880 until 1920 land sales in the Department of La Paz were intense, with the biggest periods of activity occurring from 1881 to 1886 and again from 1905 to 1915.[48] In this first five-year period the level of fraud was outstanding: for the only time in the reported sales, Indian originarios were sometimes found selling parcels (sayañas) of other Indians as well as their own—which was both illegal and led in a few cases to the immediate confiscation of entire *comunidades*. Although data are currently unavailable for the 6,700 sales in terms of the reasons for making them, contemporary data gathered for the province of Yamparez in the Department of Chuquisaca suggest that four-fifths of the sales were made under duress—either to pay back debts contracted with non-Indians or to pay court fees for cases brought to defend their lands.[49] Thus the decision of the government in 1920 to prohibit sales for debt and to create (along with a 1916 decree) far more stringent legal requirements for sale finally ended this massive invasion of Indian lands.[50] But during this period, some 11,900 sayañas owned by originarios were sold, of which 71 percent were purchased by non-Indians, and as much as a quarter of the *ayllu* lands in the Department were alienated (see Table 6.10).

As previously noted, the seizure of lands by non-Indians was mostly concentrated in a few zones. Those areas near the city of La Paz, or containing the best of the lakeside lands, or well-connected by roads to the urban market of La Paz were especially affected. Thus the orchards of Obrajes near the city of La Paz (in the province of Cercado) suffered well over a two-thirds loss of Indian community lands. Pacajes and Omasuyos, two zones well connected by good roads to the city and close to Lake Titicaca, were also particularly affected in this respect. It was here that several entire *ayllus* were seized both in the 1881–86 period and in the 1905–15 era. In fact Bolivian President Ismael Montes, who began the termination of these fraudulent sales with his decree of 1916, was one of the key beneficiaries with his

TABLE 6.10

Sale of Communal Indian Plots (Sayañas) in the Department of La Paz,
1881–1920

Province	Sayañas sold to non-Indians[a]	Tributarios resident in 1877 padrones[b]	Estimated loss of *ayllu* plots	Relative importance of sales by prov.
Omasuyos	2,977	10,243	29.1%	25.0%
Pacajes	4,488	14,160	31.7	37.7
Cercado	2,020	2,784	72.6	17.0
Sicasica	1,397	9,290	15.0	11.7
Larecaja	228	2,019	11.3	1.9
Yungas	615	2,087	29.5	5.2
Muñecas	107	4,390	2.4	0.9
Caupolican	68	3,116	2.2	0.6
TOTAL	11,900	48,089	24.7%	100.0%

SOURCE: Greishaber, "Hacienda Espansion," p. 54, table 3.

[a]This includes both full and partial plots.

[b]This figure includes both originarios and agregados, which is roughly equivalent to the total number of sayañas a community might possess, since it was the norm for an originario to have more than one sayaña and for these extra parcels to be worked by an agregado and his family. Thus including the agregados gives a rough approximation to the total number of sayañas.

purchase of Indian lands in the canton of Taraco in the province of Pacajes in 1907. The norm, however, was for a more piecemeal breakup of the Indian *comunidades*, or their reduction in size. It was common for some Indians to sell one of their sayañas, then, losing their ability to generate income, to be forced into selling the remaining lands over the next several years. As more land of the community was sold, less land was available for redistribution and in turn more community landowners were forced to sell their sayañas until little was left. Most of the sales were to the new urban elite of La Paz, who became absentee owners of their new estates.[51]

Some zones, like the distant semitropical valleys of Larecaja and most of the Yungas, were less affected, since creating haciendas here meant a major investment in capital. Also more interior zones, and those with poorer lands and/or poorer linkages to urban markets, tended to be ignored in the land rush. When this whole process ended by 1920, there had been a major shift of power to the hacendados, who now definitively dominated the countryside of the Department of La Paz, both in terms of

TABLE 6.11

Breakdown of Farm Area and Cultivated Fields by Type of Ownership,
Department of La Paz, 1950

Type of Ownership[a]	Farms	Total farm area (in ha.)	Total culti-vated area (in ha.)	Percentage of		
				Farms	Area	Cultivo
Comunidades	1,131	3,000,561	79,337	15%	40%	42%
Haciendas	1,958	3,311,167	96,032	27	45	51
Small farms	3,496	400,509	7,072	48	5	4
Others	767	709,092	5,687	10	10	3
TOTAL	7,352	7,421,329	188,127	100%	100%	100%

SOURCE: Instituto Nacional de Estatistica, "I Censo Agropecuario 1950," pp. 142–43.

[a]Haciendas are defined as "Haciendas con colonos" by the 1950 agricultural census; "Small farm are owner-operated units without hired workers; and "Others" are basically renters and sharecroppe

their labor force, the value of their estates, and the amount of land they controlled (see Table 6.11).

As recent detailed local studies have suggested, this process of expansion was not a smooth one in which the Indians remained passive actors. Constant violence was used against the *revisitadores*, or land surveyors, who were measuring the plots of the Indians. This occurred everywhere, and it would appear that the surveying, which began in the 1880's, was not completed until the 1920's.[52] There were also many cases of local violence against the peones of the hacendados from *ayllu* Indians, as well as sometimes very bloody local rebellions, with the 1920 revolt in Jesús de Machaca being outstanding.[53] Finally, the displaced Indians and their *comunidades* were constantly having recourse to the courts to protect their interests. From the 1880's virtually to the 1950's there was massive litigation over this whole process.

The fact that the Indians resisted so strongly goes a long way toward explaining the results of the first national agricultural census of 1950. For despite all the hacienda expansion and violence, Indian communities—still officially illegal until 1953—retained an impressive quantity of land in the Department of La Paz (see Table 6.11). Moreover, the *comunidades* of La Paz continued to exercise a predominant role within the national scene. Although they accounted for only 30 percent of communal farms in the republic, they controlled 42 percent of national communal acreage and 47 percent of the lands under cultivation by these communal organizations.[54]

All of this agitation, conflict, and organizational activity among even the landless Indians created a climate among Bolivian peasants, especially in the Department of La Paz, that made them a major revolutionary force.[55] It is probably no exaggeration to say that this constant land tension is the single most important factor explaining the impressive mobilization of the Indian peasants after the National Revolution of 1952. It also explains why the postrevolutionary government, against its will, was forced to accept both the idea of the legality of the free community and the total liquidation of the hacienda in most of Bolivia, but above all in the Department of La Paz. Thus the Agrarian Reform of 1953 terminated the legality of the 1874 Ex-Vinculación decree and once more recognized the corporate nature of the community and its legal identity.

Conclusion

My ANALYSIS OF eighteenth- and nineteenth-century rural Bolivia has shown the responsiveness of this supposedly "feudal" society and economy to market forces. That not all factors were completely market oriented is obvious in a society as poor and backward as was Bolivia in the nineteenth century. Subsistence agriculture was an important part of this economy, large land areas were held in corporate units that could not be alienated and were therefore outside the land market, and an important part of rural labor costs was paid for by non-monetary arrangements. Yet ultimately, all factors responded to changes in the needs of the local, regional, and even international markets.

This study has been defined by two major censuses, the royal Indian tribute census of 1786 and the republican cadastral survey of 1881–82. In this century of growth and decline, the haciendas and *ayllus* of the Department of La Paz were forced to respond to a constantly changing economic scene and also adapt themselves to a difficult ecological environment. It is this dynamic of response I have analyzed in an attempt to determine the mechanisms which they used to maintain their societies and economies intact.

The large landowners responded in both traditional and original ways to changing conditions. The market for land was an open one, and between partible inheritance, very active land sales, and land rentals, there was constant turnover of owners, and changes in the size of production units. Declining markets reduced the number of units of production, and often led to more land rentals on the larger estates. Increasing demand for farm products led to expansion of estate production, increasing number of units, and growth in the workforce. Landlords in both the colonial and republican periods were urban merchants and professionals as well as rural landlords, and their control of land was primarily for its economic return, rather than for any special social status that land ownership might confer.

Hacendados also responded in a traditional Andean way to the ecological constraints on production. Wealthy owners combined high plateau and upper and lower valley estates so as to maximize their product mix. There was also vertical integration of individual producers in some cases, with coca haciendas supplying the coca needs of the owner's grain estates and these and the livestock estancias of the upper valleys and *altiplano* supplying the food requirements for the coca hacienda workforce.

In this context, it is obvious that rural landed estates were held by owners primarily for economic reasons, and that these owners certainly responded to changing economic conditions. As the detailed examination of the real estate holdings of Don Tadeo Diez de Medina showed, these rural properties were highly productive and formed a majority of the landed wealth of this very active La Paz merchant. When these estates were no longer productive, they were either sold, rented out to smaller producers whose costs were lower and could remain in the market for longer times, or simply abandoned, as the constant reference to estates without workers indicates in the early-nineteenth-century tribute censuses. That the system of *pongueaje* provided a free servant class to these landowners is not to be denied, but this was not a fundamental need of the landowners. A large and cheap source of urban labor existed in the growing *chola* population of the cities, which has always been available for urban domestic labor in Bolivia and could have easily replaced the *pongos* at relatively little cost. Even Don Tadeo maintained slaves as servants to supplement these workers. Nor was there ostentatious construction of large rural homes to entertain on a lavish scale and create the "paternalistic" world that was supposed to have defined the slave plantation regimes of Brazil and the United States. Most estates were held by absentee landlords and were run by paid overseers, or *mayordomos*.

That the expanding economic conditions resulting from the advent of the railroad and modern silver mining led to violence on the part of the landed elite does not in fact negate the conclusion that the hacienda system was market responsive. No elite will restrain itself if it has the ideological consensus and political power to control market forces. In the intense period of political and economic change that was the last quarter of the nineteenth century, the elite decided to force the large land areas held by the Indians in inalienable estates onto the land market, profiting mightily by this political change.

Much of this land aggression was in fact due to the ability of the communities over this century of change to respond to market conditions in defense of their fundamental aim—land preservation. Without the law of 1874, it is evident that these communities would have successfully survived the transition of the national economy from silver to tin and the even more rapid growth of La Paz in the twentieth century. Even with all the seizures of lands, and the use of troops and fraud to break up the communities, what is impressive is the amount of land these now "illegal" communities still retained into the modern period. As recent work has suggested, the *originarios* of the rejected communities fought a never-ending battle to preserve their lands, their community organizations, and their traditional culture, all of which resulted in a return to a legalization of these communities in 1953.

As I have stressed throughout this work, my fundamental finding is that the Indian peasant communities successfully responded to the market economy in a number of complex ways. Not all Indian communities were equal, and like the hacendado class, there were rich and poor communities. Those in the coca-producing lower valleys were among the richest in the Andes, and some of those on the *altiplano* among the poorest. Some communities owned only land in their immediate environment, while others held estates in other ecological zones far from their original places of concentration. Especially impressive in this regard were the communities near Lake Titicaca, which held "haciendas" producing grains and tropical products in far distant provinces.

Variations of wealth between *ayllus* were also matched by an increasing internal stratification among the Indian peasants themselves. Not all Indians were economically equal. From the earliest resettlement plans of the Spaniards in the sixteenth and seventeenth centuries, a class of landless Indians had developed. But these Indians were to be found both on the estates of the non-Indian hacendados and on the lands of the Indian communities themselves. These forasteros or agregados were a permanent part of the rural scene in the late eighteenth century, but still a minority population on the *ayllus*. As the market forces grew more intense in the following century, their numbers expanded greatly until they became the majority element on the *ayllus*. It was this reserve work force which provided the originarios with the means to meet their economic obligations. These landless or only partially landed Indians could be used to cultivate the lands of the originarios who were then free to migrate to the cities, construction sites, or mines to work on a part-time basis for money wages. These same workers could also be used to expand production of marketable products beyond the subsistence needs of the community. Jealously guarding their land, these communities often had large parcels at their disposal to "rent" to migrating forasteros to attract them and their families to labor on the core parcels of the originarios. Even when the distinctions began to blend between semi-landed forasteros and originarios, the latter still retained exclusive political power and also were the only members of the *ayllus* to have access to multi-ecological land parcels.

All this responsiveness and ability to adapt to changing conditions does not preclude the fact that the Indian community members also responded in a non-market manner. When state exactions became too oppressive, or when officials were too exploitative, or when their elected officials were rejected or re-placed or their land threatened by hacienda expansion, the com-munity Indians responded with violence. Peasant rebellions and protests were a constant part of the rural scene. But these pro-tests were not about the basic structure of exchange and market arrangements. These were always against violations of the rec-ognized order. As several scholars have noted, the community Indians voluntarily paid their tribute tax in exchange for state recognition of their special land status. Thus a tacit "colonial pact" evolved whereby the Indians supported the state's right to tax them in return for its recognition and protection. But the abandonment of this protection, like the violation of their tradi-tional political or land rights by the state or private individuals, led to violent protests, rebellions, massacres, and lawsuits by the score, some of which were resolved in their favor.

Integrated into this system of communities with their dual land groups were the yanacona or colono Indian labor force on the estates of the non-Indians. These landless workers also had the same characteristics as the agregado population on the *ayllus*. They also originated as migratory Indians who had settled on the estates of the hacendados to escape the tribute obligation, and to obtain access to their own lands for subsistence and mar-ket crops. The lands they eventually worked were fairly exten-sive, if poor, and they sometimes were able to produce commer-cial crops for sale. In the case of the wealthy coca haciendas of the Yungas valleys, these resident estate workers were major producers of coca that was sold outside the zone. Given their part-time labor obligations for the hacendados, some of these colonos were even available for wage labor, either on their own estates for special tasks, or as minga or part-time wage workers on the estates of others. There are even cases of colonos who hired these landless migrating workers for labor on their own parcels of land. Clearly all rural populations sought access to land on some reasonably permanent basis as a basic means of survival, but almost all had recourse to wage-labor arrange-ments to supplement their basic subsistence activities.

These different rights of access to land also had their demographic consequences. The more secure the land claims and the larger the land resources, the larger were the family sizes, the fewer the number of widows, and the more balanced the sexual division of the population. With land securing basic subsistence, and that right not being a universal one, women who had claims on land did not lack for male partners if their husbands died. Equally, the guarantee of adequate food supplies and the security of tenure meant that families were larger, and that adults probably migrated less frequently in search of employment. Given the lack of detailed age breakdowns over a long period of time, and the limits of the parish registers for births and deaths, it is difficult to generalize about the demographic changes that were occurring among the various populations during the course of this century, but the general tendencies would appear to be that land access was the primary variable influencing demographic structure.

That Bolivia was a poor nation with an illiterate Amerindian rural population enmeshed in an exploitative social and economic system cannot be denied. But what is most impressive is the extraordinary ability of these non-Spanish-speaking Indians to survive and even prosper in this context. Some have argued that a closed economy would have favored the welfare of these Indian peasants, and that the government abandoned the colonial pact when it abandoned mercantilism and permitted the importation of wheat and foodstuffs from neighboring countries. That such a policy might have favored a few hundred Indian families in Chayanta and Cochabamba at the expense of peasants elsewhere cannot be denied. But the Indians of the province of La Paz had no difficulty accumulating capital and producing for the market, even under conditions of an open economy, which essentially defined the Bolivian market for most of the nineteenth century. Whether working on the haciendas or living on free communities, they were able to adapt to changes in these very competitive market forces. Given the constraints of the market, the response was often a complex one, and freedom to respond was not always total. Nevertheless the traditional models of a manorial, paternalistic, closed, corporate, and ultimately anti-capitalist market world that some have applied to "traditional" Latin American rural society cannot be applied to the Bolivian Andes in the eighteenth and nineteenth centuries.

Reference Matter

The Wealth of
Don Tadeo Diez de Medina

The tables that follow offer a more detailed look at the sources of wealth summarized in Table 2.1, section IA. They also include detailed estate information for properties not listed in his joint estate with his wife, which includes some he granted as dowry, some he sold before terminating his estate, and some he purchased after his wife's death. Some of this information also comes from his dispute with his son-in-law Captain Juan Fernando Iturralde. Given the lack of private estate records and account books, all of this information provides some of the most complete data we have on hacienda production and costs in the Bolivian Andes for any period. Finally, I offer a table of sampled mortgages which I generated on Chulumani coca estates, in order to provide a base from which to compare Diez de Medina's own policy of leveraging his estates.

Table A1 provides the most detailed listing from the numerous sources already cited in the text of all the relevant information I could obtain on his basic rural properties. Here all figures are given in rounded pesos. Table A2 does the same for all the known urban properties I found in the numerous sources used for this study. Table A3 provides a detailed evaluation of five of his estates—the only such complete evaluations available for any of his properties—in terms of the relative value of lands, houses, improvements, tools, animals, crops, and output. In this table, I have not rounded the figures to the nearest peso, but have left all figures in pesos and reales (there were 8 reales for each peso), since most items were given a unit evaluation and their total value was obtained from multiplying the unit value by the number of items held. Tables A4 and A5 were produced from the information Don Tadeo was forced to provide in his extensive judicial dispute with his son-in-law Captain Iturralde, and provide one of the best unpublished sources on the seasonal sales and prices available for eighteenth-century coca pro-

(continued on p. 173)

The Value of Rural Properties Owned by Don Tadeo Diez de Medina
(In pesos a 8)

Name of property	Pueblo	District	Current value	Original value	Mortgages	Annual production (cestos de coca)	Annual rent	Animals	Yanaconas	
									Total	Tributario
1. Incapampa	Coroyco	Chulumani	90,000	–	35,500	1,500	12,000	–	137	36
2. Chicalulo	Pacallo	Chulumani	65,000	98,000	–	1,500	12,000	–	184	33
3. Ataguallani	Cohoni	Chulumani (Rio Abajo)	10,667	–	3,500	–	} 4,000	–	56	13
4. Mutuguaya	Cohoni	Chulumani (Rio Abajo)	15,281	–	1,500	–		–	192	29
5. San Lorenzo de la Vina	Cohoni	Chulumani (Rio Abajo)	27,437	–	–	–	–	–	–	–
6. Estancia Cara-guaya y Cunapata	Timuse	Larecaja	10,500	3,000	3,000	–	–	–	136	19
7. Estancia Pallina Chica	Laja	Omasuyos	8,588	–	–	–	–	3,000	139	23
8. Estancia Capire	Laja	Omasuyos	10,060	1,300	–	–	–	2,600	–	–
9. Ypari y Mullu-marca	Palca	Chulumani	–	–	–	–	–	–	42	8
10. Huri (half owner)	Cohoni	Chulumani	–	–	–	–	–	–	130	23
11. Monte	Pacallo	Chulumani	10,000	–	–	300	2,400	–	77	12
12. Elena/Coripata	Pacallo	Chulumani	10,000	–	–	–	–	–	–	–
13. Cielocaguasi, Taracoca, etc.	Ambana	Larecaja	–	3,000	–	–	–	–	159	24
14. Pongo y Chucuna	Sta. Barbara	La Paz[a]	–	10,140	–	–	–	–	229	53
15. Calacoto	Palca	Chulumani	–	–	–	–	–	–	12	3

SOURCES: The revistas of 1786 to 1797 in AGN, as cited in Table 1.2.
NOTE: In addition, Don Tadeo held mortgages of 4,000 pesos each, producing 200 pesos each in annual rent, on the properties of Colopampa (in Chulumani pueblo, Chulumani district) and Tejar (in San Sebastian pueblo, in the rural parishes of La Paz).
[a]The three rural parishes of the city of La Paz.

The Value of Urban Properties Owned by Don Tadeo Diez de Medina
(In pesos a 8)

Property	City	Street	Current value	Original value	Mortgages	Annual rent
1. Tambo (Warehouse/market)	La Paz	Esq. Calle Abajo de Calle Comercio	50,000	–	–	500
2. House with ground level stores (residence of Don Tadeo)	La Paz	Calle Comercio	48,654	–	–	800
3. House (residence of Iturralde)	La Paz	Calle Comercio	7,000 ⎫	–	6,500	–
4. House (residence of Guillen)	La Paz	Calle Comercio	7,500 ⎬			
5. House	La Paz	Behind Cathedral	6,000 ⎭			
6. House with ground level stores	Coroyco	Chulumani		–	1,000	50
7. Tambo (purchased 1796)	La Paz	Plazuela de San Sebastian		20,010	8,000	1,000

SOURCES: The revistas of 1786 to 1797 in AGN, as cited in Table 1.2.

APPENDIX TABLE A3
Assessments of Some Rural Properties of Don Tadeo Diez de Medina
(Pesos/reales)

Hacienda Mutuguaya (Cohoni) in Oct. 1787	
Houses, land, improvements, implements	13,000/0
20 *cargas* of corn seed @ 20 reales	50/0
45 *cargas* potato seed @ 12 reales	67/4
251 sheep @ 10 reales	313/6
6 *cargas* of wheat @ 3 pesos	18/0
6 *cargas* of oca @ 6 reales	4/4
1 *carga* of beans @ 2 pesos	2/0
15 plowshares of 4 lbs @ 20 reales	37/4
20 mules @ 5 pesos	100/0
16 yoke of oxen @ 40 pesos	640/0
25 cows @ 18 pesos	450/0
25 calfs @ 12 pesos	300/0
Corrals and an old house	300/0
TOTAL	15,283/2
Hacienda Ataguallani (Cohoni) in Oct. 1787	
Houses, land, etc.	10,000/0
8 yoke of oxen @ 40 pesos	320/0
6 cows @ 18 pesos	108/0
6 calves @ 12 pesos	72/0
6 burros @ 5 pesos	30/0
14 *cargas* of corn seed @ 20 reales	35/0
10 *cargas* of oca @ 6 reales	7/4
44 *cargas* of potatoes @ 12 reales	66/0
1 *carga* of barley @ 28 reales	3/4
10 plowshares of 4 lbs @ 20 reales	25/0
TOTAL	10,667/0
Hacienda San Lorenzo de la Vina (Cohoni) in Oct. 1787	
Houses, land, etc.	6,000/0
127 apple trees @ 8 reales	127/0
564 peach trees @ 8 reales	564/0
217 plum trees @ 8 reales	217/0
100 quince trees @ 4 reales	50/0
12 fig trees @ 4 reales	6/0
A "new house"	1,200/0
A garden with fruit trees and flowers	300/0
9,000 vines of wine grapes @ 16 reales	18,000/0
6 farm implements @ 6 pesos	36/0
10 plowshares @ 20 reales	25/0
1 axe @ 5 pesos	5/0
TOTAL	26,530/0

APPENDIX TABLE A3 (*continued*)

Estancia Pallina Chica (Laja) in June 1788	
Houses, land, etc.	6,000/0
2,200 female sheep @ 6 reales	1,650/0
800 rams @ 5 reales	500/0
700 rams born this year @ 5 reales	437/4
TOTAL	8,587/4
Estancia Capire (Laja) in June 1788	
Houses, land, etc.	8,000/0
2,000 female sheep @ 6 reales	1,500/0
625 rams @ 5 reales	390/5
5 yoke of oxen @ 25 pesos the pair	125/0
20 native cameloids @ 3 pesos	60/0
TOTAL	10,075/4

SOURCE: AGI, Audiencia de Charcas, legajo 556, expendiente 10, document 5 [*Mayorazgo*].

NOTE: The sums are mine, since there are several arithmetic errors in the original document.

(*continued from p. 169*)

duction in the Bolivian Andes. Table A6 also comes from these judicial records and gives some of the best information available on food-producing Andean estates. Table A7 comes from an extensive examination of wills and testaments in the notarial records of the La Paz notaries of the eighteenth century. Since most Chulumani landowners were absentees and lived in the city of La Paz, these records are the best single source for the wills of the Chulumani landed class. From these wills I have extracted all the information I could find on indebtedness of estates. This is presented here to give a base for comparison both with Don Tadeo's policies in this area and with other colonial landed classes in Latin America.

APPENDIX TABLE A4
Output of the Coca Haciendas of Don Tadeo Diez de Medina, 1782–92
(In cestos)

	Chicalulo			Incapampa			Cedromayo[a]		
	June	Nov.	Mar.	June	Nov.	Mar.	June	Nov.	Mar.
1782	120	200	358	60	100	200	40	100	150
1783	308	320	400	150	250	300	120	200	250
1784	377	537	508	306	298	400			
1785	513	389	473	300	232	246			
1786	419	358	483	306	298	382			
1787	449	429	421	302	400	433			
1788	386	461	474	335	400	408			
1789	424	559	536	300	450	300			
1790	491	520	485	300	423	350			
1791	408	584	550	256	419	336			
1792	465	586	n.a.	272	378	n.a.			
TOTAL	4,360	4,943	4,688	2,887	3,648	3,355	160	300	400
AVERAGE	396	449	469	262	332	336	80	150	200

SOURCE: ANB, Tierras e Indios, Año 1795, no. 26; also found in *ibid.*, Año 1795, no. 84, folios 197–203.

[a]Cedromayo was sold by Don Tadeo in 1784.

APPENDIX TABLE A5
Prices of Coca Received by Don Tadeo Diez de Medina, 1782–92
(In reales per cesto)

	June	November	March
1782	140	72	56
1783	56	56	56
1784	68	72	64
1785	72	72	66
1786	74	74	64
1787	74	74	72
1788	68	68	68
1789	76	64	62
1790	62	58	58
1791	62	56	52
1792	46	46	n.a.
AVERAGE	73	65	62

SOURCE: ANB, Tierras e Indios, Año 1795, no. 26; also found in no. 84, folios 197–203.
NOTE: All haciendas obtained the same prices for their production.

APPENDIX TABLE A6

Output of the Foodstuffs Haciendas of Don Tadeo Diez de Medina, 1782–92
(In cargas)

Property and produce	Annual production					
	1782	1783	1784	1785	1786	1787
Lipari						
Wheat[a]	20	30	46	48	52	44
Ataguallani						
Corn	40	120	200	250	200	270
Chuño	0	50	80	100	80	60
Beans	0	0	0	0	20	15
Mutuguaya						
Corn	60	260	200	266	360	266
Chuño	0	45	30	60	80	50
Wheat	0	30	25	50	90	40
Beans	0	15	20	12	0	30
Caruga						
Corn	30	120	150	200	150	150
Chuño	30	60	100	120	100	119
Wheat	0	15	20	20	30	12
Beans	0	10	20	25	12	20
Tunta	0	0	20	15	20	15
Caya	0	60	120	80	130	120
Taracoca y Palomani						
Corn	30	60	80	70	—	—
Chuño	20	80	70	80	—	—
Wheat	0	12	10	20	—	—
Tunta	0	12	15	12	—	—
Caya	40	80	100	100	—	—
Capiri						
Chuño	20	50	60	80	80	60
Quinoa	5	10	15	20	20	10
Palina Chica						
Chuño	15	25	40	40	80	100
Quinoa	5	20	12	20	25	25
Tunta	0	0	10	15	20	20

SOURCE: ANB, Tierras e Indios, Año 1795, no. 26. Hacienda Taracoca was ceded by Don Tadeo to his daughter Doña Francisca Diez de Medina in 1786 (f. 160). Lipari and Caruga were properties that seemed to be in joint ownership dispute with Iturralde, and thus are not listed in Table A1.

NOTE: Chuño and tunta are dehydrated and frozen potatoes; caya is dehydrated from oca; and quinoa is a food grain unique to the Andes.

[a] This production is given in fanegas (= 62 kilos, or 1½ cargas).

Property and produce	Annual production					
	1788	1789	1790	1791	1792	Total
Lipari						
Wheat[a]	45	0	0	0	0	285
Ataguallani						
Corn	210	200	200	180	210	2080
Chuño	90	110	50	80	120	820
Beans	30	20	15	30	30	160
Mutuguaya						
Corn	400	270	350	420	300	3152
Chuño	100	90	80	80	50	665
Wheat	60	80	80	60	40	555
Beans	30	30	40	30	25	232
Caruga						
Corn	160	120	200	120	180	1580
Chuño	120	114	80	100	110	1053
Wheat	25	20	20	15	30	207
Beans	15	20	15	25	20	182
Tunta	20	30	15	20	30	185
Caya	80	100	110	90	120	1010
Taracoca y Palomani						
Corn	—	—	—	—	—	240
Chuño	—	—	—	—	—	250
Wheat	—	—	—	—	—	42
Tunta	—	—	—	—	—	39
Caya	—	—	—	—	—	320
Capiri						
Chuño	90	60	100	70	80	750
Quinoa	15	20	20	15	20	170
Palina Chica						
Chuño	80	100	80	100	60	720
Quinoa	14	20	10	25	10	186
Tunta	12	15	12	12	15	131

APPENDIX TABLE A7
Selected Yungas Haciendas, Their Values and Mortgages

Name of property	Location	Value	Censos & capellanias	No. of censos	Date[a]
Tabacal Cota	Coripata	30,000	9,000	2	1791
Yrpave	Palca	13,000	7,500	–	1791
Stgo de Chiquini	Chirca	3,000	2,000	2	1787
Colopampa	Coroyco	7,000	2,900	2	1787
San Antonio de Coloni	Coripata	26,000	6,500	3	1790
Tagnapata	Pacallo	10,000	400	–	1791
Santa Ana	Pacallo	27,000	2,000	–	1795
Capellania	Coroyco	25,000	8,000	–	1795
Tarila (no cocales)	Chirca	6,500	6,500	–	1795*
Minachitambo	Coroyco	8,500	0	–	1795
Yavichuco	Pacallo	15,000	5,737	–	1795
Sta. Gertrudiz	Coripata	9,000	5,000	–	1799
Cachimayo	Chirca	1,200	1,200	–	1795*
Ymanaco	Irupana	5,000	4,000	–	1801
Cachapa (huerta)	Mecapaca	2,130	2,130	–	1804*
Islas de Munaypata	Coroyco	3,500	0	–	1799
Tajna y Liquimpaya	Suri	22,000	0	–	1795
San Agustin de Peri	Coripata	50,000	9,800	–	1795
San Juan del Asomado	Chirca	9,000	2,200	–	1800
Santa Ana y Almanza	Chupe	12,000	0	–	1802
Nogalini y Tabacalani	Coroyco	25,000	4,000	–	1802
Chila	Irupana	26,000	5,000	2	1798
Viluma	Pacallo	7,010	7,010	–	1798
Guarinilla	Pacallo	9,000	7,500	–	1796
Charbina	Irupana	5,000	0	–	1801
Tirata	Cohoni	7,500	4,500	–	1800
San Lorenzo de Peri	Coripata	18,000	3,800	3	1800
Stgo. de Tacna (panllevar)	Palca	8,000	0	–	1794
San Jose de Churaca	Chirca	38,400	3,000	–	1792
Pacallo	Pacallo	16,000	2,000	–	1799
Vicua	Irupana	15,000	1,000	–	1800
Nogolani	Coripata	35,000	4,000	2	1800
Aritapa	Chirca	10,000	1,300	–	1801*
San Agustin de Melgar	Chirca	4,000	16,800	3+	1796
Bagnate	Coroyco	20,000	9,000	2	1797
Chocana	Chupe	20,000	6,000	–	1796
Santa Barbara	Coroyco	80,000	21,500	2	1803
TOTAL		628,740	171,277		

SOURCES: AHLP and AHMLP, selected notarial records for the relevant years.
[a]An asterisk after the year indicates this was an auctioned sale (*remate*).

Population Statistics for Chulumani and Pacajes, 1786–1838

The tables overleaf present detailed breakdowns of the populations of the two colonial districts (republican provinces) that are the focus of my attention in Chapter 4. The data are found in the following archives: 1786, in AGN, 13-17-6-5, legajo 24, libro 2; 1803, in AGN, 13-17-9-4, legajo 36, libro 4; 1829, in ANB, ATNC, no. 166; and 1838, in ANB, ATNC, no. 177.

APPENDIX TABLE B1
Complete Population Statistics on Chulumani, 1786–1838

Year	No. of haciendas or *ayllus*	Women				
		Niñas	Solteras	Casadas	Viudas	Total
Originarios						
1786	37	491	83	689	78	1,341
1803	37	490	125	663	67	1,345
1829	36	421	64	577	26	1,088
1838	37	466	107	503	42	1,118
Forasteros						
1786	37	478	131	923	142	1,674
1803	37	486	83	719	60	1,348
1829	36	457	38	683	29	1,207
1838	37	476	69	655	38	1,238
Total *ayllu*						
1786	37	969	214	1,612	220	3,015
1803	37	976	208	1,382	127	2,693
1829	36	878	102	1,260	55	2,295
1838	37	942	176	1,158	80	2,356
Yanaconas						
1786	276	2,051	471	3,394	397	6,313
1803	237	1,715	302	2,670	123	4,810
1829	235	1,884	205	2,462	111	4,662
1838	231	1,833	397	2,437	242	4,909

Year	No. of haciendas or *ayllus*	Men					
		Niños	Proximos	Tribu-tarios	Reser-vados	Ausentes	Total
Originarios							
1786	37	569	0	867	48	0	1,484
1803	37	570	58	906	56	2	1,590
1829	36	520	46	877	25	–	1,468
1838	37	491	91	839	63	0	1,484
Forasteros							
1786	37	569	99	1,436	144	16	2,248
1803	37	540	68	1,131	57	7	1,796
1829	36	437	46	1,033	72	–	1,588
1838	37	550	48	1,239	45	0	1,882
Total *ayllu*							
1786	37	1,138	99	2,303	192	16	3,732
1803	37	1,110	126	2,037	113	9	3,386
1829	36	957	92	1,910	97	0	3,056
1838	37	1,041	139	2,078	108	0	3,366
Yanaconas							
1786	276	2,568	440	4,049	615	45	7,672
1803	237	2,249	325	2,825	504	11	5,903
1829	235	2,041	209	3,065	258	–	5,573
1838	231	2,064	395	3,395	313	34	6,167

APPENDIX TABLE B2
Complete Population Statistics on Pacajes, 1786–1838

Year	No. of haciendas or *ayllus*	Women				
		Niñas	Solteras	Casadas	Viudas	Total
Originarios						
1786	88	3,008	1,851	3,298	720	8,877
1792	88	2,703	934	3,048	5	6,690
1803	94	2,641	1,534	3,359	173	7,707
1838	91	1,805	716	1,984	30	4,535
Forasteros						
1786	89	2,414	1,486	2,305	1,225	7,430
1792	93	2,881	1,800	3,301	1,262	9,244
1803	96	2,636	1,688	3,517	732	8,573
1838	91	3,878	1,733	4,553	703	10,867
Total *ayllu*						
1786	89	5,422	3,337	5,603	1,945	16,307
1792	93	5,584	2,734	6,349	1,267	15,934
1803	96	5,277	3,222	6,876	905	16,280
1838	91	5,683	2,449	6,537	733	15,402
Yanaconas						
1786	74	1,138	718	1,212	440	3,508
1792	74	1,222	463	1,434	314	3,433
1803	76	975	703	1,518	204	3,400
1838	66	1,673	592	1,730	181	4,176

Year	No. of haciendas or *ayllus*	Men					
		Niños	Proximos	Tribu-tarios	Reser-vados	Ausentes	Total
Originarios							
1786	88	3,533	590	3,103	913	131	8,139
1792	88	3,131	484	3,153	454	205	7,222
1803	94	3,339	842	3,602	524	125	8,307
1838	91	2,021	413	2,403	196	38	5,033
Forasteros							
1786	89	2,554	391	2,711	564	880	6,220
1792	93	3,345	579	3,489	1,204	1,053	8,617
1803	96	3,537	921	4,250	787	290	9,495
1838	91	4,422	1,030	6,550	1,087	238	13,089
Total *ayllu*							
1786	89	6,087	981	5,814	1,477	1,011	14,359
1792	93	6,476	1,063	6,642	1,658	1,258	15,839
1803	96	6,876	1,763	7,852	1,311	415	17,802
1838	91	6,443	1,443	8,953	1,283	276	18,122
Yanaconas							
1786	74	1,357	225	1,278	308	185	3,168
1792	74	1,413	200	1,476	314	257	3,403
1803	76	1,472	360	1,717	260	121	3,809
1838	66	1,891	343	2,120	398	64	4,752

———

The Male Tributary Population in the Nineteenth Century

The tables overleaf detail the rapid increase in the *ayllu* populations vis-à-vis the yanacona populations in Bolivia in the nineteenth century. Table C1 gives the total tributary population of the Department of La Paz for eight separate years, and Tables C2–C4 then break down the *ayllu* and hacienda populations for three specific years both for La Paz and for the other districts of the republic. These tables show that, over forty years in the mid-nineteenth century, growth in the tributary population was centered in the *ayllu* population; the hacienda population actually decreased slightly overall, though it did show slight increases in some departments.

APPENDIX TABLE C1
*Adult Male Tributarios of All Categories in the
Department of La Paz, 1852–77*

Province	1852	1856	1858	1863
Cercado	5,750	n.a.	5,058	5,263
Pacajes	14,750	n.a.	13,943	14,395
Larecaja	4,168	3,952	3,616	3,731
Omasuyos	19,066	n.a.	19,358	19,483
Inquisivi	3,317	n.a.	2,553	2,955
Yungas	5,714	n.a.	5,731	5,444
Sicasica	9,566	–	9,560	10,001
Muñecas	5,579	–	7,788	5,897
TOTAL	67,910		67,607	67,169

Province	1867	1869	1871	1877
Cercado	4,583	n.a.	n.a.	4,986
Pacajes	14,616	11,920	15,348	15,613
Larecaja	3,081	3,450	3,718	3,816
Omasuyos	20,222	n.a.	20,307	21,001
Inquisivi	3,905	3,488	3,252	3,467
Yungas	n.a.	4,226	4,794	4,800
Sicasica	7,546	7,182	10,846	11,335
Muñecas	5,949	–	5,736	5,736
TOTAL				70,754

SOURCE: Oficina Nacional de Inmigración, Estadística y Propaganda Geográfica, *Boletin*, I (1901), pp. 515–16.

APPENDIX TABLE C2
The Male Tributary Population of Bolivia, 1838

Department	Total	Male tributarios on	
		Ayllus[a]	Haciendas[b]
La Paz	61,289	38,329	22,308
Cercado	5,801	2,847	2,778
Omasuyos	15,667	8,790	6,877
Pacajes	13,791	11,162	2,417
Yungas	5,968	2,151	3,662
Sicasica (1842)	10,864	7,648	3,216
Larecaja	3,879	1,724	2,046
Muñecas (1826)	5,319	4,007	1,312
Potosí	30,802	26,441	3,675
Oruro	14,217	10,448	3,656
Cochabamba	11,163	6,783	4,284
Chuquisaca	5,083	3,379	1,517
TOTAL REPUBLIC	122,554	85,380	35,440

SOURCE: Grieshaber, "Survival . . . A Regional Comparison," table 1.
NOTE: I have excluded from the table the figures for Caupolican plus the small number of town (pueblo) Indian tributarios.
[a]Originarios plus forasteros.   [b]Yanaconas.

APPENDIX TABLE C3
The Male Tributary Population of Bolivia, 1858

| Department | Total | Male tributarios on | |
		Ayllus[a]	Haciendas[b]
La Paz	67,825	44,512	22,704
Cercado	5,486	2,991	2,401
Omasuyos	19,356	11,447	7,909
Pacajes	15,423	12,606	2,498
Yungas (1852)	5,825	2,246	3,464
Sicasica	12,215	8,772	3,443
Larecaja (1863)	3,731	2,089	1,561
Muñecas	5,789	4,361	1,428
Potosí	31,183	27,573	3,204
Oruro	17,700	13,345	4,206
Cochabamba	8,245	5,380	2,821
Chuquisaca	5,636	4,129	1,284
TOTAL REPUBLIC	130,589	94,939	34,219

SOURCE: Grieshaber, "Survival of Indian Communities . . . A Regional Comparison," table 2.
NOTE: I have excluded from the table the figures for Caupolican plus the small number of town (pueblo) Indian tributarios.
[a] Originarios plus forasteros.
[b] Yanaconas.

APPENDIX TABLE C4
The Male Tributary Population of Bolivia, 1877

| Department | Total | Male tributarios on | |
		Ayllus[a]	Haciendas[b]
La Paz	70,821	47,358	22,774
Cercado	4,832	2,784	1,939
Omasuyos	21,129	12,628	8,504
Pacajes	17,326	14,160	2,785
Yungas	4,800	2,019	2,737
Sicasica	13,182	9,290	3,892
Larecaja	3,816	2,087	1,574
Muñecas	5,736	4,390	1,346
Potosí	36,857	32,391	4,096
Oruro	20,015	15,410	4,457
Cochabamba	6,900	4,985	1,843
Chuquisaca	5,387	4,238	940
TOTAL REPUBLIC	139,980	104,382	34,110

SOURCE: Grieshaber, "Survival of Indian Communities . . . A Regional Comparison," table 3.
NOTE: I have excluded from the table the figures for Caupolican plus the small number of town (pueblo) Indian tributarios.
[a] Originarios plus forasteros.
[b] Yanaconas.

Notes

For full forms of citations shortened in the Notes, see the Bibliography following.

Introduction

1. This is the influential model developed by Françoise Chevalier in *La formation des grandes domaines au Méxique*.

2. See, e.g., Macera, "Feudalismo colonial americano." A more complete and complex statement of this model is found in Kula, *Teoría económica del sistema feudal*.

3. In the case of Mexico, see Taylor, *Landlord and Peasant in Colonial Oaxaca*, and Van Young, *Hacienda and Market in Eighteenth-Century Mexico*. For Peru, see, e.g., Burga, *De la encomienda a la hacienda capitalista*, and Glave and Remy, *Estructura agraria y vida rural en un región andina*.

4. Two of the more interesting of such studies are Spalding, *Huarochirí, An Andean Society Under Inca and Spanish Rule*, and Stern, *Peru's Indian Peoples and the Challenge of Spanish Conquest*.

5. See Bauer, "Rural Workers in Spanish America." Even for Mexico the use of debt peonage and physical coercion is now said to exist only for the Southwest coast and Yucatan; see Katz, ed.; *La servidumbre agraria en México en la época porfiriana*.

6. The *ayllu* is defined as a land-owning corporate unit whose members work the lands in individual plots. In the pre-conquest period the *ayllu* was the basic fictive kinship group, and its land claims were often not on contiguous plots. Under Spanish resettlement plans *ayllus* became more like communal villages, with a fixed and well-defined land area. It is the norm for several *ayllus* to make up one Indian *comunidad*, or free Indian community, as I often refer to it in this text. In the Andes, the several *ayllus* of a community are traditionally grouped into a moiety—with half of them being part of an "upper" division and half a "lower" one (or *urinsaya* and *anansaya*). This, in fact, was the way the colonial and republican census-takers registered the *ayllus* of a *comuni-*

dad. In this work, when I use the term *comunidad*, I am referring to a multi-*ayllu* community, which typically has a central administration representing all the autonomous *ayllus*. It was often these *comunidades* rather than individual *ayllus* that owned haciendas in other districts.

7. Among the most important works of reevaluation have been Murra, *Formaciones económicos y políticas del mundo andino*, Sánchez-Albornoz, *Indios y tributos en el Alto Peru*, Saignes, *Los Andes Orientales*, Larson, *Colonialism and Agrarian Transformation in Bolivia*, Rivera, "La expansión del latifundia en el Altiplano boliviano," Platt, *Estado boliviano y ayllu andino*, Grieshaber, "Survival of Indian Communities in Nineteenth-Century Bolivia," and Langer, *Economic Change and Rural Resistance in Southern Bolivia*.

8. The 1900 figures for area and Indian population are found in Bolivia, *Censo general de la población de la República de Bolivia . . . 1900*, vol. 1, p. 160; vol. 2, p. xliii.

Chapter One

1. This latter zone, Caupolican, or Apolobamba, was in the eastern frontier region far from traditional settlement areas. Because of its recent conversion from missions to settled villages, it contained no haciendas. For this reason, I have excluded it from all the following tables.

2. In the *padrones* of 1785/87 and of 1803/7, the estimates of the Indian population of the province were 199,003 and 219,842, respectively. This meant that La Paz was the most populous Indian province in both Upper and Lower Peru in the late colonial period. See Santamaría, "La propiedad de la tierra y la condición social del indio en el Alto Perú, 1789–1810," p. 254; and Vollmer, *Bevölkerungspolitik und Bevölkerungsstructur*, p. 267. By 1827 it was estimated that the province's total population (including whites and cholos) consisted of some 375,000 persons, making it the most populous province of the new Republic of Bolivia. Pentland, "Report on the Republic of Bolivia, 1827," folio 81.

3. The most detailed linguistic survey of the region is the listing of 1580 found in Bouysse-Cassagne, "Pertenencia étnica, status económico y lenguajes en Charcas." On the Urus, see Harriet Klein, "Los urus: el extraño pueblo del altiplano"; and Wachtel, *Le retour des ancêtres*.

4. Luis Crespo, *Geografía de la República de Bolivia*, pp. 145–46. This figure excludes Caupolican.

5. Saignes, "De la filiation à la residence."

6. Contemporary descriptions of these districts can be found in Alcedo, *Diccionario geográfico-histórico de las indias occidentales o América*; for a modern analysis of this region, see Muñoz Reyes, *Geografía de Bolivia*.

7. Pentland, "Report," folio 82.

8. The province was the second wealthiest in Alto Peru and thus in the entire viceroyalty, generating over 280,000 pesos in 1790. It was also consistently the most profitable for the Crown (in terms of producing revenues over costs) of all the viceregal provinces. Herbert Klein, "Structure and Profitability of Royal Finance," table V.

9. Sánchez-Albornoz, *Indios y tributos*, p. 43n.

10. Here and throughout the rest of the book, peso is understood to signify the *peso a 8* (or the peso worth 8 reales), which was the standard unit of currency used in colonial Spanish America.

11. Much of the above discussion is based on the ideas presented in Sánchez-Albornoz, *Indios y tributos*, chaps. 1–2.

12. The best study to date on the origins of the forastero class—though concentrated on Cuzco—is Wightman, *Indigenous Migration and Social Change*. For a good description of the role of forasteros in the mining industry of Oruro, see Zulawski, "Forasteros y yanaconas," pp. 159–92.

13. This was formally developed by the Lima treasury official Jorge Escobeda y Alarcon in July of 1784. For a printed version of this "Introducción Medocia," see *Instrucción de Revisitas o matriculas formado por el señor Don Jorge Escobedo y Alarcon (. . .) en cumplimento del articulo 121 de la Real Instrucción de Intendentes* (Reimpreso en Buenos Aires, 1802), found in AGN, Biblioteca, "Folletos Varios," 87/E.

14. The censuses (or *padrones y revisitas de indios*) are found in AGN, Sala XIII, in the following locations: *Chulumani* (1786) in 13-17-6-5, libro 2; *Omasuyos* (1786) in 13-17-5-4, libros 1,2,3; *Pacajes* (1796) in 13-17-8-3, libro 1, and 13-17-8-4; *Larecaja* (1786) in 13-17-6-3, libros 1,2; 13-17-6-2, libro 2; and 13-17-7-1, libro 1; *Sicasica* (1792) in 13-17-7-2, libros 1,2; *3 Parroquias de La Paz* (1786) in 13-17-6-3, libro 1, for names of hacendados, and (1792) 13-17-7-3, libro 1, for population. The census years chosen were based on the availability of names of owners and the completeness of the account. The former information was available in only scattered documentation, and thus I could not use the same year for all districts. In my survey of all the Alto Peruvian tribute accounts available in the archives of La Paz, Sucre, Buenos Aires, and Seville, and in the Matta Linhares collection in Madrid, I have found very few lists for the eighteenth or early nineteenth centuries that contain the names of the hacienda owners.

15. This analysis of the creation of a free labor market is based on ideas developed in Sánchez-Albornoz, *Indios y tributos*, chap. 2.

16. Chayanov, *The Theory of Peasant Economy*.

17. Lema, "Production et circulation de la coca en Bolivie," p. 370. Don Tadeo Diez de Medina, the hacendado who will be examined in

Chapter 2, paid some 230 pesos per annum in tribute for 46 adult male workers (*tributarios*) on his Yungas coca estates between 1782 and 1792. This represented 2 percent of his total operating costs (of 10,871 pesos per annum), and 5 percent of his labor costs (of 4,365 pesos). *Ibid*, p. 368, Table 7.11.

18. For a fuller discussion of these labor arrangements in the nineteenth century, see Chapter 6 below.

19. The term *yanaconas* was used to designate landless estate Indians who served as *pongos* and *colonos*. Yanacona was a preconquest term used to designate the personal servants of the nobles and the Incas, and may still have been used to designate such serfs of the Indian nobility in the sixteenth and early seventeenth centuries. By the eighteenth century, however, it was used exclusively as an equivalent to landless peasants, who were also sometimes called pongos, agregados, or forasteros in other regions. For an analysis of this class in Peru, see Matos Mar, *Yanocanaje y reforma agraria en el Perú*, chap. 1.

20. ACALP, tomo 116, folios 261–77. This is one of the few extant account books of a private estate, and covers the period from 1794 to 1800. In the coca fields of the Yungas, cleaning yielded a daily wage of 3 reales and harvesting was paid 2 reales daily. On these estates the daily labor was based on a working day lasting from 6:30 A.M. to 6:00 P.M., with a total of four half hour breaks for resting, chewing the coca, and eating the rations provided by the hacendado. Lema, "Production et circulation," pp. 204–5.

21. ANB, Tierras e Indios, 1804/5, "Visita de las Haciendas del Partido de Yungas," folios 29v–30. In the vineyards of the southern zone of Tarija in the hacienda of La Angostura in the late seventeenth century there was a complex mixture of slaves (22), yanaconas (66 in all), and wage laborers (48), the latter of whom worked exclusively in the wine harvest in April and May and received 4 reales per day, less the costs of their maintenance of beef, corn, and wine. These wage laborers came exclusively from neighboring estates or even came out of the forastero group of Indians, who rented lands (either for cash, labor exchange, or both) on this very wealthy hacienda (evaluated at 117,000 pesos). Presta, "Una hacienda tarijeña en el siglo XVII."

22. These patterns seem to be universal in Alto Peruvian agriculture. The detailed records of a late-sixteenth-century wine-growing hacienda (Llanqueuma) in Sicasica show employment of resident yanaconas and even a few free black workers, along with a large number of temporary jornaleros, who worked from a few days to two months on the estate. The majority were *reparto* Indians granted to the estate by the Audiencia of Charcas, but there were also many individual migrating workers, Spanish skilled wine makers, and even yanaconas from nearby estates who were skilled in vineyard care. These temporary workers also re-

ceived the name of *mingas*, and, interestingly enough, the skilled Spanish workers—though receiving much higher wages of 4 pesos per day (as compared to 1 peso per day for Indians performing the same skilled tasks)—also received part of their wages in foodstuffs. Sebill, *Ayllus y haciendas*, pp. 79–81.

23. On the coca haciendas of Don Tadeo Diez de Medina, food supplied to resident workers amounted to about 1,250 pesos per annum, or 12 percent of his total operating expenses and 29 percent of his labor costs (see n. 17). To this should be added another 2,175 pesos expended in just moving the foodstuffs from his highland haciendas to the coca estates. Lema, "Production et circulation," p. 368, Table 7.11. An 1805 account written by the *mayordomo* of the coca hacienda of Cochuna claimed that 40 cestos of coca were consumed by workers producing 1,500 cestos per annum. Bergana, "Demonstración Matematica," folio 22. From this I have estimated coca costs at 3 percent of Don Tadeo's output (coca was from his own output and not listed in his labor costs).

24. Bergana, "Demonstración Matemática," folios 31–32.

25. One of the few records on colon and jornalero debts comes from the hacienda of Pacallo (in Pacallo) in the mid-eighteenth century. Some two-thirds of the yanaconas at Pacallo had outstanding debts to the owner, ranging from 1 real (less than a day's labor) to 11 pesos, 5 reales (between 31 and 46.5 days of work, depending on the wage rate, which varied from 2 to 3 reales per day). The remaining third were owed sums by the hacendado. Only 20 percent of the minga workers had any claims or obligations with the hacendado, suggesting a much more immediate payment arrangement. Lema, "Production et circulation," pp. 207–8.

26. Van Young, *Hacienda and Market in Eighteenth-Century Mexico*, pp. 253ff.

27. An excellent recent survey of this literature is contained in Konrad, *A Jesuit Hacienda in Colonial Mexico*, pp. 326ff.

28. See Chapter 6 below for further discussion of these arrangements.

29. For the description of the land arrangements, see Birbuet D., *Tierra y ganado en Pacajes*, pp. 21–22; Albó, "Dinámica en la estructura inter-comunitaria de Jesús de Machaca," pp. 785–86; and Mamani, "Agricultura a los 4000 metros," pp. 75–132. The best description of relative control over lands on the pre-1953 haciendas is Turvosky, "Bolivian Haciendas Before and After the Revolution."

30. Detailed descriptions of such pongo and colono labor obligations are found in the notes of the sub-delegados, or royal officials who were in charge of taking the censuses (or *revisitas*). Thus the Omasuyos subdelegado reported in 1792 that the "Yanaconas are defined as those Indians who live on the estates of the Spaniards and who do not possess royal lands," (i.e., do not reside like the forasteros on the *ayllu* lands).

Such Indians also "provide weekly domestic services [in the homes] of the Patrons . . . , and others pasture the herds of the landowners, sowing and harvesting the owner's crops, for which they receive usufruct lands on the estates." AGN, 13-17-7-4, libro 3, folios 348v–49. This same document is also duplicated in AGN 13-17-7-3, libro 4, folio 2-2v.

31. This was the consistent pattern seen in the special census of absent male tributarios carried out in Chulumani from June 1786 to December 1790. See AGN, 13-17-5-3, "Padron de Ausentes y Muertos."

32. The only qualification to this generalization has to do with the important coca-growing district of Chulumani. Here the physical limitations on hacienda size due to the extraordinarily steep valleys kept down the average size of the hacienda labor force, so using the number of yanaconas alone as a proxy for wealth creates a bias in the data. No weighting scheme has been adopted to compensate for this bias.

33. A partial census of hacendados in the partido of Chulumani in 1796 found 240 of the local hacendados to be living in the city of La Paz, two who lived in Oruro, and 133 who were resident on their estates in the Yungas. See AGI, Audiencia de Buenos Aires, legajo 513, "Estado que manifiesta el numero de haciendas . . . en el Partido de Yungas," dated La Paz, 17 Noviembre 1796.

34. In the census of 1846, Dalence estimated the provincial population of La Paz at 90,662 whites and 295,442 Indians (*Bosquejo estadístico de Bolivia*, p. 222). Using this ratio for the 207,369 Indians of the province in the late eighteenth century yields a total of estimated whites in the province of 63,635 persons. Accepting an approximation of five persons per hacendado family (and including the institutional, cholo, and *ayllu* owners in this total compensates for the relatively low multiplier), we arrive at a total hacendado class of 3,610 persons, who thus represent 5.7 percent of the total white population. In the U.S. South in 1790, it has been estimated that 35 percent of the free population were slaveowners (this figure calculated from Gray, *History of Agriculture in the Southern United States to 1860*, vol. 1, p. 482). It would thus appear that the hacendado class was a much more restricted one than the contemporary slaveowner group in the United States, despite their identity—as will be seen below—in wealth distribution patterns.

35. This figure was calculated from data provided in Soltow, "Economic Inequality in the United States in the Period from 1790 to 1860," pp. 828–29. The GINI coefficient measure for inequality for these 1790 slaveowners is 0.602.

36. The GINI coefficient for the 721 hacendados and their 82,465 yanaconas was 0.583. This is virtually the same figure as for the United States. It is also close to the figure for concentration of slave ownership in the Brazilian province of São Paulo in the 1820's; see Klein and Vidal

Luna, "Slaves & Masters in Early Nineteenth Century Brazil." A similar concentration was found in the distribution pattern of ownership of urban real estate in the city of New York in 1789 (GINI = 0.588); see Klein and Willis, "The Distribution of Wealth in Late 18th Century New York City," p. 267. A slightly higher GINI rate (0.635) was found for the distribution of land among 265 cattle ranchers in a frontier zone of rural Buenos Aires in the late eighteenth century, though the actual distribution of cattle among these same *estancieros* was substantially lower (0.483). Azcuy Ameghino and Martinez Dougnac, *Tierra y ganado en la campaña de Buenos Aires*, p. 142.

37. There is a statistically significant negative correlation of −.2033 between the ratio of the economically active population (here measured as the percentage of tributarios in the total yanacona population) and the total population on the 1,099 private estates contained in the Intendencia of La Paz in the 1780's and 1790's.

38. Turvosky, "Bolivian Haciendas Before and After the Revolution," p. 81, and Table V-8, p. 315. In fact, the large haciendas of the northern *altiplano* districts (Omasuyos and large parts of Pacajes and Sicasica) had an even higher percentage of their lands devoted to peasant plots—the average being 90 percent.

39. *Ibid.*, pp. 82–83.

40. This figure appears to be close to the norm for the importance of women among hacendados in other parts of the Andes. Thus in a sample of 705 haciendas in ten districts of the province of Cuzco in 1689, women were found to account for 15 percent of the 492 hacendados who owned these estates. Mörner, *Perfil de la sociedad rural del Cuzco a fines de la colonia*, p. 35.

41. For an analysis of the restricted role of elite women in colonial commercial wealth, see Socolow, *The Merchants of Buenos Aires, 1778– 1810*, chap. 2. Women of the lower classes, especially those in small-scale trading and petty retail commercial activities, however, seem to have been far more independent. See Lavrin and Couturier, "Dowries and Wills," pp. 300–302.

42. Sánchez-Albornoz, *Indios y tributos*, pp. 105ff. Indian officials testified that the free communities of Omasuyos at one time in the early colonial period had possessed 170 haciendas, which the kurakas subsequently alienated to private Spanish owners or to themselves. See "Informe de 14 marzo 1690," in *ibid.*, p. 123.

43. Larson, *Colonialism and Agrarian Transformation in Bolivia*.

44. AGN, 13-17-8-2, libro 2 (libro no. 3 of Revisita), folios 294–94v.

45. This material was first analyzed in Santamaria, "La estructura agraria del Alto Peru a fines del siglo XVIII," and subsequently refined in his *Hacendados y campesinos en el Alto Perú colonial*. I am grateful to him

for showing me the original documentation, and I have also adopted his calculations for size and output of estates in my own statistical analysis.

46. AGN, 9-31-6-2 (Justicia), legajo 29, expediente 873, folios 46–58v. I have only counted divided estates when a second owner was listed in the document in the following standard formula: "en la dicha hacienda de . . . posee Don . . . un pedaso de tierras. . . ." In his study of these same documents, Daniel Santamaria chose to treat each citation as a separate hacienda.

47. The coefficient of variation on the undivided estate values was 0.95, and on the multiple estates 1.3.

48. The indices of size and output are similarly related: the average size of the 18 haciendas was 1,197.6 hectares; the 12 undivided estates averaged 3,865.8 hectares; and the multiple-owner ones were 92.1 hectares, with the 23 secondary owners having just 88.1 hectares. Output in kilograms was respectively 20,804 kgs. (mostly of corn, with some potatoes and a small quantity of wheat) per annum on the undivided properties, and 3,697 on the six multiple estates, and just 3,282 kgs. (or only 23 *cargas* per annum) for the secondary owners of parcels on the multiple-owner properties.

49. On the estate of Sayani the *jilakata* Blas Mamani rented some orchards from the hacienda for 24 pesos for the year 1794. There were also three other persons who rented orchards for a varying annual fee ranging from 10 to 3 pesos. ACALP, Tomo 116, folio 262.

50. In 1950, haciendas possessed 45 percent of the land and 51 percent of the cultivated acreage in the department of La Paz. The comunidades held 40 percent of the total area and 42 percent of the area under cultivation. This left small family-run farms with just 5 percent and 4 percent, respectively, of land held and land under cultivation. In the nation as a whole, such small farms had 29 percent of the acreage and 19 percent of the cultivated lands. While the haciendas and comunidades of La Paz represented 33 percent and 47 percent, respectively, of the cultivated lands in the entire republic, the small farms of the department only accounted for 6 percent of the national total. Bolivia, Instituto Nacional de Estadística, *I Censo agropecuario, 1950*, pp. 25–26, 142–43.

Chapter Two

1. This is the position of two major recent Peruvian writers who have done considerable work on Andean haciendas. See Macera, "Feudalismo colonial americano"; and Polo y La Bora, "La hacienda Pachacachaca."

2. This figure represents his maximum holdings by the last decade of the century. In the combined 1786–97 listings, which are primarily for the previous decade, his total holdings are less than this figure.

3. The standard model describing the multi-ecological "arquipeligo" system of preconquest and early colonial times can be found in Murra, *Formaciones económicas y políticas del mundo andino*.

4. The two major sources of data for the wealth of Don Tadeo Diez de Medina are the *mayorazgo-hijuela* documents dated 1789–92 and found in AGI, Audiencia de Charcas, legajo 556, expediente 10, documentos 1–13 (hereafter cited as *Mayorazgo* and document number); and the testament that he dictated after a long illness but many years before his death on October 30, 1792, found in AHLP, Registro de Escrituras Notariales, Registro 3 del año 1793 de Escribano Crispin de Vera y Aragon, folios 234–47v (hereafter cited as *Testamento* and clause or item number).

5. In all his documents, Don Tadeo never lists any prominent relative, nor does he even mention his parents. It appears likely, however, that he was at least a distant relation of the *oidor* (judge) of the Chilean Audiencia (High Court) Dr. Francisco Tadeo Diez de Medina, given the similarity of their names and the fact that the latter took Don Tadeo's two sons under his care when he traveled to Spain. See *Testamento*, item 60.

6. *Ibid.*, items 6, 12.

7. *Ibid.*, item 5.

8. The house with the ground floor stores in Coroyco, the haciendas Ypari and Husi, and the estancias Palina Chica and Cielocaguasi all came to him from the estate of Don Diego Solis. *Ibid.*, items 17–26. He also obtained his title of *regidor* on the La Paz cabildo from his father-in-law in the early 1770's. AGN (Buenos Aires), Justicia, 9-31-3-6, legajo 9, expediente 160; and 9-31-3-8, legajo 11, expediente 212.

9. *Testamento*, items 50, 51.

10. *Mayorazgo*, documento 6 (1789).

11. Don Tadeo held two large mortgages for a total of 8,000 pesos. *Testamento*, items 28, 49. *Censos* by law carried an automatic 5 percent annual interest charge. Escriche y Martin, *Diccionario razonado de legislacion*, p. 105, n. 3.

12. A detailed analysis of this type of activity as carried on by the merchants of Cochabamba in this period is contained in Larson, *Colonialism and Agrarian Transformation in Bolivia*, pp. 272ff. The fact that Don Tadeo had very significant political ties can be seen in his role as official bondsman (*fiador*) for the outgoing intendant, Don Fernando de la Sota y Aguirre, during his official *residencia*. AHLP, Registro 1 del año de 1796, Crispin de Vera y Aragon, folios 111–11v.

13. *Mayorazgo*, documento 13 (1790).

14. *Ibid.*, unnumbered document, letter dated March 7, 1791; and Crespo et al., *La vida cotidiana en La Paz*, p. 73.

15. *Testamento*, items 7–11.

16. *Ibid.*, f. 236.

17. *Ibid.*, item 75.

18. Aside from the information in the will of 1792, see ANB, Tierras e Indios (hereafter TI), Año 1795, documento 26; ANB, TI (1803), no. 13. An alternative set of these papers, found in ANB, TI (1795), no. 84, was used extensively by Lema for her "Production et circulation."

19. *Testamento*, items 52, 56.

20. ANB, TI (1803), no. 43, folio 7.

21. *Ibid.*, no. 13.

22. Socolow, *The Merchants of Buenos Aires, 1778–1810*.

23. Some idea of Don Tadeo's relative landed wealth can be obtained by comparing his estates with those owned by the Jesuits in the nearby district of Cuzco in the southern Peruvian sierra. There the Jesuits owned nine haciendas for foodstuff production (*panllevar*), whose value averaged 28,390 pesos (ranging in size from 2,000 pesos for the smallest to 92,000 for the largest), and four livestock (*ganado*) estates, which averaged 20,563 pesos (16,159 standard deviation). Their three sugar estates were worth 44,000, 49,000, and an extraordinary 247,000 pesos. Macera, "Haciendas Jesuitas del Peru," pp. 16–25, 34–35. By these standards, Don Tadeo can be considered to have a well developed set of properties. His ten estates for which a value was given averaged 35,352 (12,528 standard deviation). His panllevar farms and ganado estates were poorer than those of the Jesuits, with the former averaging only 17,795 pesos, and the latter just 9,715 pesos. His coca plantations however ranged from 10,000 to 90,000 pesos, quite comparable to their sugar estates. In turn both these sets of Peruvian sierra properties were richer than those found in the northern sierra, such as the Jesuit properties of New Granada (see Germán Colmenares, *Las haciendas de los jesuitas en el Nuevo Reino de Granada, siglo xviii* [Bogotá, 1969]); but all these properties were distinctly inferior in value to those of Mexico. In New Spain the Jesuit colegios held 31 haciendas which averaged 95,354 pesos (105,313 standard deviation). Hermes Tovar Pinzón, "Elementos constituitivos de la empresa agrícola jesuita en la segunda mitad del siglo xviii en Mexico," in CLACSO, *Haciendas y plantaciones en America Latina* (Mexico, 1975), pp. 158–59.

24. These statistics are found in ANB, TI (1795), no. 26. Though agricultural production is fully listed, livestock production is not, so Don Tadeo was apparently not forced to list the results of his *estancias*.

25. *Ibid.*, item 75; and *Mayorazgo*, documento 7 (1789). For an estimate of Chulumani's coca production, see AGI, Audiencia de Buenos

Aires, legajo 513, "Estado que manifiesta el numero de haciendas . . . en el Partido de Yungas," La Paz, May 17, 1796.

26. *Mayorazgo*, documento 5 (1789).

27. In the 1796 survey of the Yungas coca zone, it was found that 308 haciendas were owned by 240 hacendados, 105 who resided in La Paz. Only 133 hacendados were resident on their own estates. See AGI, Audiencia de Buenos Aires, legajo 513, "Estado que manifiesta el numero de haciendas . . . en el Partido de Yungas," La Paz, May 17, 1796.

28. Aside from the various statements made in his 1792 will, note also his purchases made to expand the coca fields of Incapampa in AHLP, Registro 1 del año de 1794, Crispin de Vera y Aragon, La Paz, Feb. 28, 1784, unpaginated. On his purchase of Yanarani in Larecaja, see AMLP, Registro 1 del año de 1786, Pedro de Mariaca (Escribano), La Paz, Mar. 24, 1786, folios 38–38v.

29. *Mayorazgo*, documento 6 (1789); and *Testamento*, item 31.

30. AHLP, Registro 2 del año de 1792, Crispin de Vera y Aragon, folios 214–15.

31. AHLP, Registro 1 del año de 1794, Crispin de Vera y Aragon, folios 116v–17v. In 1795 he also provided a twelve-month loan to a La Paz merchant of 2,311 pesos, 2½ reales for another importation of Castillian textiles. AHLP, Registro 1 de 1795, Crispin de Vera y Aragon, folios 291–92.

32. Crespo et al., *La vida cotidiana*, p. 173.

33. Herbert S. Klein, "Structure and Profitability of Royal Finance," pp. 458–59, appendix table 1.

34. Arze, "Las haciendas jesuitas de La Paz," p. 120; Ladd, *The Mexican Nobility at Independence*.

35. There were three basic types of mortgages (*censos*) held on rural properties: first, *censos redimibles*, whose principal could be paid off when the borrower wished to do so; second, *censos perpetuos*, or *irredimibles*, in which the principal was never paid off, but produced a constant rent from a fixed property so long as that property existed; and third, *censos a plazos* (of which the life *censos* was one type), where the death of the borrower required a liquidation of the principal of the loan. A good contemporary description of these types appears in a dispute over mortgages held on the hacienda of Pongo in Calacoto in the Yungas district in 1806, between the owner and the Junta de Temporalidades. See AGN, 9-21-9-1, "Relativo de la Instancia seguida sobre la Hacienda de Pongo . . . 25 Nov. 1806."

36. This would give him an approximate ratio of rent to capital on his rural properties of 11 percent, which would appear to be quite a reasonable return. On his urban properties, however, his ratio of rent to capital was just under 1 percent, suggesting that most of this urban property was in fact used either for living space or, as in the case of the

tambos, for storing his own commercial merchandise. There is no indication from these records of the return on his commercial activities.

37. This is an approximate estimate. The original 30,000 pesos figure comes from calculating the income from his known coca output (worth 26,400 pesos), plus the 4,000 pesos in rents generated from his three Cohoni estates. Independently, estate assessors for the Crown estimated at the time of the *mayorazgo* request that the value of the two sons' income from their respective rural and urban properties would come to approximately 15–16,000 pesos on their approximately 170,000 pesos of inherited assets. *Mayorazgo*, documento 7. Assuming this same 9.5 percent ratio of rent to capital, we add approximately 5,500 pesos per annum for each of the other two inheritors of the estate (their share coming to 120,000 pesos in assets), plus another 4,500 for his second wife's rents. This yields a minimum total of 31,500 pesos. Given this minimum, and the various unknowns, a reasonable estimate would be the 35,000 to 45,000 figure.

38. *Testamento*, item 48.

39. *Mayorazgo*, documento 6.

40. Brading, *Haciendas and Ranchos in the Mexican Bajio*, pp. 92–93. On a small sample of estates in the declining sugar region of Lambayeque on the northern Peruvian coast, the ratio of mortgages to total value was 40 percent between 1650 and 1719 and rose to almost 65 percent in the 1720–1810 period. Ramírez, *Provincial Patriarchs, Land Tenure, and the Economics of Power in Colonial Peru*, p. 219.

41. *Testamento*, item 55. The 11 stores (six facing on Calle Comercio and the five others apparently inside) on the ground floor of his La Paz residence were worth 22,000 pesos. He granted his daughter an "assignación de renta vitalica" (or life income) of 700 pesos per annum based on the rent from these stores. *Mayorazgo*, documento 6, nota 1. To calculate this he assigned her a special type of *capellanía* worth 14,000 pesos out of the total 22,000 pesos value. AHLP, Registro 1 del año de 1787, Crispin de Vera y Aragon, La Paz, Mar. 9, 1787, no pagination. The rest of the rents from the store and the tambo—some 800 pesos—were variously assigned to a *capellanía* for masses to be said for his deceased first wife, and for various religious expenses.

42. A printed biography of the elder son, Don Juan Josef, called "Relacion de los meritos de servicios," is found in *Mayorazgo*, documento 13.

43. *Testamento*, item 12; *Mayorazgo*, documento 6.

44. The sum of 40,000 pesos seems to have been close to the standard for a *mayorazgo* in this region in the colonial period. See Amunategui Solar, *Mayorazgos i títulos de Castilla*. On the origins of the institution, see Clavero, *Mayorazgo. Propiedad feudal en Castilla (1369–1836)*.

45. See the side notes and inserted addendum pages (dated May 8, 1819, and July 22, 1828) added to a document of Don Tadeo in 1796 granting a *capellanía* to the Dominican Order, in AHLP, Registro 3 de 1796, Crispin de Vera y Aragon, folios 254v and following. In 1828 the new republican government of Bolivia extinguished the order and assigned its rent from the *capellanía* to a government agency known as La Beneficencia.

46. AHLP, Registro 1 del año de 1796, Crispin de Vera y Aragon, folios 107–7v. Don Tadeo "sold" his office for the same price that he paid for it, that is for 910 pesos. Crespo, *La vida cotidiana*, p. 73.

47. By 1803, Juan Josef was listed as the owner of Incapampa, while the haciendas of Chicalulo, Ypari, Ataguallani, Mutuguaya, and a new one called Guaguasi of the pueblo of Mecapa were listed as belonging to his father Don Tadeo. Don Tadeo's granddaughter Doña María Vicencia Eguino owned Choxlla Grande in Pacallo, and one of his sons-in-law, Francisco Guillen, held the Monte estate in the same pueblo. In all they controlled some 188 male tributarios on their estates, and a total Indian population of 575—a considerable reduction from the 1786 period. AGN, Seccion Contaduria, Padrones de La Paz, 1802–3, legajo 36, libro 4 (13-7-9-4).

48. By 1817 Don Tadeo Antonio controlled the estate formerly owned by his father and elder brother. ANB, Archivos del Tribunal Nacional de Cuentas, no. 162, "Ano de 1817, Padron gral. de indios . . . Partido de Chulumani." Don Tadeo must have died sometime before December of 1806, for in that month his second wife, Doña Manuela Mireles, was obtaining legal assistance to deal with the inheritance of her recently deceased husband, AHLP, Registro de 1805–8, Mariano de Prado (Escribano), La Paz, Dec. 16, 1806, unnumbered. Don Tadeo had remarried in mid-1786, shortly after the death of his first wife. ACALP, tomo 90, folio 160.

49. The testament of Dr. Don Francisco Tadeo Diez de Medina is found in AHLP, Registro de 1803, Mariano del Prado (Escribano), La Paz, Sept. 25, 1801, folios 167–78v.

50. *Testamento*, items 19–20, 26, 54, and 56 for the *capellanías*, and 46, 47, and 55 for the gifts.

51. The costs of educating his two sons in Spain up to 1789 came to 28,422 pesos, or approximately 2,600 pesos per annum for those first 11 years. The two sons seem to have remained in Spain at least until 1795, thus adding another six years, or 15,600 pesos. The various offices and honors probably cost between 3,000 and 5,000 pesos for the two. Thus a figure of 50,000 pesos seems to be the upper limit, excluding the *mayorazgo* purchase.

52. Her dowry was 6,000 pesos, and he specifically excluded her

from his formal *hijuela*, saying that she had renounced her claims. *Mayorazgo*, documento 6, nota 1.

53. He in fact assigned his daughter's convent a *capellanía* of 1,000 pesos fixed on his house/store in Coroyco in the Yungas, with an annual rent of 50 pesos for a *novena* on his saint's day. *Testamento*, item 19.

54. María Antonia was also to be given 10 pesos on Don Tadeo's death. His daughter María Magdalena was specifically prohibited from selling María Antonia. *Testamento*, item 39; and item 54 (for weekly food provisions).

55. His interest in sugar imports from Lima is mentioned in *Testamento*, item 34.

56. ANB, Archivos del Tribunal Nacional de Cuentas, no. 166, "Revista de 1829" of Chulumani.

57. This would appear to be in sharp contrast to the central Chilean landed elite, which seemed able to work out complex family arrangements so as to prevent the rules of partible inheritance from destroying the integrity of large rural holdings. See Borde and Góngora, *Evolución de la propiedad rural en el valle de Puangue*, vol. 1, pp. 59ff. The authors argue that land as a consequence never entered the market. Such family unity and inhibitions to market sales were not the norm in Alto Perú.

Chapter Three

1. An older survey of this literature is found in Mörner, "The Spanish American Hacienda." A more recent assessment is Van Young, "Mexican Rural History since Chevalier."

2. The classic study on Chile is Borde and Góngora, *Evolución de la propiedad rural en el valle de Puangue*. On Peru, see Macera, *La hacienda peruana colonial*, and Glave and Remy, *Estructura agraria y vida rural en una región andina*.

3. In the last two decades a number of studies have finally begun to appear on rural institutions and their labor force in Bolivia in the colonial period and the nineteenth century. These include Arze Aguirre, "Las haciendas jesuítas de La Paz"; Santamaría, *Hacendados y campesinos en el Alto Perú colonial*; Larson, *Colonialism and Agrarian Transformation in Bolivia*; Langer, *Economic Change and Rural Resistance in Southern Bolivia*; Platt, *Estado boliviano y ayllu andino*; A. Crespo et al., *Siporo, historia de una hacienda*; and most recently Sebill, *Ayllus y haciendas*.

4. See, above all, the report of Francisco Viedma, the able intendant of Cochabamba and Santa Cruz, in de Angelis, ed., *Colección de obras y documentos*, vol. 6, pp. 511–736. Several of Viedma's unpublished reports are in the Colección Mata Linhares, Academia Real de Historia (Madrid).

5. The most complete of such accounts so far published are those of Joaquin de la Pezuela, *Memoria de gobierno,* and Manuel de Amat y Junient, *Memoria de gobierno.*

6. On Pacajes, see Alcedo, *Diccionario geográfico-histórico de las indias occidentales de América,* vol. 3, p. 85. Alcedo noted that "Previously Pacajes was celebrated for being a rich and opulent mining center . . . but none of these mines is now worked." The Spanish population formerly supported by the mining had largely disappeared by 1780, and the only mineral export from the region was some talcum produced in one remaining mine.

7. An extensive survey of the Yungas in 1798 reported that "in the territory of Chulumani are nine parishes which have fifteen townships inhabited by thousands of persons, half of them being Spaniards." Report of the Oidor Honorario de Charcas, Don Pedro Vicente Cañete, in his Visita to the Real Caja de Aduana of La Paz, dated Potosí, July 26, 1798, in AGI, Audiencia de Buenos Aires, legajo 511.

8. In his 1798 report, Visitador Don Pedro Vicente Cañete noted that in the sixteenth century little coca was produced in the Yungas, and that what there was came from the *ayllus.* In this period, the province of Cuzco was the prime supplier for all of Peru. In the seventeenth century a few *paceños* began to purchase land and begin coca plantings in the Yungas, but even so it was not until the 1730's that major haciendas were finally established in the region. AGI, Audiencia de Buenos Aires, legajo 511.

9. The major areas that have been excluded are the mining centers of Oruro and Potosí, which were overwhelmingly Aymara, and some of the cereal-producing valleys to the south and the west, especially in the province of Chuquisaca. While there were some Aymara in the cereal center of Cochabamba, this was primarily a Quechua Indian area.

10. A recent, if limited, review of this debate is found in Rasnake, *Domination and Cultural Resistance,* pp. 49–51.

11. Skar, in *The Warm Valley People,* argues that *ayllus* were not really closed (chapter 5). See the review of the literature on this subject in Johnsson, *Food and Culture Among Bolivian Aymara,* pp. 30–31, 89–91. Though Spanish documents all speak of primogeniture and male descent as the rule of inheritance among *ayllu* members, some anthropologists challenge this as a European distortion. See Platt, "Pensamento politico Aymara," pp. 376, 379. Finally, much of the ritual life in the *ayllu* seems to assume a common ancestral origin for both *ayllu* and individual lineages. See Bastien, *Mountain of the Condor.*

12. Carter and Albó, "La comunidad aymara," pp. 451ff.

13. Fiestas, sponsored by officials known as *cabezas* and *prestes,* were fundamental for the holding of office and the ratification of community

powers. See Rasnake, *Domination and Cultural Resistance*, pp. 173ff. For an analysis of *colono* fiestas held on the haciendas, see Buecher, *The Masked Media*, chap. 11.

14. This description of *ayllu* land tenure is based principally on Buecher, *The Masked Media*, pp. 465ff; and Mamani, "Agricultura a los 4000 metros," pp. 8off. Also see Birbuet D., *Tierra y ganado en Pacajes*, Albó, "Dinámica en la estructura inter-comunitaria," and Turvosky, "Bolivian Haciendas."

15. For the best description of the forastero-originario relationship in the contemporary period, see Godoy, *Mining and Agriculture in Highland Bolivia*, pp. 80–84.

16. It is obvious that detailed micro-analyses could be developed using the individual listings in the tribute censuses to study family structure and to construct male age pyramids that could then be used to test for various demographic variables—notably migration patterns—at the local *ayllu* and hacienda level. There also exist a few pre-1786 *revisitas* in which the ages of all women are listed. See, e.g., the Pacajes censuses of 1724 and 1767 in AGN, 13-17-3-5 and 13-17-10-3.

17. The age breakdowns are found in Escobedo y Alarcón, the official *Instrucción de Revisitas o matrículas*, pp. 17, 21, 33.

18. Though both the terms forastero and agregado are used interchangeably in the documents of the eighteenth century, henceforth I will use forastero as the standard term to avoid confusion.

19. This was the conclusion reached by Carter in his study of a series of haciendas and free communities in Pacajes in the mid-1950's after they were seized by the central government. From pre-1952 surveys and from his own studies, he concluded that the haciendas in what in the colonial era was the Pacajes region had only some 30 percent of the total arable land and grazing fields in the owner's crops and 70 percent in usufruct for the peons. Carter, *Aymara Communities and the Bolivian Agrarian Reform*, pp. 65ff.

20. While the above tables of sex ratios have been calculated for the entire populations, it is worth pointing out that calculating these ratios for the adult populations alone (here estimated to be over fourteen years of age) yields similar results. Thus in Chulumani the overall figure for the adult population is 111.5 males per 100 females, and for Pacajes it is 76.4 males per 100 females (see data in Tables 3.5 and 3.6, and 3.9 and 3.10).

21. Letter of the ex-corregidor of the Yungas district, Jose de Albizuri, to Sebastian de Segurlo, La Paz, June 22, 1784, AGN, Manuscritos de Biblioteca Nacional, Libro 190, pieza 1930. This migratory labor pattern continued up to the time of the Agrarian Reform in the 1950's and was as much promoted by the local yanaconas as by the hacendados themselves. Burke reported that the Yungas coca haciendas

still accounted for 80 percent of local exports and were the most intensively farmed haciendas in the region. "There has never been population pressure upon the land in this region," he noted, and therefore "labor, prior to the agrarian reform, was always somewhat scarce in the Yungas and thus was able to command a money wage." He also noted that because the yanaconas (or colonos) produced a cash crop, aside from the traditional subsistence ones, and had to pay labor time to the hacendados, they also "utilized migratory labor from the over-populated Altiplano on both their usufruct lands and those of the hacendado." Burke, "An Analysis of the Bolivian Land Reform," p. 117.

22. On this complex transition see Platt, "Acerca del sistema tributario pre-toldeano en el Alto Perú," pp. 33–46.

23. Sebill, *Ayllus y haciendas*, chap. 1.

24. Fortunately the Pacajes census of 1786 gives the total of all persons definitively missing from the community, aside from the ausente males of tributary age. To the 1,209 absent tributarios are added 139 missing proximos and 103 male children under 14. Also missing were 443 married women, 5 single women, 20 widows, and 17 girls under 13. Thus the grand total of missing was 1,970 persons, of whom 1,485 were males and 485 were females. If this breakdown were the norm, then it would appear that two-thirds of all persons missing were males, and well over half of the total missing were tributarios—that is, double their share in the resident population. It should be stressed that these ausentes were not temporary migrants or miners, nor were they deceased, since all such persons were carefully recorded, the former listed as if in residence, and the latter noted in the *libros de difuntos* of the parish. Several of these eighteenth-century parish registers for Pacajes and Chulumani have been preserved and can be found in the Archivo de la Curia del Arzobispado de La Paz.

25. Though Mecapaca had no *ayllu*, its location in the center of the poorer zone and its consistent identity of demographic features with the poorer pueblos led me to include it in the poorer zone.

26. The simple correlations between the dummy variable created to represent the wealthy pueblos and these three factors were +.422 for the economically active male population, −.311 for fertility, and +.240 for sex ratio.

27. See Whitehead, "Altitude, Fertility and Mortality in Andean Countries."

28. In Pacajes only 12 percent of the adult women were widows among the originarios, compared to 24 percent among the forastero families. In turn in Chulumani, the originario adult women were only 8 percent widowed compared to 18 percent among the forasteros.

29. Of the 72 hacendados who made up the top 10 percent of the province's landowners, 28 (or 38 percent) had one or more cocales in

the Yungas of the Chulumani district. In terms of districts, however, Omasuyos came in ahead, with over half of the owners (38 out of the 72) having estates in this lakeside district. See Chapter 1 above.

30. AGI, Audiencia de Buenos Aires, legajo 513, "Estado que manifiesta el numero de Haciendas . . . en el Partido de Yungas . . . ," dated La Paz, May 17, 1796.

31. AGN, 13-17-7-4, libro 1, folio 9–9v.

32. The combined Chulumani and Pacajes districts, which contained 426 haciendas, had a correlation between EAP and size even more significantly negative—at −.2851—than it was for the entire province (see Chapter 1 above).

33. AGN, 13-17-6-3, libro 1, folios 97ff for the population of the estate and its ownership. The kuraka of Timusi informed the royal officials that the free community Indians of Jesus de Machaca lived 50 leagues distant from his town and came every year to collect their crops. Their haciendas, he claimed, had been purchased from the Crown by the community for between 5,000 and 10,000 pesos in one of the traditional royal sales of public lands (*composición de tierras*), and he complained that they occupied the best lands of the village, to the detriment of local producers. AGN, 13-17-7-1, libro 3, folios 38–40v.

34. Langer, *Economic Change*, p. 54.

35. Coroyco participated in virtually every export leaving the Yungas valleys and was the largest single producer in three-quarters of the categories of goods shipped from the region. AGI, Audiencia de Buenos Aires, legajo 513, "Estado," 1796.

36. The region around Coryoco is currently less suitable for coca growing than lands in the Coripata and Chulumani districts (personal communication from Professor Barbara Leons, dated Dec. 10, 1974). This may also have been the case in the eighteenth century.

37. In fact, grazing may have been the richest source of income for the *altiplano* populations. In the province of Chuquito, just to the north of Pacajes, royal officials in the sixteenth century noted the great wealth of the region, which was evident from the rich ornamentation of the local churches and was based on "a vast quantity of community herds." Cited in Murra, "An Aymara Kingdom in 1567," p. 120. Chuquito and Pacajes both more or less conformed to the ancient boundaries of the pre-Incan Aymara kingdoms of Lupaqua and Pacajes, respectively.

Chapter Four

1. The most detailed study of the demographic and economic impact of the epidemics, though with data mostly from the region of Potosí, is provided in Tandeter, "Crisis in Upper Peru, 1800–1805." The La Paz area was badly affected as well. In Omasuyos in the year 1804, some 786

forasteros (or 17.6 percent of the tributarios registered in 1803) and 29 originarios died, making an average of about 15 percent of the total tributary population. Clearly this was an epidemic which differentially affected the population in terms of wealth. Moreover, as the local royal officials noted, adults were more affected than children (f.34): the average age of the dead tributarios was 31. For this special analysis of deaths due to the plague in Omasuyos province, see AGN, 9-23-6-2, legajo 15, expediente 466; and for the 1803 population of the province, see AGN, 13-17-10-1, libro 1.

The best single source for the economic decline over this entire period remains the classic study of José María Dalence, *Bosquejo estadístico de Bolivia*.

2. See Herbert S. Klein, "Coca Production in the Bolivian Yungas."

3. In 1790 the Chulumani *Manuales de Alcabala* listed some 65,000 *cestos* of coca for the year—which probably represented a third of the total Yungas output—of which 28,577 *cestos* (or 44 percent) were shipped to Potosí alone. AGN, 13-3-3-6, legajo 66, libros 1 and 2. If we take 200,000 *cestos* as a reasonable production estimate for coca for this era (it comes from a royal survey carried out in 1796, found in AGI, Audiencia de Buenos Aires, legajo 513, dated La Paz, May 17, 1796), then it would appear that Potosí alone absorbed between 10 and 20 percent of total output (or 20,000–40,000 *cestos* per annum). With the addition of Oruro and the other mining centers, mine workers probably absorbed as much as a third of Yungas production. These estimates thus disagree with that reported by a local royal official in 1796 of 96,000 pesos' worth of coca (or some 11,294 *cestos*) imported into Potosí. See RAH, Tomo xxxvii, folio 368 (9-9-3 1692).

4. Calculated from the *Manuales de Alcabala* (Caminos de Arriba y Abajo) of Potosí for 1777–78. AGN, 13-6-4-5, legajo 23, libros 4 and 5; and 13-6-5-1, legajo 24, libro 3.

5. Dalence, *Bosquejo estadístico*, p. 315. Dalence estimated exports at a very high 441,927 *cestos*, of which only 8,500 were shipped outside the country—some 7,300 to Peru and 1,200 to Argentina.

6. These four censuses were the earliest complete population listings for the Yungas. Though officially required to be taken every five years, no census was made at all in the 1790's. Censuses were taken in 1817 and 1828, but they were incomplete and listed only male tributarios. There again appears to have been none taken in the 1840's, which makes 1838 the last census before those of 1852 and 1857. By this decade Suri was eliminated from the district, along with several smaller hamlets, which makes direct comparisons difficult. The 1850's were also badly disrupted by a cholera epidemic in 1855–56, which makes it difficult to isolate the economic factors from the disease ones influencing population change. On the cholera epidemic, see Sánchez-Albornoz,

Indios y tributos, pp. 35–36; and Greishaber, "Survival of Indian Communities in Nineteenth Century Bolivia," p. 178.

7. The data for Figure 4.1 are found in Rück, *Guía general,* pp. 170–71. I have supplemented Rück's numbers with the original Banco de Rescate manuscripts for the period 1810–1820. See ACM, Banco de San Carlos, nos. 19, 113.

8. These data were calculated from Pentland (1826) and Dalence (1846) by Prado Robles, "Politica monetaria y patrón de articulación comercial," p. 116.

9. Dalence, *Bosquejo,* pp. 302ff.

10. Mitre, *El monedero de los Andes.*

11. Mitre, *Los patriarcas de la plata,* p. 48. In 1840–44 the debased "moneda feble" accounted for 40 percent of minted silver coins, and rose to 50 percent in the next quinquenium. By 1850 over 80 percent of minted coins were of this category.

12. Although Bolívar tried to abolish the *tributo* and replace it with a *contribución directo* on all citizens in his Chuquisaca decree of Dec. 22, 1825, this was opposed by everyone, including the Indians, who appeared to want the retention of the old tribute as a guarantee of their land ownership status. Mariscal Antonio José de Sucre tried to carry out the change but finally was forced to concede defeat, and the Bolivian government reestablished the tribute in July 1826. From the time of its reestablishment the tribute was the single most important source of government revenue. Lofstrom, *El Mariscal Sucre en Bolivia,* pp. 331–46. The nineteenth-century *padrones* were based on the 1784 royal decree, modified somewhat in 1831. For the modifications, see Bolivia, *Colección Oficial de leyes, decretos, órdenes y resoluciones,* vol. 5, pp. 84–97.

13. The only males excluded were the six in each community who worked for the church; all infirm men of tributary age who could not work; "caciques" (*kurakas*) and their eldest sons; alcaldes and their assistants (*jilakatas*), who were temporarily exempt during their term of office; and the few local Indians destined for mail service (*potillones*). Reglamento de Feb. 28, 1831, item no. 24 in Bolivia, *Colección Oficial de leyes . . . ,* vol. 5, pp. 89–90.

14. Although the term was not too common in the subsequent census volumes, the 1831 decree did distinguish between *originarios con tierras, forasteros con tierras,* and *forasteros sin tierras.* The landed *forasteros* are specifically mentioned. *Ibid.,* p. 89.

15. The only other republican change from the colonial formula was the category of *vagos,* listed for both *ayllus* and haciendas from the 1838 *padron* on. Although there is no clear definition of what distinguished a vago from a forastero or a yanacona, their position must have been comparable, since they paid the identical tribute of 5 pesos per annum. I therefore assume that they were newly arrived yanaconas or foras-

teros on *ayllus* who had no immediate or direct access to land. Indeed, the *padron* of 1871 listed many "vagos" as having "passed over" into regular forastero status since the last census. ANB, ATNC, no. 181. I have therefore listed these 1838 vagos (who are relatively few in number) as forasteros or yanaconas in order to make the figures comparable with the three previous censuses. This category of "vago," moreover, was only used by the Bolivian government in its listings for the Yungas region, and not applied elsewhere (personal communication from E. Greishaber, Aug. 15, 1978).

16. Inheritance of originario status was based on the principle of primogeniture, with the male heir preferred, in contrast to traditional partible inheritance practices that were the norm for the rest of the population. In fact this inheritance pattern seems to have predominated among the Indian populations on the *ayllus* until this century (Maldonado, *Derecho agrario*, pp. 283–84). On inheritance and residency rules, see the decrees of Nov. 22, 1838 (on primogeniture), Feb. 28, 1831 (two-year residence required), and Nov. 15, 1838 (residence requirement reduced to one year) in Bolivia, *Colección Oficial*, vol. 3, pp. 284–85, vol. 5, p. 91, and vol. 5, pp. 98–99, respectively.

17. Averanga Mollinedo, *Aspectos generales de la población boliviana*, pp. 22–23.

18. Dalence, *Bosquejo*, p. 208.

19. *Ibid.*, p. 222. In the republican period, what had been the province or intendencia of La Paz became the Department of La Paz. The former districts were now known as provinces.

20. *Ibid.*, p. 199.

21. Grieshaber, "Survival of Indian Communities in Nineteenth Century Bolivia, A Regional Comparison," pp. 226–31.

22. This is the position of Antonio Mitre in *El monedero de los Andes* and of Tristan Platt in *Estado tributario y librecambio en Potosí (siglo XIX)*. This argument is challenged by Prado Robles (in "Política monetaria"), who argues that regional exports did not expand in the period from the 1820's to the 1840's, and that the debased currency offered no protection to local markets but in fact promoted an inflation of prices.

23. Nevertheless, there was an unusual development among some 5 percent of the free communities—they seem to have lost their originario populations. This may mean that these *ayllus* were actually dependent units of larger *ayllus*—the most likely explanation—or that their poverty was such that the government downgraded their taxes to those of only forasteros.

24. See Mitre, *El monedero de los Andes*, Prado Robles, "Politica monetaria."

25. Prado Robles, "Politica monetaria," pp. 120–23.

26. The finding in 1786 that the ratio of widows in the total popula-

tion was less for originarios than for any other group still held true for both Pacajes and Chulumani for all censuses studied, although the declining population of Chulumani had a higher percentage of widows than did Pacajes in the censuses of the early nineteenth century (see Appendix B).

Chapter Five

1. For the Bolivian experience, see Sánchez-Albornoz, *Indios y tributos*; Grieshaber, "Survival of Indian Communities in Nineteenth-Century Bolivia: A Regional Comparison"; and Rivera, "La expansión del latifundio en el Altiplano boliviano."

2. The ideological underpinnings of the various land decrees of the late 1820's, 1831, 1866, and 1874 are analyzed in Maldonado, *Derecho agrario, historia—doctrina—legislación*.

3. The economic liberalization movement is analyzed in Mitre, *Los patriarcas de la plata*.

4. All these facts were discussed in great detail in the pamphlet literature of the period. Several of the most important and informative of these from 1871 have been reproduced in a special issue of the La Paz journal *Illimani*, nos. 8–9 (1976). Also see the fine documentary collection edited by Honorio Pinto H., *Contribución indígena en Bolivia, 1829–1911 (Documentos)*.

5. Article 7 unequivocally declared that once titles to land were granted to individual Indians, "the law will no longer recognize communities. No individual or group of individuals will henceforth be able to take the name of *comunidad* or [aillo], nor represent such entities before any authority." República de Bolivia, *Anuario de leyes y disposiciones supremas, 1874*, pp. 187–91 (law of 5 Oct. 1874).

6. Condarco Morales, *Zárate El "Temible" Wilka*.

7. This new elite and its land purchases in Pacajes province are analyzed in Rivera, "La expansión del latifundio."

8. [Aspiazu], *Informe*, pp. 16–18.

9. Typical of some of these cases was the judicially forced repayment of the principal of a 3,400 peso *censo* that Dionicio Montes had to make on his hacienda San Juan de Yaicquate, which originally came from the caja de comunidad of an *ayllu* in Palca. AHLP, Registro 2 (1792), Crispin de Vera y Aragon, no pagination, document dated March 23, 1792. The Indians of the pueblo of Sapaaqui in Rio Abajo region near La Paz had granted a 5,000 peso *censo* to the hacienda de cocales named Paco e Islas in Coroyco, Chulumani, which collected 5 percent annual interest (or 250 pesos). AHLP, Registro 1 (1790), Crispin de Vera y Aragon, April 28, 1791, folio 263. The antiquity of some of these arrangements is indicated in a *censo* given also by a Palca *ayllu* to a hacienda de cocales

named Guariqui in Chupe, Chulumani. This small *censo* of 800 pesos principal was given in October of 1735, 57 years earlier. AHLP, Registro 2 (1792), Crispin de Vera y Aragon, folio 105.

10. Herbert S. Klein, "Structure and Profitability of Royal Finance"; Gölte, *Repartos y rebeliones*.

11. A discussion of some of these churches is provided in Gisbert and de Mesa, *Arquitectura andina*, pp. 252ff; an even more recent work is Fraser, *The Architecture of Conquest*, pp. 160ff.

12. All the colonial revisitas are taken from the padrones collection housed in Sala XIII of the AGN. All the nineteenth-century ones are found in the special revisita collection in Sucre in the ANB, except for the following found in AHLP: Omasuyos (1863), Inquisivi (1855), and Cercado (1852). The calculations were made from the revisitas of the following years:

Province	1780's	1830's	1850's	1870's
Pacajes	1786	1838	1852	1871
Omasuyos	1792	1832	1858	1863
Sicasica	1786	1838	1858	1877
Inquisivi	*a*	*a*	1858	1877
Larecaja	1786	1838	1858	n.a.
Munecas	*a*	1848	1858	n.a.
Chulumani	1786	1838	1858	1877
Cercado	n.a.	1838	1852	1877

*a*Not then in existence.

13. See above, Chapters 1 and 4.

14. The best lands on the *altiplano* are located in Omasuyos. This is the most densely populated highland region, with the warmest climate and the best water resources. It appears that the growth in the economy led to an increase both in the number of haciendas in this entrenched hacienda zone (from 173 units in the 1780's to 196 in the 1870's) and in total yanaconas and in average labor force per hacienda.

15. The traditional view is that the miners came primarily from the free communities, which exported temporary and seasonal labor in order to obtain tribute income. Mitre, *Los patriarcas*, pp. 140–41.

16. See above, Chapter 4.

17. [Aspiazu], *Informe*.

18. Herbert S. Klein, *Bolivia, the Evolution of a Multi-ethnic Society*, pp. 105, 297. For a recent study of the development of the city of La Paz in the nineteenth century, see Barragán, *Espacio urbano y dinámica étnica, La Paz en el siglo XIX*.

19. In Greishaber's figures the general pattern that emerges is the same for most of Bolivia as it is for the Department of La Paz. Total *ayllu*

population in the latter grew at an annual average rate of .52 percent, compared to .53 percent nationally in this same period. The hacienda population grew at .05 percent annually (and −.10 percent nationally) and the total departmental tributary population at .36 percent (and .36 percent nationally). His figures also reveal a similar trend in growth rates between the 1830's–50's and the 1850's–70's.

20. The major study on this transformation is Larson, *Colonialism and Agrarian Transformation in Bolivia*.

21. This occurs even today in communities in northern Potosí: see Godoy, *Mining and Agriculture in Highland Bolivia*, chap. 5.

22. Platt, *Estado boliviano y ayllu andino*.

23. Data from a zone of northern Potosí close to the area studied by Platt challenge his assertion. The Jukumani of Northern Potosí, whose population grew extremely fast in the nineteenth and twentieth centuries, saw rates of density go from only 3 persons per square kilometer in the first quarter of the nineteenth century to 5 persons per square kilometer at the end of the century. In the second half of the twentieth century the figure rose to 28 persons per square kilometer. Godoy, *Mining and Agriculture*, p. 33.

24. In the first national census (1900), the rural Indian population of the Department of La Paz numbered only 212,000, out of 315,000 Indians for the entire department. A more realistic definition of rural raises that figure to 312,000. Bolivia, Oficina Nacional de Inmigración, Estadística y Propaganda Geográfica, *Censo general . . . de 1900*, vol. 2, pp. 41, 129, 132, 138. In the third national census of 1976, the rural population of the Department numbered 768,000, of whom 63 percent spoke Aymara (21 percent as their only language). Bolivia, Instituto Nacional de Estadística, *Resultados del censo nacional de población y vivienda, 1976* (La Paz, 1978), vol. 2, pp. 25, 28.

25. Bolivia, *Censo general . . . de 1900*, vol. 2, pp. xliii, 132; and Bolivia, Direccion General de Estadística y Censos. *Censo Demográfico, 1950* (La Paz, 1950), pp. 7ff.

Chapter Six

1. For these debates see Langer, "El liberalismo y la abolición de la comunidad indígena."

2. According to the director of the cadastral survey, Augustín Aspiazu, agricultural and land prices in the Department of La Paz had doubled between 1860 and 1880, largely due to growing demand for food from the expanding urban population. He also credited the recent export to Europe of Bolivian wool from the *altiplano* flocks of sheep as another factor contributing to increasing the value of *puna* estates. See [Aspiazu], *Informe*, p. 16.

3. For a recent detailed study of these sales, see Erwin P. Grieshaber, "Modernization and Indian Land Sales in Bolivia, 1880–1886" (paper presented at the 44th International Congress of Americanists, 1982). On the Indian response to these land seizures, see Rivera, *Oprimidos pero no vencidos*; and Demelas, "Jacqueries indiennes, politique créole."

4. For a good survey of the legislation and conflicts, see the discussion in Bolivia, *Memoria del Ministerio de Hacienda . . . 1882*, pp. 15–18. By the decree of December 30, 1881, the government in essence recognized that most Indians opposed sales to individuals and recognized their right to hold lands *proindiviso*. For these Indians, the old tribute tax was still in effect, while for those who purchased their lands as private individuals, the new *impuesto rural* applied. This decree is reprinted in *ibid.*, Anexo no. 7.

5. A good survey of the pattern of community survival as seen in 1920 is given in McBride, *The Agrarian Indian Communities of Highland Bolivia*, pp. 10–12. A full discussion of Indian land sales is found in Grieshaber, "Hacienda Expansion." Some 74 percent of the 16,000 *sayañas* and partial *sayañas* sold were to non-Indians (see Table 6.10). It is worth recalling, as Gustavo Rodriguez has pointed out, that the destruction of comunidades was far more dramatic in a few selected zones, especially in the Department of La Paz, and that the assault was more attenuated elsewhere. See Rodriguez, *Expansión del latifundio*.

6. Sánchez-Albornoz, *Indios y tributos*; and Ovando Sanz, *El tributo indígena*. Although central government revenues were no longer influenced by tributary income, the same was not the case with departmental income. As late as 1918, the tribute tax (now called the "contribución territorial" and producing some 202,000 bolivianos) was the third most important source of revenues to the provincial government, just after a special recently established import tax initiated for the construction of the Yungas railroad (at some 392,000 bolivianos) and the traditional tax on coca exports from the Yungas (at 375,000 bolivianos). Pérez Velasco, *Informe del Prefecto . . . del Departamento de La Paz . . . 1918*, pp. 27ff.

7. Law of August 15, 1880, in Bolivia, *Anuario de leyes y supremas disposiciones de 1880*, pp. 123–26. The government thus explicitly assumed direct control over funding the national Catholic church from these revenues.

8. The details on how this registration of titles, properties, and values was to be undertaken is contained in the "Decree of October 26, 1880," in *ibid.*, pp. 218–28.

9. On the delays and problems in the registration, see Bolivia, *Memoria del Ministro de Hacienda . . . 1883*, pp. 40–42. But on the whole the government seemed pleased with the results. The Minister estimated that the total "impuesto territorial" (as the tax on "predios rusticos y urbanas" was sometimes called) generated about 20 percent more than

the old *diezmos*—for a total estimated at 260,000 bolivianos (excluding the province of Chuquisaca, where registration was still delayed).

10. [Aspiazu], *Informe*, pp. 31–42.

11. AHLP, Padrones y Revisitas (hereafter PR) contains the extant set of materials (see notes to Table 6.1 for greater details). The manuscript volumes are usually entitled "Libro de inscripciones de las propiedades urbanos y rusticas de la provincia de. . . ."

12. The only provinces excluded are the Amazonian frontier zone of Caupolicán, which was only lightly settled, and the crucial comunidad-dominated *puna* province of Pacajes. The former zone, which held 92 estates with a total worth of 61,851 bolivianos, was of relatively minor importance and far from the major centers of production. In contrast, Pacajes was on the lake and was a prime target for new hacienda expansion and comunidad destruction. Unfortunately, no manuscript volumes have survived for Pacajes in 1881–82. Pacajes, according to the published results of the cadastre, contained 94 estates with a high valuation of 932,440 bolivianos. See [Aspiazu], *Informe*, pp. 35–36.

13. While the studies of the region of the Norte de Potosí have yielded valuable insights into local regional variations in comunidades (see, e.g., Platt, *Estado boliviano y ayllu andino*), it should be recalled that the Indian tribute censuses of 1877, the so-called *padrones* or *revisitas* of 1877, show that this zone held only 11 percent of the landless yanaconas and only 30 percent of the originarios and forasteros on the comunidades. La Paz, by contrast, held 63 percent (or 22,774) of the yanaconas and 43 percent of the originarios and forasteros in all of Bolivia. The second-largest department in terms of landless workers in 1877 was the Department of Oruro, with just 12 percent of the total of 36,110 landless workers.

14. In general, the manuscript cadastre shows higher valuations than those in the published summary.

15. Grieshaber, "Hacienda Expansion," appendix table IV, p. 66. This rhythm was not the same for all Bolivia. Langer found that the most intense periods of land sales in the Department of Chuquisaca came later, between 1895 and 1898. Langer, *Economic Change*, pp. 66–67.

16. For the 167 estates that contained sheep, the correlation with the value of the estate was .63 and was significant (here and elsewhere only significant correlations of less than 0.01 are reported).

17. The correlation between barley and value of estates was .64, with the 13,300 *cargos de papas amargas* produced on 164 of the haciendas also being highly correlated with value (at .53).

18. On 141 of the province's estates coca was produced—averaging 323 *cestos* per annum. Coffee was produced on 108 estates, averaging 18 arrobas per estate. When correlated with estate values, coca correlated with values at a high .86 and coffee at .47.

19. Interestingly enough, the key variable determining differences in worker output was the canton where the *cocales* were located, and not the value of the hacienda (which was not significantly correlated with annual *cesto* output per *peon*). Thus land quality was clearly the key factor influencing productivity and not size of estate.

20. An average of 29 cargos of corn per annum were produced on 307 estates and 21 cargos of potatoes on 123 different estates. Corn was correlated with estate values at .81 and potatoes at .67—the two crops themselves were not correlated.

21. Sweet potatoes were produced on 116 of the province's estates and averaged 63 cargos per estate—with this production correlating with estate values at .65.

22. Some 117 estates produced a wide variety of fruits, whose total values correlated with estate values at .77.

23. In Larecaja over 600 estates raised corn and produced almost 5,000 fanegas and 7,200 cargos per annum. Unfortunately, the census-takers here and in other provinces reported maize production on some estates in both fanegas and cargos and at other times just used the one measure or the other. The correlations of both, however, are highly correlated with estate values in Larecaja, at .73 (cargos) and .84 (fanegas).

24. One of the few exceptions to this was a Carmelite monastery that had professional administrators running its hacienda Millocato in Cohoni (Cercado province). The farm was worth 120,000 bolivianos and its orchards produced an extraordinary 8,000 Bs. worth of fruit every year. AHLP/PR, libro 26 (Cercado 1881), f.25.

25. AHLP/PR, Libro 10 (Sicasica 1881) ff. 45v–46. It was customary for the church to auction (*remate*) its estates off to the highest bidder for a fixed multiyear term with options for one-year or longer extensions. A typical case was the hacienda Chacarilla in Coroyco, which in 1793 received four bids ranging from 805 pesos to 1,100 pesos per annum rental, with the winning bid being the high one for three years. ACALP, tomo 103, ff. 258–66.

26. AHLP/PR, libro 10 (Sicasica 1881), f. 15v.

27. AHLP/PR, libro 26 (Cercado 1881), ff. 29–29v, f. 53.

28. Larson, *Colonialism and Agrarian Transformation in Bolivia*, pp. 188ff.

29. In the cadastral survey of the Yungas carried out in 1895, there were 281 haciendas registered, of which only 209 had validated titles. Of this total of known cases, the basis of ownership of only 25 was inheritance, whereas 141 had been purchased from another owner, and 8 had been purchased from the state (*remate*). Thus estates which had their origin in purchase represented 71 percent of the total known cases. Soux Muñoz Reyes, "Produccion y circuitos mercantiles de la coca yungueña," p. 75.

30. Going back to the colonial period, there even existed standard credit arrangements for sales of estates. Thus, for example, the ranch (*estancia*) of Caraxaran in Guarina in the province of Omasuyos was sold—without its sheep herds—for 3,000 pesos in cash (plus another 1,000 recognized as a mortgage transfer) in three stages, with 1,000 due in 2 months, another 1,000 in 8 months, and the final 1,000 to be paid at the end of 18 months. A varying interest rate was charged on these moneys, going from 0.2 percent in the first installment to 7.5 percent in the last one. AHMLP, Registro de Escrituras de Pedro de Maraca, Caja 58, ff. 248–52. In another case, a coca hacienda called Coloni in Coripata in the Yungas was sold in 1790 for 19,500 pesos in cash, with 6,000 pesos down and the rest paid in annual installments of 3,000 to 4,000 pesos. The 13,500 delayed payment funds were charged an interest of 5 percent. AHLP, Registro de Escrituras, Crispin de Vera y Aragon, 1 de 1790, ff. 60–62.

31. The correlations between value and percentage rent were −.09. A dummy variable created for provinces also produced no significant correlation between place, value, rent, or percentage income. The figure of 8 percent comes close to the calculations of net income made for some wealthy Yungas coca haciendas in the twentieth century, where the return on investment was estimated at 10 percent per annum. Soux Muñoz Reyes, "Producción y circuitos mercantiles," p. 161.

32. APSMR, "Inventario que se hace de la casa de hacienda de ANGUIA . . . 15 Nov. 1851."

33. Lema, "Production et circulation de la coca en Bolivie, 1780–1840," p. 204. It should also be remembered that work was not done on 52 Sundays and 27 holidays, and there was an average of two weeks of rain when no work was performed anywhere in the Yungas. These estimates come from the mayordomo of the coca hacienda of Cochuna, who wrote a detailed critique on the use of slave labor in the Yungas. Bergana, "Demonstración Matemática," ff. 25–25v, and 28v. The manuscript was made available to me by Alberto Crespo, who used it in his study *Esclavos negros en Bolivia*, pp. 143ff.

34. ANB, Expedientes Coloniales, 1808, no. 11, ff. 35–35v.

35. ACALP, tomo 116, ff. 261–77. In these accounts, it is reported in 1799 that to sow the wheat it was necessary to pay 4 "jornaleros" and 8 Indians from off the estate a daily wage of 2 reales "por falta que hubo de gente en la hacienda. . . ." The administrator also reported that because the oxen of the yanaconas were incapacitated, he had to rent other oxen teams at 2 reales per day. He also was required to pay all Indians "segun costumbre" during the harvest a ration of coca which cost 17 reales for 10 days' worth of labor; there was also 12 reales for food for this group of wheat harvesters. Another 3 reales worth of coca was given to those who harvested various root crops.

36. Lema, "Production et circulation," p. 207.

37. APTS, "Cuenta liquido que yo Juan Andres Martinez instruio al Sr. Dn. Diego Antonio del Portillo, pertenientes a las mitas de Santos, Marzo y San Juan del año 1803 en la Hacienda de Chimasi," Chimasi, 2 Oct. 1804. I am grateful to Philip Parkerson for providing me with a copy of this document.

38. *Ibid.*, p. 208.

39. The largest payment, to Andres Tapia, was 57 pesos, 6 reales; the smallest, 14 pesos, 2 reales, was to Mariano Carrasco.

40. It has been argued that on Cuzco estates in the eighteenth century, the food and clothing advances to workers—which in fact were quite large and complex—were insufficient to maintain a family for a year. This meant that almost all workers must have had access to some lands for the production of subsistence crops. Glave and Remy, *Estructura agraria y vida rural en un región andina*, pp. 348–49.

41. *Ibid.*, pp. 205–6.

42. *Ibid.*, p. 370.

43. This was the case of the Cercado hacienda Lullu in the canton of Mecapaca. Though it was worth 12,000 pesos, the surveyors were forced to rely on the jilakata Miguel Poma for information on its ownership and production. AHLP/PR, libro 26 (1881), f. 45v. In the neighboring canton of Obrajes, the equally valued estate of Sipari y Mollomarca also seemed to have only the jilakata Damaso Gonzalez in charge. *Ibid.*, f. 49.

44. There were a total of 1,100 functioning estates (i.e., those with peones or yanaconas working on them) in 1786/92. See Chapter 1.

45. The detailed statistics for the late colonial period are contained in Chapter 1.

46. [Aspiazu], *Informe*, pp. 17–18.

47. Langer, *Economic Change and Rural Resistance in Southern Bolivia*, chapter 4.

48. Communication from Erwin Greishaber, March 3, 1991.

49. In Chuquisaca Langer found that some 54 percent of sales were for debt and 34 percent to pay court costs—usually in land dispute cases with whites. Langer, *Economic Change*, p. 64. Unfortunately, the causes for sales in the Department of La Paz have not been studied.

50. See Bolivia, *Anuario de leyes y disposiciones supremas de 1916*, pp. 448–50, for the Decree of October 12, 1916, which defined the stricter legal requirements for sale, and the *Anuario de . . . 1920*, pp. 116–17, for the Decree of October 2, 1920, which prohibited sales for debt.

51. Rivera, "La expansion del latifundio"; and Grieshaber, "Indian Resistance to Communal Land Sales."

52. This was the case in Yamparaez province in Chuquisaca. See Langer, *Economic Change*, p. 66.

53. Choque, *Las masacres de Jesús de Machaca*.
54. Bolivia, Instituto Nacional de Estatística, *I Censo Agropecuario, 1950*, pp. 25–26, 142–43. In all the republic, *comunidades* contained 22 percent of total acreage and 26 percent of the cultivated lands.
55. See Albó, *Achacachi*, for the activity in the Department of La Paz. For the special role of the peasants in Cochabamba, see Dandler, *El sindicalismo campesino en Bolivia*.

Bibliography

Archival Sources

AALP	Archivo de la Curia del Arzobispado de La Paz.
ACALP	Archivo de la Catedral del Arzobispado de La Paz, Archivo Capitular.
ACM	Archivo de la Casa de Moneda (Potosí), Banco de San Carlos.
AGI	Archivo General de Indias (Seville), Audiencia de Buenos Aires; and Audiencia de Charcas.
AGN	Archivo General de la Nación (Buenos Aires) Salas IX (División Colonial-Sección Gobierno); and XIII (División Colonial-Sección Contaduria); and Manuscritos de Biblioteca Nacional.
AHLP	Archivo Histórico de La Paz (Universidad Mayor de San Andrés), Fondo-Prefectura de La Paz, Padrones y Revisitas; and Registro de Escrituras Notariales.
AHMLP	Archivo Historical de la Municipalidad de La Paz, Registro de Escrituras Notariales.
ANB	Archivo Nacional de Bolivia (Sucre), Tierras e Indios; Audiencia de Charcas; Archivos del Tribunal Nacional de Cuentas; Expedientes Coloniales.
APSMR	Archivo Particular de María Luisa Soux Muñoz Reyes (La Paz).
APTS	Archivo Particular de la Familia Tejada Sorzano (La Paz).
RAH	Real Academia de Historia (Madrid), Colección Mata Linhares.

Books, Articles, and Manuscripts

Albó, Xavier. *Achacachi: medio siglo de lucha campesina*. La Paz, 1979.
———. "Dinámica en la estructura inter-comunitaria de Jesús de Machaca," *América Indígena*, 32, no. 3 (July–Sept. 1972).

————, ed. *Raíces de América: El mundo Aymara*. Madrid, 1988.

Alcedo, Antonio de. *Diccionario geográfico-histórico de las indias occidentales o América*. 4 vols. 2d ed.; Madrid, 1967.

Amat y Juninet, Manuel de. *Memoria de gobierno*. Seville, 1947.

Amunategui Solar, Domingo. *Mayorazgos i títulos de Castilla*. 3 vols. Santiago de Chile, 1901–4.

Angelis, Pedro de, ed. *Colección de obras y documentos relativos a la historia antigua y moderna de las provincias del Río de la Plata*. 2d ed.; Buenos Aires, 1970.

Arze, René. "Las haciendas jesuitas de La Paz en el siglo XVIII," *Historia y Cultura* (La Paz), 1973, no. 1.

[Aspiazu, Augustín]. *Informe que presenta al Señor Ministro de Hacienda el Director General de Contribuciones Directas del Departamento de La Paz*. La Paz, 1881.

Azcuy Ameghino, Eduardo, and Gabriela Martínez Dougnac. *Tierra y ganado en la campaña de Buenos Aires según los censos de hacendados de 1789*. Buenos Aires, 1989.

Averanga Mollinedo, Astenio. *Aspectos generales de la población boliviana*. La Paz, 1974.

Ballivian, Manuel V., and Eduardo Idiaquez. *Diccionario Geográfico de la República de Bolivia*, Vol. 1, *Departamento de La Paz*. La Paz, 1890.

Barragán, Rossana. *Espacio urbano y dinámica étnica, La Paz en el siglo XIX*. La Paz, 1990.

Bastien, Joseph W. *Mountain of the Condor. Metaphor and Ritual in an Andean Ayllu*. St. Paul, Minn., 1978.

Bauer, Arnold J. "Rural Workers in Spanish America: Problems of Peonage and Oppression," *Hispanic American Historical Review*, 59, no. 1 (Feb. 1970).

Bergana, Francisco Xavier de. "Demonstración Matemática." Unpublished ms. La Paz, dated July 30, 1805, in the APTJ.

Birbuet D., Gustavo. *Tierra y ganado en Pacajes. Estructura de tenencia de la tierra y tamaño del hato ganadero familiar en la economía campesina de Caquiaviri y Comanche*. La Paz, 1986.

Bolivia, República de. *Anuario de leyes y disposiciones supremas, 1874*. La Paz, 1875.

————. *Anuario de leyes y disposiciones supremas de 1880*. La Paz, 1881.

————. *Anuario de leyes y disposiciones supremas de 1916*. La Paz, 1917.

————. *Anuario de leyes y disposiciones supremas de 1920*. La Paz, 1921.

————. Oficina Nacional de Inmigración, Estadística y Propaganda Geográfica, *Censo general de la población de la república de Bolivia, 1 de setiembre de 1900*. 2 vols. La Paz, 1902–4.

————. Instituto Nacional de Estadística. *I Censo Agropecuario, 1950*. La Paz, 1985.

———. *Colección oficial de leyes, decretos, órdenes y resoluciones vijentes de la República Boliviana [1825–1845].* 5 vols. Sucre, 1846–47.

———. Instituto Nacional de Estadística. *Resultados del censo nacional de poblacion y vivienda, 1976.* La Paz, 1978.

———. *Memoria del Ministro de Hacienda e Industria presentada al Congreso Ordinario de 1883.* La Paz, 1884.

———. *Memoria del Ministerio de Hacienda correspondiente al año 1881 presentada al honorable Congreso Nacional en 1882.* La Paz, 1882.

Borde, Jean, and Mario Góngora. *Evolución de la propiedad rural en el valle de Puangue.* 2 vols. Santiago de Chile, 1956.

Bouysse-Cassagne, Thérèse. "Pertenencia étnica, status económico y lenguajes en Charcas a fines del siglo XVI," in David Noble Cook et al., eds., *Tasa de la Visita General de Francisco Toledo.* Lima, 1975.

Brading, David A. *Haciendas and Ranchos in the Mexican Bajío. Leon, 1700–1860.* Cambridge, Eng., 1979.

Buecher, Hans C. *The Masked Media: Aymara Fiestas and Social Integration in the Bolivian Highlands.* The Hague, 1980.

Burga, Manuel. *De la encomienda a la hacienda capitalista en el Valle de Jequetepeque, del siglo XVI al XX.* Lima, 1976.

Burke, Melvin, "An Analysis of the Bolivian Land Reform by Means of a Comparison Between Peruvian Haciendas and Bolivian Ex-Haciendas." Ph.D. diss., University of Pittsburgh, 1967.

Carter, William E. *Aymara Communities and the Bolivian Agrarian Reform.* Gainesville, Fla., 1964.

———, and Xavier Albó. "La comunidad aymara: un mini-estado en conflicto," in Xavier Albó, ed., *Raíces de América: El mundo Aymara.* Madrid, 1988.

Chayanov, A. V. *The Theory of Peasant Economy.* Ed. D. Thorner et al. Homewood, Ill., 1966.

Chevalier, Françoise. *La formation des grandes domaines au México: Terre et société au XVI–XVIIe siècles.* Paris, 1952.

Choque, Roberto. *Las masacres de Jesús de Machaca.* La Paz, 1986.

Clavero, Bartolomé. *Mayorazgo. Propiedad feudal en Castilla (1369–1836).* Madrid, 1974.

Colmenares, Germán. *Las haciendas de los jesuitas en el Nuevo Reino de Granada, siglo XVIII.* Bogotá, 1969.

Condarco Morales, Ramiro. *Zárate El "Temible" Wilka. Historia de la rebelión indígena de 1899.* La Paz, 1966.

Crespo, Alberto, et al. *La vida cotidiana en La Paz, 1800–1825.* La Paz, 1975.

———. *Siporo, historia de una hacienda.* La Paz, 1984.

———. *Esclavos negros en Bolivia.* La Paz, 1977.

Crespo, Luis S. *Geografía de la República de Bolivia.* La Paz, 1910.

Dalence, Jose María. *Bosquejo estadístico de Bolivia*. Chuquisaca, 1851.

Dandler, Jorge. *El sindicalismo campesino en Bolivia: los cambios estructurales en Ucureña*. Mexico City, 1969.

Demelas, Marie-Danielle. "Jacqueries indiennes, politique créole: la guerre civile de 1899," *Caravelle*, 44 (1985).

———. *Nationalisme sans nation? La Bolivie aux XIXe–XXe siècles*. Paris, 1980.

Escobedo y Alarcón, Jorge. *Instrucción de Revisitas o matrículas formado por el señor Don Jorge Escobedo y Alarcón . . . en cumplimento del artículo 121 de la Real Instrucción de Intendentes*. Buenos Aires, 1802.

Escriche y Martín, Joaquín. *Diccionario razonado de legislación civil, penal, comercial y forense. . . .* Mexico City, 1837.

Fraser, Valerie. *The Architecture of Conquest. Building in the Viceroyalty of Peru, 1535–1635*. Cambridge, Eng. 1990.

Gagliano, Joseph A. "The Coca Debate in Colonial Peru," *The Americas*, 20, no. 1 (July 1963).

Gisbert, Teresa, and José de Mesa. *Arquitectura andina. Historia y análisis*. La Paz, 1985.

Glave, Luis Miguel, and María Isabel Remy. *Estructura agraria y vida rural en una región andina, Ollantaytambo entre los siglos XVI y XIX*. Cuzco, 1983.

Godoy, Ricardo A. *Mining and Agriculture in Highland Bolivia: Ecology, History, and Commerce Among the Jukumanis*. Tucson, Ariz., 1990.

Gölte, Jurgen. *Repartos y rebeliones. Túpac Amaru y las contradicciones de la economía colonial*. Lima, 1980.

Gray, Lewis C. *History of Agriculture in the Southern United States to 1860*. 2 vols. Washington, D.C., 1932.

Grieshaber, Erwin P. "Survival of Indian Communities in Nineteenth Century Bolivia." Ph.D. diss., University of North Carolina, 1977.

———. "Survival of Indian Communities in Nineteenth-Century Bolivia, A Regional Comparison," *Journal of Latin American Studies*, 12 (1980).

———. "Hacienda Expansion in the Department of La Paz, Bolivia, 1850–1920: A Quantitative Review." Paper presented at the American Historical Association meeting, Dec. 1988.

———. "Indian Resistance to Communal Land Sales in the Department of La Paz, 1881–1920." Paper presented at FLACSO, Quito, Mar. 1989.

Johnsson, Mick. *Food and Culture Among Bolivian Aymara*. Uppsala, 1986.

Katz, Friedrich, ed. *La servidumbre agraria en México en la época porfiriana*. Mexico City, 1976.

Klein, Harriet E. Manelis. "Los urus: el extraño pueblo del altiplano," *Estudios Andinos*, 3 no. 1 (1973).

Klein, Herbert S. *Bolivia, the Evolution of a Multi-ethnic Society.* New York, 1982.

———. "Coca Production in the Bolivian Yungas in the Colonial and National Periods." In D. Pacine and C. Franquemont, eds., *Coca and Cocaine: Effects on People and Policy in Latin America.* Boston, 1986.

———. "Structure and Profitability of Royal Finance in the Viceroyalty of the Rio de la Plata in 1790," *Hispanic American Historical Review,* 53, no. 3 (Aug. 1973).

———, and Francisco Vidal Luna. "Slaves & Masters in Early Nineteenth Century Brazil: São Paulo in 1829," *Journal of Interdisciplinary History,* 21 no. 4 (Spring 1991).

———, and Edmund P. Willis. " The Distribution of Wealth in Late 18th Century New York City," *Histoire Sociale/Social History* (Ottawa), 18, no. 36 (Nov. 1985).

Konrad, Herman W. *A Jesuit Hacienda in Colonial Mexico, Santa Lucia, 1576–1767.* Stanford, Calif., 1980.

Kula, Witold. *Teoría económica del sistema feudal.* Buenos Aires, 1974.

Ladd, Dorris M. *The Mexican Nobility at Independence, 1780–1826.* Austin, Tex., 1970.

Langer, Erick D. *Economic Change and Rural Resistance in Southern Bolivia, 1880–1930.* Stanford, Calif., 1989.

———. "El liberalismo y la abolición de la comunidad indígena en el siglo XIX." *Historia y Cultura,* 14 (Oct. 1988).

Larson, Brooke. *Colonialism and Agrarian Transformation in Bolivia: Cochabamba, 1550–1900.* Princeton, N.J., 1988.

Lavrin, Asunción, and Edith Couturier. "Dowries and Wills: A View of Women's Socio-Economic Role in Colonial Guadalajara and Puebla, 1640–1790," *Hispanic American Historical Review,* 59, no. 2 (May 1979).

Lema, Ana María. "Production et circulation de la coca en Bolivie, 1780–1840." Paris, Thèse de doctorat, EHESS 1988.

Lofstrom, William Lee. *El Mariscal Sucre en Bolivia.* La Paz, 1983.

Macera, Pablo. "Feudalismo colonial americano, el caso de las haciendas peruanas," and "Haciendas Jesuitas del Peru," in his *Trabajos de Historia.* 3 vols. Lima, 1977. Vol. 3.

———. *La hacienda peruana colonial (siglo XVIII).* Lima, 1969.

Maldonado, Abraham. *Derecho agrario, historia—doctrina—legislación.* La Paz, 1956.

Mamani, Mauricio. "Agricultura a los 4000 metros." In Xavier Albó, ed., *Raíces de América: El mundo Aymara.* Madrid, 1988.

Matos Mar, José. *Yanocanaje y reforma agraria en el Perú.* Lima, 1976.

McBride, George McCutchen. *The Agrarian Indian Communities of Highland Bolivia.* New York, 1921.

Mitre, Antonio. *El monedero de los Andes. Región económica y moneda boliviana en el siglo XIX.* La Paz, 1986.

————. *Los patriarcas de la plata. Estructura socioeconómica de la minería boliviana en el siglo XIX.* Lima, 1981.

Mörner, Magnus. *Perfil de la sociedad rural del Cuzco a fines de la colonia.* Lima, 1978.

————. "The Spanish American Hacienda: A Survey of Recent Research and Debate," *Hispanic American Historical Review,* 53, no. 2 (May 1973).

Muñoz Reyes, Jorge. *Geografía de Bolivia.* La Paz, 1977.

Murra, John. *Formaciones económicas y políticas del mundo andino.* Lima, 1975.

————. "An Aymara Kingdom in 1567." *Ethnohistory,* Vol. 15, no. 2 (Spring 1968).

Ovando Sanz, Jorge Alejandro. *El tributo indígena en las finanzas bolivianas del siglo XIX.* La Paz, 1986.

Pentland, Joseph Barclay. "Report on the Republic of Bolivia, 1827." In *Great Britain, Foreign Office, Reports,* F.O. 61/12. Public Record Office, London.

Pérez Velasco, Néstor. *Informe del Prefecto . . . del Departamento de La Paz . . . 1918.* La Paz, n.d.

Pezuela, Joaquín de la. *Memoria de gobierno.* Seville, 1947.

Pinto H., Honorio. *Contribución indígena en Bolivia, 1829–1911 (Documentos).* Lima, 1979.

Platt, Tristan. "Acerca del sistema tributario pre-toldeano en el Alto Perú," *Avances* (La Paz), 1978, no. 1.

————. *Estado boliviano y ayllu andino: tierra y tributo en el norte de Potosí.* Lima, 1982.

————. *Estado tributario y librecambio en Potosí (siglo XIX).* La Paz, 1986.

————. "Pensamento político Aymara," in Xavier Albó, ed., *Raices de América: El mundo Aymara.* Madrid, 1988.

Polo y La Bora, Jorge. "La hacienda Pachacachaca (segunda mitad del siglo XVIII)," *Histórica* (Lima), 1, no. 2 (Dec. 1977).

Prado Robles, Gustavo Adolfo. "Política monetaria y patrón de articulación comercial: un ensayo sobre el proceso decimonónico de apertura de la economía boliviana al comercio mundial." M.A. thesis, Universidade Federal do Rio de Janeiro, 1986.

Presta, Ana María. "Una hacienda tarijeña en el siglo XVIII: La viña de 'La Angostura'." Unpublished ms., 1988.

Ramírez, Susan E. *Provincial Patriarchs, Land Tenure, and the Economics of Power in Colonial Peru.* Albuquerque, N.M., 1986.

Rasnake, Roger Neil. *Domination and Cultural Resistance. Authority and Power Among an Andean People.* Durham, N.C., 1988.

Rivera, Silvia C. "La expansión del latifundio en el Altiplano boliviano: elementos para la caracterización de una oligarquía regional." *Avances* (La Paz), 1978, no. 2.

———. *Oprimidos pero no vencidos: luchas del campesinado aymara y qhechwa de Bolivia, 1900–1980.* La Paz, 1986.

Rodriguez, Gustavo. *Expansión del latifundio o supervivencia de las comunidades indígenas? Cambios en la estructura agraria boliviana del s. XIX.* Cochabamba, n.d.

Rück, Ernesto. *Guía general de Bolivia, Primer Año.* Sucre, 1865.

Saignes, Tierry. *Los Andes Orientales: Historia de un olvido.* La Paz, 1985.

———. "De la filiation à la residence: Les ethnies dans les valées de Larecaja." *Annales, E.S.C.* 33, no. 5-6 (1978).

Sánchez-Albornoz, Nicolás. *Indios y tributos en el Alto Perú.* Lima, 1978.

Santamaría, Daniel J. "La estructura agraria del Alto Perú a fines del siglo XVIII. Un análisis de tres regiones maiceras del Partido de Larecaja en 1795," *Desarrollo Económico* (Buenos Aires) 18, no. 72 (1979).

———. *Hacendados y campesinos en el Alto Perú colonial.* Buenos Aires, [1989].

———. "La propiedad de la tierra y la condición social del indio en el Alto Perú, 1780–1810," *Desarrollo Económico,* no. 66 (1977).

Sebill, Nadine. *Ayllus y haciendas. Dos estudios sobre la agricultura colonial en los Andes.* La Paz, 1989.

Skar, Harald O. *The Warm Valley People, Duality and Land Reform Among the Quechua Indians of Highland Peru.* Oslo, 1982.

Socolow, Susan Migden. *The Merchants of Buenos Aires, 1778–1810: Family and Commerce.* Cambridge, Eng., 1978.

Soltow, Lee. "Economic Inequality in the United States in the Period from 1790 to 1860," *Journal of Economic History,* 31, no. 4 (Dec. 1971).

Soux Muñoz Reyes, María Luisa. "Producción y circuitos mercantiles de la coca yungueña, 1900–1935." Tesis de Licenciatura, Universidad Mayor de San Andrés, La Paz, 1987.

Spalding, Karen. *Huarochirí: An Andean Society Under Inca and Spanish Rule.* Stanford, Calif., 1984.

Stern, Steve J. *Peru's Indian Peoples and the Challenge of Spanish Conquest: Huamanga to 1640.* Madison, Wisc., 1982.

Tandeter, Enrique. "Crisis in Upper Peru, 1800–1805," *Hispanic American Historical Review,* 71, no. 1 (1991).

Taylor, William B. *Landlord and Peasant in Colonial Oaxaca.* Stanford, Calif., 1972.

Tovar Pinzón, Hermes. "Elementos constituitivos de la empresa agrícola jesuita en la segunda mitad del siglo XVIII en México." In CLACSO, *Haciendas y plantaciones en América Latina.* Mexico City, 1975.

Turvosky, Paul Robert. "Bolivian Haciendas Before and After the Revolution." Ph.D. thesis, University of California at Los Angeles, 1980.

Van Young, Eric. *Hacienda and Market in Eighteenth-Century Mexico. The*

Rural Economy of the Guadalajara Region, 1675–1820. Berkeley, Calif., 1981.

————. "Mexican Rural History since Chevalier: The Historiography of the Colonial Hacienda," *Latin American Research Review*, 18, no. 3 (1983).

Vollmer, Günter. *Bevölkerungspolitik und Bevölkerungsstructur im Vizekönigreich Peru zu ende der kolonialzeit (1741–1821).* Bas Homburg von der Hohe, 1967.

Wachtel, Nathan. *Le retour des ancêtres. Les Indiens Urus de Bolivie XXe–XVIe siècle. Essai d'histoire regressive.* Paris, 1990.

Whitehead, Lawrence. "Altitude, Fertility, and Mortality in Andean Countries," *Population Studies*, 21, no. 3 (Nov. 1968).

Wightman, Ann M. *Indigenous Migration and Social Change: The Forasteros of Cuzco, 1570–1720.* Durham, N.C., 1990.

Zulawski, Ann. "Forasteros y yanaconas: la mano de obra en un centro minero en el siglo XVII." In Olivia Harris et al., *La participación indígena en los mercados surandinos.* La Paz, 1987.

Index

Agrarian Reform, 131, 159
Agregados, 12, 61. See also
  Forasteros
Agriculture, 3–4, 57; multi-
  ecological farming and, 23, 161;
  rotation practices in, 60–61;
  ayllus and commerce in, 128;
  late-eighteenth-century,
  138–40. See also Coca production; Usufruct land
Alcabala, 57
Altiplano region, 7, 9. See also
  specific locations
Amat, Viceroy Manuel de, 38
Ancoryames, 116
Anguia, 143
Aspiazu, Augustín, 117, 136,
  210n2
Ataguallani, 54
Ayllus: internal government in,
  10, 16, 59–60; hacienda ownership by, 29–30, 77, 204n33;
  population of, 57, 64–83 passim, 183–85; definition and
  basic structure of, 58–62,
  187n6; groups of (comunidades),
  59–60, 157, 187–88; land distribution and, 60–62; and production, 67, 79, 81, 98f, 126,
  128; transformed into haciendas, 98; market influences on,

112, 162–63; and attacks on
  property rights, 115–18,
  132–37 passim, 156–58; government revenues from, 119–20;
  church construction and, 120;
  in the modern era, 158, 162;
  wealth of, 163. See also Forasteros; Originarios
Aymara Indians, 3, 7. See also
  Ayllus; specific Indian subgroups

Balance of trade, 87, 134
Banking system, 134, 155–56
Birth rates, 72, 74, 105
Bolívar, Simón, 113, 206n12
Bolivian government, and Indian
  property rights, 132–37,
  156–58, 115–18

Caciques, 60
Cadastral surveys, 117, 135–37,
  148, 160
Capire, 36
Capital, access to, 79
Carazo, Diego, 39
Catholic church, 30, 32, 75;
  hacienda ownership by, 30,
  75, 145, 153–54, 196n23; Don
  Tadeo's grants to, 51; ayllus in-
  vestment for, 120; wealth of,
  154, 196n23

Cedromayo, 43
Censuses, 10–13 *passim*, 62–64, 85, 88, 121, 160, 205n6; republican, 88–89, 113; cadastral surveys, 117, 135–37, 148, 160; and Indian status legitimacy, 131; modern, 158; sources for, 189n14, 209n12. *See also* Tribute taxes
Cercado, 137–42 *passim*
Chaqui, 69
Charapacci, 98
Chicalulo, 37–43 *passim*
Children-to-women ratios, 71f, 83, 100, 106, 110, 121, 129
Chile, war with, 135
Chirca, 98
Choclla, 98
Cholera epidemics, 90, 105, 121, 127, 204n1
Chulumani, 5f, 9; distribution of haciendas in, 17–19; wealthy hacendado investments in, 23; multiple-owner farms in, 30–31; Don Tadeo's estates in, 37–38, 43; Indian population of, 56–58, 64–74, 89–102, 109–10, 180; and tribute taxes, 71; hacendado class in, 74–76; immigration to, 81–82; distribution of wealth in, 137–40, 155; wage labor in, 145. *See also* Yungas; *specific locations*
Chupe, 95
Church, *see* Catholic church
Coca production, 9, 18, 57–58, 77–85 *passim*, 138, 164, 201n8, 205n3; on Don Tadeo's estates, 37–38, 43f, 54; labor force for, 67, 69; of *ayllus*, 79, 81, 98f, 126; mining industry decline and, 85, 94–100 *passim*, 122; and vertical integration, 161

Coca rations, 15, 147, 191n23, 214n35
Cochabamba valley, 31, 128
Coinage, 87–88
Colonos, 11, 16, 43. *See also Yanaconas*
Comunidades, 116, 157, 187–88. *See also Ayllus*
Convents, 30, 49, 52, 153
Coripata, 95, 102
Coroyco, 81, 95, 102
Credit, 214n30
Crop rotation, 60–61

Debts, 15–16, 191n25
Demographics, *see* Children-to-women ratios; Population; Sex ratios
Diez de Medina, Don Tadeo, 34–38, 161; marriage alliances of, 38–42, 53, 55; urban real estate of, 41, 44; businesses of, 43–45, 53; wealth and income of, 45–48, 169–78, 196–98; sons of, 50–54
Diez de Medina, Francisco Tadeo, 50f, 195n5

Eguino, Francisco Xavier, 41
Eguino, Vicente, 54
Elders, 10, 16, 59–60, 148
Elena hacienda, 39, 42
Epidemics, 90, 105, 121, 127, 204n1
Exports, 87, 103, 105, 134f
Exvinculación decree, 117, 159

Fallowing, 60f
Family size, 26, 77
Fertility, 71
Feudal models, 1–2, 34
Food rations, 15, 147, 191n23, 214n35

Forasteros, 11–12, 61–64 *passim*, 89, 92, 131; and *originario* population ratios, 69; market influences on, 97, 100–110 *passim*, 121–32 *passim*, 163; sex ratios of, 107; migrations of, 127, 129; and status legitimation, 131
Forced labor, 6, 10, 14, 128
Free Indian communities, *see* *Ayllus*

Guancapampa, 98
Guaqui, 108
Guaycho, 116
Guillen, Patricia, 54
Guillen, Ramón, 39–41

Hacendado class, 6; multiple property ownership of, 20–23, 149; relative size of, 20; women landowners in, 27–29, 32, 75–76, 154, 165; in Chulumani, 74–76; population of, 192n34. *See also* Diez de Medina, Don Tadeo
Haciendas: non-market models, 1–2, 34; market responsiveness of, 2, 89–95 *passim*, 110–11, 160–62; distribution of, 17–20, 57; productivity of, 17, 67, 76, 79, 81, 126, 139, 161; size of, 19, 76, 140–41, 194n48; wealth distribution and, 20–23, 29, 137–55 *passim*; Indian ownership of, 29–30, 77, 204n33; joint ownership of, 30–31, 54; church ownership of, 30, 32, 75, 145, 153–54, 196n23; as rental property, 32, 141–42, 161; and *ayllu* comparisons, 56, 64–83; and population density, 75f; productivity of, 76, 79, 81,

126, 161; and ownership changes, 93; and *ayllu* transformations, 98; late nineteenth century growth of, 117–18; and cadastral surveys, 135–37; *ayllu* property rights vs., 136–37; sales of, 142–43, 213n29, 214n30; modern, 159, 194n50. *See also* Hacendado class; *Yanaconas*; *specific haciendas*

Import-export ratio, 87, 134
Incapampa, 43, 199n47
Indian free communities, *see* *Ayllus*
Indian peasantry, *see* *Forasteros*; *Originarios*; *Yanaconas*
Infrastructure, 134
Inheritance, 144, 207
Inquisivi, 139
Intendencia of La Paz, *see* La Paz (province)
Iturralde, Juan Fernando, 39, 41–42, 169

Jesuits, 196n23
Jilakatas, 10, 16, 59–60, 148
Joint ownership, 30–31, 54

Kurakas, 10, 60

Labor, 15; forced (*mita*), 6, 10, 14, 59, 128; non-compensated personal service, 11, 17, 147–48, 161; and wages, 15–16, 144–47, 164, 190n21, 203n21, 214n35; and coca harvest, 67, 69; mining crisis and, 89–110 *passim*; *ayllu*-hacienda competition for, 129. *See also* *Forasteros*; *Yanaconas*
Land distribution, in *ayllus*, 60–62

Landowners, see Hacendado class
Land scarcity, 130–31
Land use, labor exchange for, see Usufruct land
La Paz (city), 4, 9, 30, 127; Don Tadeo's real estate in, 41, 44; nineteenth century growth of, 134
La Paz (province), 3, 6–9; population, 3, 7, 8, 35, 90, 188n2, 192n34, 210n24; demographic survey of, 81–83; cadastral survey of, 136. *See also* Chulumani; Pacajes; *specific districts and haciendas*
La Purissima Concepción, 49, 52
Larecaja, 6, 9, 18, 30f, 36–37, 82–83, 139f
Latifundias, 140–41. *See also* Haciendas
Liberals, 117

Machaca, Jesus de, 77, 108
Machaca, San Andres de, 108
Market forces, 2; hacienda responses to, 110–11, 160–62; Indian peasantry response to, 112, 133, 165–66. *See also* Mining industry
Marriage alliances, 38–42, 53, 55
Marxist models, 1–2
Mayorazgo, 50ff
Medina, Tadeo Diez de, see Diez de Medina, Don Tadeo
Melgarejo government, 115–16, 128, 133f
Mestizos, 11, 128
Mexico, 2, 15–16, 47
Migration, 127, 129
Minga labor, 145–47, 164
Minifundia, 32
Mining industry, 35; forced labor for, 6, 10, 14, 59; decline of,

84–88; coca production linkages to, 85, 122; Chulumani demographic correlations with, 89–102, 109–10; hacienda populations and, 89–95 *passim*; *ayllu* population and, 96–98; Pacajes demographic correlations with, 103–10; tribute revenues and, 115; revival of, 134
Mita labor, 6, 10, 14, 59, 128
Monasteries, 30, 153
"Moneda feble," 88
Montes, Ismael, 156
Mortgages, 38, 119, 169, 197n35
Mutuguaya, 54

Omasuyos, 6, 9, 18f, 82–83, 209n14; wealthy hacendado investments in, 23; distribution of wealth in, 137f, 155; *ayllu* seizures in, 156
Originarios, 11–12, 60–64, 89, 122ff; and widow remarriage, 74; market influences on, 96, 102–10 *passim*, 122–32 *passim*; sex ratios and, 107; and status legitimation, 131, 207n16. *See also Ayllus*
Oruro, 134

Pacajes, 5f, 9, 18, 64–83, 90, 103–10, 181; Indian-owned haciendas in, 30; *ayllu* distributions in, 57; tributary taxes in, 71; relative wealth in, 83; *ayllu* seizures in, 156
Pacallo, 145
Padron de indios, 10, 62, 85, 88. *See also* Censuses; Tribute taxes
Palomar, 141
Pentland, George, 87, 105
Peones, 15. *See also Yanaconas*
Platt, Tristan, 130

Pongueaje labor, 11, 17, 147–48, 161

Population: of La Paz province, 3, 7f, 35, 90, 130, 210n24, 188n2, 192n34; of La Paz city, 9, 127; of Chulumani, 56–58, 81–82, 180; of *ayllus*, 65–67, 96–98; density of, 65–67, 75f, 130; and coca production relationships, 77–81 *passim*; mining industry changes and, 89–110 *passim*; of Pacajes, 103–10 *passim*, 181; and market influences, 121–32 *passim*; land scarcity and, 130–31; and nineteenth century tributarios, 183–85; of hacendado class, 192n34

Potosí: forced labor for, 6, 14; coca imports of, 85, 205n3; mint at, 87; and mining industry revival, 134; population of, 210n23

Productivity, 17, 67, 76, 79, 81, 126, 139, 161

Property rights, government assaults on, 115–18, 132–37 *passim*, 156–58

Property tax, 135, 143

Quechua speakers, 7

Rebellions, 38, 60, 116ff, 158f, 164

Rentals, 32, 141–42, 161

Retana, Fernando, 39

Revisitas, 10, 62, 113, 120f, 131, 209n12. *See also* Censuses; Tribute taxes

Rio Abajo zone, 23

Sales tax, 57

San Francisco de Paulo del Monte, 39

San José, 144

San Pablo, 144

San Roque, 98

Santiago el Grande, 147

Sex ratios: of Indians, 27–29, 71f, 81f, 100f, 107, 121, 165; of landowners, 27–29, 32, 75–76, 154, 165

Sicasica, 6, 9, 18, 30f, 82–83, 137, 139

Silver production. *See* Mining industry

Siripaya, 98

Sucre, Mariscal Antonio José de, 206n12

Tahana, 15, 144

Taxes, 57, 135, 143. *See also* Censuses; Tribute taxes

Tax farming, 38

Tiahuanaco, 108

Tliquina, 116

Toriri, 98

Trade deficits, 87

Tribute taxes, 10–14, 62–63, 83, 88–89, 147; seasonal workers and, 69; of Chulumani and Pacajes compared, 71; government revenues from, 113, 115, 119–20, 135, 206n12, 211n6; and Indian status legitimation, 131, 164, 206n12. *See also* Censuses

Tupac Amaru rebellion, 60

Ulloa y Solis, Antonia de, 36

Upper Peru, 6. *See also* La Paz (province); *specific locations*

Uprisings, 38, 60, 116ff, 158f, 164

Urban real estate, 41, 44, 135

Usufruct land, 14–17 *passim*, 26, 63–64, 77, 94, 143f; coca production on, 79; inheritance of, 144

Vidal, Pastro, 141
Vilavila, 41
Village elders, 10, 16, 59–60, 148
Village(s), *see Ayllus*
Vineyards, 190n21

Wage labor, 15–16, 144–47, 164, 190n21, 203n21, 214n35
Wars, 84, 113, 134
Wealth, 13, 20–23, 29, 83, 137–41, 148–55; of Don Tadeo Diez de Medina, 38–39, 45–48, 169–78, 196–98; of Church, 154, 196n23; of *ayllus*, 163; of Jesuits, 196n23
Widows, 74
Women landowners, 27–29, 32, 75–76, 154, 165
Women workers, 143–44

Yalaca, 144
Yanacachi, 89f, 95, 98
Yanaconas, 11, 164, 190–92; work obligations of, 11, 17, 147–48, 161; tax obligations of, 12, 63, 89, 147; land use rights of, 14–17 *passim*, 63–64; debts of, 15–16, 191n25; and wage labor, 15–16, 144–47, 164, 190n21, 203n21, 214n35; and authority structures, 16–17, 148; productivity of, 17, 67, 79, 81, 126, 139; and family size, 26, 77; on Don Tadeo's estates, 43; population of, 92–93, 100–110 *passim*, 183–85; hacienda ties of, 94–95, 110–11; sex ratios of, 107; and women workers, 143–44
Yungas, 85, 201nn7–8; Don Tadeo's investments in, 37, 54; labor sources for, 67, 94–95, 110; and *yanacona* mobility, 94–95; and response to market changes, 99; distribution of wealth in, 137ff; land rentals in, 142. *See also* Chulumani; Coca production

Zuri, 98